THE
FAST-FOOD
GUIDE

What's good,
what's bad,
and how to tell
the difference.

MICHAEL JACOBSON, PH.D.
Executive Director
Center for Science in the Public Interest

SARAH FRITSCHNER

Workman Publishing, New York

Library of Congress Cataloging-in-Publication Data

Jacobson, Michael F.
   Fast food.
   1. Fast food restaurants—United States.
2. Convenience foods. I. Fritschner, Sarah.
II. Title.
TX945.J3   1986   647'.9573   86-40226
ISBN 0-89480-351-4

Cover design: Charles Kreloff
Cover illustration: Karen Kluglein
Book design: Heather Gilchrist
Book illustration: Kenneth Spengler

Workman Publishing Company, Inc.
1 West 39th Street
New York, NY 10018

Manufactured in the United States of America
First printing September 1986

10 9 8 7 6 5

ACKNOWLEDGMENTS

We acknowledge, with gratitude, the efforts of our friends and colleagues who contributed to this book in one way or another. Bonnie Liebman, CSPI's nutrition director, wrote several articles in *Nutrition Action Healthletter* identifying key problems with fast foods; she also helped insure the accuracy of the health information in this book. D'Anne DuBois, assistant to the director of CSPI, has made countless phone calls and written innumerable letters, alternately pleading and demanding information from reluctant fast-food companies. Svetlana Bekman and Jim Gollin were very helpful in getting the information, accurately, into CSPI's computer. And Svetlana, with unmatched cheerfulness and attention to details, helped maintain all of our files and proofread endlessly. CSPI's legal staff, Bruce Silverglade and Mitch Zeller, have done yeoman work in support of ingredient labeling. And, in Louisville, Chris Yeager helped Sarah Fritschner survive the ordeal of simultaneously writing a book and editing a newspaper food section. We'd also like to thank Frank Sacks, Sara Sloan, Stephanie Turner, Max Sharbach, Mary Ann Griese, Robert Hall, Marge Blumberg, Jean Czerwinski, Linda Goldstein, Eric Kilburn, Ronald Collins, Richard Cotton, Ann Rust, Harriet Sobel-Roth, Judith Stern, Frensch Niegermeier, and several industry officials who, understandably, prefer anonymity. They each provided useful information about fast foods or helped conduct several studies on fast-food fats.

Finally, we would like to sing the praises of Peter Workman, Susan Gough Henly, Suzanne Rafer, Shannon Ryan, and others at Workman Publishing whose wisdom, enthusiasm, and hard work made it possible to produce this book in record time. They don't make publishers like that anymore. Thank you, Fran Collin, for connecting us with these gems.

Michael F. Jacobson
Washington, DC

Sarah Fritschner
Louisville, KY

August 1986

Before You Eat Your Next Burger and Fries 9

CHAPTER ONE

A Fast Survey of Fast Food 11

Today's Seducers 12

*The Biggest Franchised
Restaurant Chains* 15

*Restaurant Television
Advertising (1985)* 24

A Glimpse into the Future... 30

CHAPTER TWO

The Health You Save May Be Your Own 39

Dietary Guidelines 40

Fast Foods Highest in Calories 45

Eschewing the Fat: A Look at Heart Disease, Cancer, and Diabetes 46

Fast Foods Highest in Fat ... 49

*Shortening Used
Restaurant Chains* 50

Fast Foods Lowest in Fat 53

Dietary Fiber 58

*Dietary Fiber Content of
Common Foods* 61

Sodium 63

*Fast Foods Highest in
Sodium* 65

Sugar..................... 68

Fast Foods Highest in Sugar . 69

Fast-Food Thirst Quenchers.. 70

Vitamins and Minerals 71

*Fast Foods Highest in
Calcium* 75

Fast Foods Highest in Iron... 77

Adding It All Up 78

*Fast Foods With Highest
Gloom Factor* 79

Chemical Cuisine: Colorings,
Preservatives, and Other
Additives 80

CHAPTER THREE

WHAT'S IN THIS STUFF, ANYWAY? 89

Ingredient Labeling 90

Petitioning for Better
Labeling 95

The Need for Nutrition
Labeling 98

Labeling Breakthroughs..... 99

CHAPTER FOUR

CHOOSING A FAST-FOOD MEAL 103

Coping in the Fast-Food
Jungle 103

*Daily Dietary Goals for
Healthful Eating* 104

*Fat and Protein Content of Roast
Beef and Hamburger Meat...107*

*An Explanation of the Gloom
Rating* 111

Fast Food: French Fries.....112

Fast Food: Shakes, Malts....113

*Fast Food: Hamburgers,
Cheeseburgers* 114

Fast Food: Chicken 116

Fast Food: Fish 118

Fast Food: Roast Beef 119

Arby's 120

Arby's Ingredients 122

Arby's Complete Nutritional Values 124

Arthur Treacher's 128

Arthur Treacher's Complete Nutritional Values 128

Arthur Treacher's Ingredients...............129

Burger King 130

Burger King Ingredients 134

Burger King Complete Nutritional Values 136

Carl's Jr. 138

Carl's Jr. Ingredients 141

Carl's Jr. Complete Nutritional Values 142

Church's Fried Chicken.....144

Church's Fried Chicken Complete Nutritional Values 146

Church's Fried Chicken Ingredients 147

Dairy Queen.............148

Dairy Queen Complete Nutritional Values 150

Dairy Queen Ingredients....151

D'Lites 154

D'Lites Complete Nutritional Values 156

D'Lites Ingredients 157

Domino's Pizza...........160

Domino's Pizza Complete Nutritional Values 160

Domino's Pizza Ingredients..161

Hardee's 162

Hardee's Ingredients 163

Hardee's Complete Nutritional Values 164

Jack in the Box...........168

Jack in the Box Complete Nutritional Values 170

Jack in the Box Ingredients ..171

Kentucky Fried Chicken 174

Kentucky Fried Chicken Ingredients 175

Kentucky Fried Chicken Complete Nutritional Values 176

Long John Silver's 178

Long John Silver's Complete Nutritional Values 180

Long John Silver's Ingredients 181

McDonald's...............184

McDonald's Ingredients.....188

McDonald's Complete Nutritional Values 190

Popeyes..................196

Popeyes Ingredients........196

Roy Rogers...............197

Roy Rogers Complete Nutritional Values..........198

Roy Rogers Ingredients.....199

Taco Bell.................204

Taco Bell Ingredients.......206

Wendy's..................207

Wendy's Ingredients........210

Wendy's Complete Nutritional Values.........210

APPENDIX 221

The Restaurants............221

Further Resources.........223

Now That You've Read the Book 224

BEFORE YOU EAT YOUR NEXT BURGER AND FRIES

Fast food is certainly the eating phenomenon of the mid-twentieth century. Good-bye home-cooked meal; hello hamburger heaven.

For better or worse, American highways and cities are dotted with tens of thousands of fast-food restaurants. Starting out as hamburger joints or ice-cream stands, these restaurants have evolved into international chains, comprised of thousands of outlets, that feature everything from the ridiculous (triple cheeseburgers) to the sublime (fresh fruit and vegetable salad bars).

While tens of millions of people pass through the portals of fast-food restaurants every day, they have had little guidance other than their taste buds to help them with their menu choices. Ingredients and nutrients are not listed on wrappers or on wall charts. Instead, it's pay your money, gulp it down, and hope for the best.

With Americans spending some $50 billion a year on fast foods, and with a growing number of people deeply concerned about the quality of their own diets and their kids' diets, we believe that anyone considering a visit to a fast-food restaurant should have comparative information about the products. This book gives that and much more. We have obtained every bit of information that we could possibly cajole out of the major companies, we got some more from occasional co-operative clerks, we commissioned laboratory studies on the fat content of hamburgers and french fries, we calculated the approximate sugar content of foods, and we even searched through a few trash bins to obtain ingredient information listed on bulk packaging. We generally used each company's spellings for their own products thus leading to inconsistencies such as "filet" and "fillet."

You can use this book to identify the most nutritious choices at your favorite restaurant. Or you can compare similar foods produced by different restaurant chains. And, in some cases, you can peruse ingredient information to see if foods contain something to which you're allergic.

Unfortunately, this book is not as complete as we'd like it to be for the simple reason that some companies refuse to disclose information about their products. Some companies have never even conducted nutritional analyses of their products. For this information, you'll have to wait for a second edition.

You should be forewarned that ingredient and nutrition information supplied by companies may contain errors or be out-of-date, that companies may change their recipes from time to time, and that individual outlets sometimes have a choice of several ingredient options for a particular product. Consequently the food that you purchase may not be precisely what is indicated here.

The Center for Science in the Public Interest (CSPI) is urging companies to provide more information and at the same time advocating legislation that would require ingredient information to be printed right on the fast-food packaging.

We also urge readers to help turn on the lights in the fast-food world. First, use this book. Customer preferences guide restaurants to produce either nutritious or nonnutritious foods. Our buying dollars can spur the spread of salad bars, low-fat baked chicken and fish, and other healthful products. Second, ask for skim milk, whole-wheat buns, fresh fruit, and other nutritious foods that seem to be verboten in fast-food restaurants. Third, urge your senators and representatives to support legislation that would require fast-food restaurants to disclose the ingredient and nutrition composition of their products.

The fast-food industry generally maintains a one-way line of communication with the public, relying primarily on multi-million-dollar ad budgets, form letters that don't really respond to inquiries, and the like. Responses to our calls and letters were few and far between. To help fill the information gap, we took full advantage of trade journals, such as *Advertising Age, Restaurants and Institutions,* and *Restaurant Business,* whose fact-filled pages are rarely read by the general public: the people who most need to know the secrets bared therein. We also thank Burger King and McDonald's for providing us with information on ingredients prior to its general availability.

A FAST SURVEY OF FAST FOOD

When Ray Kroc opened the doors of that first McDonald's restaurant in Des Plaines, Illinois, in 1955, he opened a whole new world for busy parents, fussy eaters, and people who just plain did not like to cook.

It has come to be a world of burgers and quick-fried chicken ready before the kids begin to yank on each other, ready to pick up on the way home from work, ready without dirtying that first pan or laying the first piece of flatware. Kitchen cleanup is just a trash can away.

It started a love affair with the french fry—one that increased per capita consumption from about two pounds in 1960 to 14 pounds in 1984. And it no doubt encouraged the love affair with soft drinks. From 1963 to 1984, soft-drink consumption per capita more than tripled.

These restaurants fueled other dietary changes occurring in America since the turn of the century. In addition to french fries and soft drinks, Americans consume more meat, fish, poultry, and cheese than they did in 1910. If we take a look at fast-food restaurant menus, we can understand one major reason why.

Changes in the foods we consume have resulted in changes in the nutrients we consume. In the past 75 years, our fat intake has increased 31 percent. Sugar consumption has increased 40 percent. We eat more processed foods that often come with high levels of salt (or other sodium-containing additives) and fat. Fast-food restaurants take things one step further by making their own distinct modifications to traditional foods. Offering a ham and Swiss cheese sandwich on a croissant, for instance, adds far more fat and calories than we would get by eating the same sandwich made with two slices of bread.

Consuming three out of five calories as fat or refined sugar, as many people do, affects more than our waistlines. It crowds out fresh fruits and vegetables, milk, and other nutrient-packed foods. In addition, we don't get the fiber we need—fiber that helps protect us against heart attacks, strokes, and cancers promoted by a diet high in fat, calories, and sodium.

Some of our dietary changes were a result of increasing affluence. And as we have prospered since World War II, other changes in society have affected the way we eat.

In 1960, Wendy's wasn't even a twinkle in David Thomas's eye and only 250 McDonald's sprinkled the landscape. In those days, Americans chose fast-food restaurants only one in 20 times when they ate out, which wasn't often. Most moms stayed home with the kids and cooked (whether they liked it or not). Dad worked and brought home the only money to support the family. When they went out to eat, they generally chose an independently run restaurant with a variety of foods offered on the menu.

But then many moms joined the work force. Since Dad was working too, time for doing chores at home diminished. When people work outside the home 40 or more hours a week, they make more money, have less time, and need to make more efficient use of the free time they have. Cooking gets short shrift in such a world. Fast foods were made to order. Nearly everyone agrees that the working woman was a phenomenon that contributed greatly to the success of the fast-food industry.

TODAY'S SEDUCERS

In a society known for its time constraints, even eating is measured carefully against other priorities. Fast foods make the desk or the car seem a suitable dining room. We'd rather sleep in the morning than eat, so many of us skip breakfast, or detour on the way to work through the drive-in window for biscuits and coffee. We spend lunch hours working or shopping or doing the odd errand so we eat standing at a kiosk, on the run, waiting at a stoplight, or back at the office. Dinner hours are diffused by all manner of distractions, from cheerleading practice to working overtime. Fast-food restaurants allow us to eat quickly without planning, without dressing up, without having to make many decisions, and without getting out of the car. For the hurried, harried, and overworked, it's eat and run at reasonable prices.

The presence of children makes fast foods even more appealing.

One or two working adults might content themselves with tuna from a can, but good parents find it difficult to impose such a diet on their children. We've always learned that children must have something hot and at least a semblance of a vegetable on their plates. So much the better if they actually eat the stuff. Contenting their children with hamburgers, fries, and a toy, parents can rest assured.

The fast-food restaurant seems remarkably resilient to anything toddlers can do to it. They can spill or smush food—tables and floors are made for mopping and wiping. Service is quick enough that you don't have to mollify your children with crackers only to find out they aren't hungry when dinner arrives. And as one mother observed, "You don't have children climbing on chairs that are going to fall over."

Restaurants have their allure for single, working parents whose quality time with children is critically low anyway. They don't need to ruin it trying to coax Jason to eat his peas. Fast-food restaurants mean hassle-free dinner with a playground oftentimes thrown in for good measure.

Our mobility accounts for no small portion of fast food's popularity. With two bored children in the backseat, a car pointed toward Disney World, and 15 hours to drive, you'd like to know that mealtime will be a pleasurable experience. Where some restaurants build their reputations on fancy French food, fast-food restaurants build theirs on uniformity and dependability. From Tacoma to Tallahassee, one Original Recipe chicken wing tastes exactly like another.

Mobility has become such a way of life it affects our eating habits. Many of us, who grew up on fast foods, have adopted the practice called "grazing"— eating small amounts of food all through the day rather than eating at three or four designated times—a feeding pattern that doesn't take much time and leaves the impression of having eaten very little.

"Grazers are largely members of the first generation to grow up on fast foods. They eat on impulse rather than three times a day," reported *The Wall Street Journal* in April 1984. As a result, people expect to eat when they are ready, not when the food is. Eating on impulse leaves plenty of opportunity for fast-food restaurants that thrive on selling snacks—chicken nuggets, a slice of pizza, and nachos to go. Now.

Fast-food dining fits in with the flexible suburban life-style that puts a premium on speed and privacy. The McDonald brothers seized on these concepts as early as 1948 when, in an effort to reduce personnel, they replaced carhops with window clerks. They used chalk to draw a floor plan of the restaurant on their tennis court "where they meticulously worked out the placement of windows and equipment to eliminate any unnecessary movement by the personnel," wrote Philip Langdon in the *Atlantic Monthly.*

These days it takes no more verbal contact than a "Help you ma'am?" and a total-bill tally, with perhaps a "Have a nice day" thrown in by especially animated clerks. The restaurants are clean, the prices low and predictable, and we can get through an entire meal without getting to know the quirks and travails of Bob, our waiter.

Many of us still turn to fast food remembering the early days when hamburgers cost 15 cents, fries a dime, and milk shakes less than a quarter. The low-cost image remains despite the fact that fast food now sometimes costs as much as the fare at a table-service restaurant. Fast-food meals can cost you more than double what it would cost to make them at home—even without the extra dollar or two for the optional toys that you can buy your children. "I have three kids," says one single mother; "by the time I feed them and feed myself, I can spend $10 or $12. That could be three days worth of meals for me if I shop economically."

As society was changing, baby boomers got older and had more money to spend. The 1980s brought an adult population that had never lived without fast foods, and children who couldn't imagine a world without Whoppers. Now, almost five out of every ten dollars we spend on restaurant food is handed across the counter of a fast-food restaurant, according to the U.S. Department of Agriculture (USDA). Each American spends an average of $200 a year on fast foods. Many people predict it will be even more in the future.

In the '50s, nobody worried much about burger joints and chicken outlets. They offered respite to Mom and a treat for the kids. Mom-and-pop restaurants offered a variety of foods sure to please every taste. The new-style restaurants reduced the pleasure to a common denominator—the hamburger—and became known in the trade as "limited-menu" establishments.

And limited they were. In 1955, your McDonald's meal could consist of nothing but a hamburger or cheeseburger, fries, and a

THE BIGGEST FRANCHISED RESTAURANT CHAINS

COMPANY	1985 SALES ($ millions)	RESTAURANTS
1. McDonald's	11000	8901
2. Burger King	3990	4225
3. Kentucky Fried Chicken	3100	6396
4. Wendy's	2700	3459
5. Hardee's	2200	2411
6. Pizza Hut	2100	4912
7. Dairy Queen	1572	4822
8. Taco Bell	1140	2173
9. Big Boy	1135	870
10. Domino's Pizza	1097	2816
11. Arby's	814	1545
12. Church's	739	1647
13. Ponderosa	681	641
14. Long John Silver's	637	1359
15. Jack in the Box	612	822
16. Dunkin' Donuts	577	1447
17. Shoney's	576	488
18. Roy Rogers	507	540
19. Sizzler	443	465
20. Baskin-Robbins	423	3305
21. Bonanza	421	542
22. Western Sizzlin'	420	500
23. Popeye's	355	540
TOTAL	$37.239 billion	54,826 units

Excerpted with permission from Restaurant Business, March 20, 1986. Figures include overseas outlets.

beverage. That formula was good enough for Wendy's, too, which opened almost 15 years later, adding only chili—a handy receptacle for unsold burgers.

But one McDonald's has grown to more than 9,000. In late 1985, one McDonald's went up every 15 hours somewhere around the world as sales topped the $11 billion-a-year mark. Other chains built more restaurants to cash in on the quest for convenience. Now, upward of 55,000 fast-food restaurants compete for the consumer's dollar.

As for cashing in, the top 50 restaurant chains (not all of them "limited menu") sold more than $43 billion worth of food in 1984, according to the trade journal *Restaurants & Institutions*. Not surprisingly, McDonald's topped the list, with Burger King, Kentucky Fried Chicken, Wendy's, and Hardee's filling out the top five. These fast-food restaurants account for half of all sales in the top 50.

It's difficult to believe that in 1979 some analysts said America had had its fill of fast-food restaurants. There were too many already, many were closing their doors, and the future looked bleak for expansion. The nation was suffering from high gasoline prices that restricted mobility. High beef prices were a scourge to those restaurants depending on ground meat to keep prices low and customers happy.

But market saturation? Pshaw. The fast-food giants were taking a deep breath and regrouping. According to USDA statistics, fast-food sales jumped by 39.8 percent (adjusted for inflation) between 1977 and 1984. Breakfast traffic is flourishing where virtually none had been before. The fast-food business "is the fastest-moving segment of the food service industry," a National Restaurant Association (NRA) spokesperson told *The Washington Times* in late 1985.

The fast-food industry feels that until all tables are full at every time of day and there's a steady stream of cars in the drive-through lane, restaurants will not be fulfilling their potential. To keep profits growing, fast-food executives will diversify, improve, advertise, and market their products, enticing us in for yet one more cheeseburger. They are building new restaurants, redecorating old ones, and even toting some around on wheels to make that cheeseburger more pleasurable and more accessible than ever before.

IMAGE FACELIFTS

In New Orleans' historic district, the Wendy's is painted a subtle gray and fitted with red awnings. Wrought iron secures the stairways and balconies. On the Chisholm Trail in Round Rock, Texas, the Wendy's restaurant is built of rough-hewn cedar and limestone. At Rockefeller Center, in New York City, McDonald's customers choose tables on carpeted platforms amid lots of glass, tile, and neon.

All over America fast-food restaurants are changing the way they look, from the gaudy candy striping of the early days to subtler and more sophisticated designs. These attempts toward tasteful design reflect two significant changes in the fast-food market.

First, fast-food patrons are getting older, and they appreciate the sophisticated look. In pursuit of individual style, "typically, operators are aiming for subtler lighting and warm, earthy environments, reminiscent of the fern bars that overtook urban areas about 10 years ago," reported *The Wall Street Journal*, which added that restaurant volume nearly always goes up after remodeling.

Burger King, undertaking what one fast-food expert called a "massive redecorating campaign," had remodeled 30 percent of its outlets by December 1985. "We're trying to get all that plastic out," Burger King spokesperson Joyce Myers told one reporter. "We're adding on greenhouses, with real plants. We're using brass railing to queue the customers. Etched glass separates dining areas. Even the trash receptacles are surrounded with oak."

Just as important as appealing to the older customers, fast-food restaurants need to attract new ones. In the old days, restaurant operators simply needed to stake out a spot on a busy corner, put up four walls, and turn on the fryer. These days, competition is tougher, and they need to attract new customers to keep production up.

Upscale designs are one lure that attracts a broader range of people, "especially those people who have traditionally said, 'I don't go into those kinds of restaurants,'" one Wendy's franchisee told *The Wall Street Journal*.

So the operator of one New Jersey McDonald's spent $650,000, a quarter-million dollars over the average, to fit his restaurant with marble, mirrors, brass, and granite. "It's what the public wants," the owner told *The Wall Street Journal*. "Even when they go for french fries they want it to be an event." Lately reorganized Arthur Treacher's, attempting to win family business away from other fast-food restaurants, has scheduled redesigns and enlargements for its restaurants, which now seat no more than 60 people. The bigger restaurants will have more comfortable seating than the hard benches of old. Expanded interiors will include solariums "and as much glass as possible," said Edward Hamrock, spokesperson for the chain.

In fact, the fast-food restaurants are so upscale some fear they will lose the one attribute that Ray Kroc perfected so well—turnover. Kroc didn't allow pay phones or cigarette machines in his restaurants because he didn't want to have to deal with the bane of the burger joint: loitering teenagers. "Kroc wanted the teenage trade," Philip Langdon wrote in the *Atlantic Monthly,* "but he hoped to keep the transactions quick and limited."

In addition, he kept restaurant seating hard and immobile. "Sitting down at a typical McDonald's," Langdon wrote, "customers felt immediate relief in the cushioning of the seat backs. A few minutes later, however, they became restless because the seat bottom consisted of hard, uncushioned plastic." In an effort to keep the restaurant neat and the customers moving, seats were screwed to the floor. After shifting in his seat once or twice, the typical customer was on his way. Since Wendy's was designed to appeal to an older crowd, restaurant design didn't need to be so austere. Still, according to Wendy's president David Thomas, the tables at his restaurants are fitted with "four not particularly comfortable chairs." A McDonald's in Washington, D.C., goes one step further than hard chairs. It has posted numerous signs warning, "No Loitering. 20 minute time limit consuming food." Next thing you know they'll put parking meters by the tables and give tickets to slow eaters.

MORE CONVENIENT

Fast-food restaurants are being spruced up, but beauty's only skin deep. Convenience is the core of fast-food business and another way to compete for more customers.

Proximity is an important aspect of convenience—nobody wants to drive far or make dangerous turns against oncoming traffic in order to get a mediocre hamburger. In fact, many of us would rather sacrifice flavor than spend time or effort getting better food, according to a 1984 *Consumer Reports* survey. Ask people what their favorite fast food is and you're likely to get a response similar to that of this Indiana diner:

"I can tell you where I eat all the time. I can't tell you I like the food they serve there."

As competition gets tougher, the restaurants strive to make their outlets more convenient. McDonald's set up McSnack stores in areas that wouldn't accommodate larger shops. McSnacks sell only ice cream, shakes, cookies, french fries, and McNuggets. Arthur Treacher's is opening in malls after 15 years of free-standing restaurants.

In some cities, Burger King now hauls its Whoppers right up to your door or playground. It's been converting $110,000 recreational vehicles into mobile restaurants that offer everything a full-size restaurant can except onion rings, shakes, and salad bars. "It's the ultimate evolution of the fast-food industry; bring the restaurant to the people," Burger King vice president Stephen Finn told *The New York Times*. Restaurants on wheels mean additional low-cost, high-volume outlets for fast-food chains. Summer crowds on New Jersey beaches don't scare these guys. If lines get too long, clerks will "work the crowd, punching in sales on a hand-held keyboard that electronically relays the message to a printer in the van. A cook fills the order just as the customer reaches the front of the line. Employees can call in special requests on a radio headset," the newspaper reported. When summer ends and the tourists go home, the restaurant operator puts the transmission in "drive" and heads for another spot. Mobile restaurant sales have been reported as high as $3,000 per day, about average for a Burger King restaurant without wheels. A Burger King official has predicted that burger-wagons will become a major part of the restaurant system.

The search for more convenient locations inspired Wendy's to set up next to the gorilla cage at the zoo in Columbus, Ohio. There are fast-food restaurants in hospitals, on military bases, on college campuses, at museums, and floating on the Mississippi River. Burger King installed shops in Greyhound Bus stations. One analyst said toll roads are "wildly successful" locations for fast foods. State governments "would much rather have a McDonald's than a Howard Johnson's because McDonald's will double the sales," he said, and higher sales mean more money for the state because of rents and sales taxes.

Anywhere there is a consumer traffic pattern and a lunch hour, there is restaurant potential. "We finally took our blinders off and realized we had captive markets in places like K-Mart," Wendy's spokesperson Denny Lynch told *The New York Times*. Captive markets allow chains to install outlets not just on street corners, but everywhere from office buildings and schools to naval ships and museums.

It should be noted, though, that not every fast-food restaurant is greeted with open arms. Forays into wealthy neighborhoods are sometimes fended off. Burger King tried to put an outlet in affluent Great Neck, New York, in early 1986 but was kept out by angry neighbors. According to Michael and Jan Wallace, leaders of the opposition, villagers feared not just the littering, traffic congestion, and smells, but also the domino effect: first Burger King, then 17 other fast-food joints that would change the character of the community. According to *Restaurants and Institutions*, Carmel, California, has banned fast-food restaurants and several other cities are considering doing so as well.

Hospitals, in particular, are surprising sites for "limited menu" restaurants. In 1985, when a McDonald's was installed in St. Joseph's Hospital and Medical Center, in Phoenix, Arizona, Kathy Rodman, a concerned citizen, was aghast. In a letter to the president of the hospital, Ms. Rodman protested, "McDonald's is not only a symbol but in the forefront of serving largely, if not only, foods that are considered inadvisable for proper nutrition and good health. . . . In an institution dedicated to relieve suffering and to promote good health, it strikes me as ironic indeed to promote something knowingly at odds with your own aims." The president of the hospital passed the buck to McDonald's, which offered the usual pamphlets and homilies. "McDonald's has demonstrated a strong concern for the health and nutrition of the customer. . . . Our intent is not to try to change your viewpoint but to inform you of the good nutrition available at our restaurant."

CONSISTENCY

Product consistency has always been a hallmark of the fast-food restaurants. It's a quality that attracts many customers and one for which the chains pay dearly. Long John Silver's (LJS), with restaurants in 37 states, saw profits decline for more than two years. This chain set aside more than $5 million to improve employee training in 1985 and "enacted stricter quality control guidelines for the food," according to a 1985 interview with LJS chief, John Tobe.

McDonald's spends many millions more, according to *Business Week*. In addition to employee training, they have "idiot-proof" cooking machinery, said one industry watcher, including a computer-controlled french fryer. McDonald's keeps tight control over its suppliers shipping frozen prepattied beef to its restaurants and drawing strict specifications for its potatoes. "If you have a good manager, nothing can go wrong," one analyst said. "Say what you will about their product, but you always know what you're getting."

DIVERSIFIED MENUS

In 1964, a brand new Arby's opened in Boardman, Ohio, selling roast beef sandwiches, potato chips, and beverages. Today, Arby's restaurants sell burgers, fries, salads, stuffed potatoes, and much, much more.

The menu expansion that took Arby's from roast beef to croissants and baked potatoes is a relatively new concept in fast food. "Five or six years ago, fast food had no interest in new products," says Wendy's Denny Lynch. "If you were a hamburger chain, all you had to do was serve a hamburger, fries, and soft drinks; that was your formula for success." It was Wendy's president who told *Business Week* in 1977, "I've always felt that menu diversification was a sign of weakness."

In the 1980s, however, it was a sign of strength. The high price of beef forced executives to look at fish, chicken, and pork possibilities. Competing for the women's market, the restaurants began offering salad options—Wendy's found it could keep costs low by using hearts of lettuce left over from their fresh lettuce-topped hamburgers. In addition, many consumer taste buds were tiring of burgers.

Restaurants galore have joined the baked-potato bandwagon, stuffing spuds with everything from chicken à la king to taco mix. Salad sales are fiercely competitive. Wendy's salad bar is "one of the industry's most prominent successes," according to *Advertising Age* magazine. And the salad bars at Burger King, Roy Rogers, and D'Lites are a great alternative to burgers, too. McDonald's, slow out of the starting gate, is testing several varieties of prepackaged salads in a thousand outlets.

Not only are burger joints diversifying their menus, but the fast-food market itself continues to broaden. The Mexican food business began to realize its potential in the early '80s. Its strong point was a culinary paradox—they offered something more than hamburgers. But not too much more. They serve the same food—beef, cheese, tomato, and lettuce—but throw in a tortilla and just enough spice so that if you close your eyes you won't think you're at Burger King. Consumers tired of burgers can choose from not-very-spicy burritos, tostadas, and tacos. "My family loves it because they don't like spicy food," says one mother about their meals at Taco Bell.

Pizza popularity continues to increase, with home delivery being the big change. *Restaurant Business* calls the growth of pizza restaurants a "significant trend," with "faster than a speeding bullet" Domino's pizza becoming the tenth largest restaurant in 1985.

Long John Silver's, the country's largest quick-service seafood chain, expanded the batter-fried menu to include breaded-fried items and nonfish entrées such as batter-fried chicken and breaded chicken nuggets. In its four-point plan to attract more customers and win loyalty among present ones, the chain has expanded its line of summer seafood salads and has tested broiled foods in three markets.

Several factors affect menu changes. If food prices go off the map, as beef prices did in the late '70s, a restaurant will naturally seek alternatives to keep costs low, as Wendy's did with the salad bar. Sometimes menus expand because corporate headquarters wants to test a trend—Pizza Hut tested the regional food trend by selling barbecued pizza in Louisville. If the product succeeds—barbecued pizza did not—it winds up on menus nationwide.

Depending on how liberal the corporate chiefs are, restaurant franchisees are sometimes permitted to test their own ideas. The McD.L.T. came from a Texan who asked a local packager to come up with a box that could hold hot food on one side and cold food on the other so that the fresh vegetables wouldn't stew when they hit hot meat. Once he proved the success of the product, corporate headquarters bought it and offered it nationwide, to the drumroll of a multi-million-dollar advertising blitz.

Does diversity mean nutrition? In some cases, yes. The McD.L.T. obviously improves on the old burger idea by adding a small amount of fiber- and vitamin-containing vegetables. The burger also helps McDonald's compete with similar products sold at Wendy's, Carl's Jr., and at other fast-food restaurants. Plain baked potatoes, salad bars, and broiled chicken and fish all potentially improve your diet—especially if you choose them over fried potatoes, fried chicken, and fried fish.

Yet it seems that with every new healthful item comes another unhealthful one. The bacon-cheese-topping syndrome spread from restaurant to restaurant, adding extra fat and sodium to sandwiches. Fatty biscuits and croissants are replacing bread and rolls. Salads are only as good as their ingredients and if you pour on the bacon bits and full-fat salad dressing you might not be doing your health a favor.

Many fast-food restaurant executives claim that what people say and what they do are two entirely different things. Fast foods are popular, the restaurateurs say, because, although people say they want nutritious foods, they actually buy for taste and convenience. But Americans' attitudes about eating are changing, and eating habits will also change, as day follows night. Ten years ago, people would have laughed if someone had suggested that hamburger joints would have handsome salad bars. Could vegetarian burgers be too far away?

Diversity generally does not mean speed. As fast-food restaurants offer more menu choices, they become decidedly less fast. It's not uncommon to stand in line for five minutes and then have to wait, standing, another five or ten minutes for an item to be prepared. The most extreme example we encountered occurred at a Popeyes. We asked for corn on the cob and were told that we would have to wait 35 minutes.

ADVERTISING

If menu diversity, convenient location, and chic decor aren't enough to lure you in, the restaurants also saturate the airwaves—and you—with commercials. From "Dallas" and "Hill Street Blues" to the Olympics, fast-food purveyors use television to create or increase your yearning for flame-broiled burgers, biscuits, and Big Macs. In 1985, the restaurant chains spent more than $1 billion on television advertising alone, according to *Advertising Age*. The budget for all forms of advertising and promotions was probably close to $2 billion.

McDonald's, the restaurant with top sales, not coincidentally spends the most on advertising. In 1985, the company spent $686 million in the United States and overseas on advertisements and promotions. More than half a billion dollars! It boggles the mind.

McDonald's runs so many commercials that it built a specially equipped "restaurant" to serve as a set for use by its ad agency and filmmakers. Burger King invested $15 million to advertise the vital message that the "Croissan'wich beat the stuffin' out of Egg McMuffin two-to-one in consumer taste tests," according to *The Wall Street Journal.* The same company spent $40 million in an—ultimately futile—effort to get America searching for Herb. And McDonald's inundated Americans with over $5 million a week in advertising for its McD.L.T. sandwich. With ad blitzes like these, it's likely that 1986

RESTAURANT TELEVISION ADVERTISING (1985)*

COMPANY	AD SPENDING ($ millions)
1. McDonald's	$302.8
2. Burger King	$155.0
3. Wendy's	$83.7
4. Kentucky Fried Chicken	$75.3
5. Pizza Hut	$63.3
6. Taco Bell	$38.7
7. Hardee's	$32.3
8. Red Lobster	$27.7
9. Long John Silver's	$26.3
10. Denny's	$23.0
11. Domino's Pizza	$17.4
12. Arby's	$15.9
13. Sizzler	$14.1
14. Jack in the Box	$12.6
15. Dairy Queen	$11.9
TOTAL	$900 million

Expenditures in the United States; excerpted with permission, from the March 17, 1986, issue of Advertising Age, *copyright © 1986 by Crain Communications Inc.*

advertising expenditures will not only greatly exceed those of 1985, but will probably drive some marginal companies out of business (for better or for worse).

Of course, paid television promotion is only one small part of the overall advertising picture. Burger King's favorite nerd, Herb, flashed $5,000 giveaways in outlets across America. And who could put a dollar amount on the exposure McDonald's got during the 1984 Olympics when the golden arches showed up on every dive during the diving competition?

And don't forget the big screen. McDonald's presence in Stephen Spielberg's "Back to the Future" was no accident, and ditto for "Moscow on the Hudson." The favor of showing McDonald's restaurants in the 1985 feature, "Santa Claus, the Movie," was repaid when McDonald's publicized the movie in its thousands of restaurants. These dollars buy an image. In "Back to the Future," for instance, McDonald's appears as the quintessential middle-class teenage work experience.

THE CHILDREN'S MARKET

During the 1985 Christmas season, a fetching young girl tells other kids how to get their own Huggletts stuffed animals from Taco Bell. All they have to do is convince Mom and Dad how useful the Huggletts are. She states several chores the Huggletts can do—walking the dog, for instance. And, if Mom and Dad don't buy the argument, kids can always get Grandma to take them to Taco Bell for a Hugglett.

Huggletts are only one of the varied and ever-changing ploys directed at children to get them into a specific fast-food restaurant: Star Wars and Star Trek, Care Bears, Masters of the Universe, and Fast Macs—the themes change with the times.

Children mean big business for the fast-food industry. Once you've hooked the children, getting their parents' business is no problem. Survey after survey shows that parents let their children make restaurant choices. "I'll say, 'what do you want to eat tonight, kids?' and it's a majority vote," said Angela Partee, a single mother whose family eats out about once a week.

Consumer Reports' readers preferred the food at Wendy's, but when they chose restaurants "to please someone else" (typically children, according to this magazine's editors) they drove into Mc-Donald's. Mrs. Partee concurs. Her children like the "happy meal" because "it makes it more like a treat . . . something more than dinner," despite the fact that, "I don't think the hamburgers are very good there; it reminds me of economy meat." Consumers prefer the taste of Burger King and Wendy's hamburgers, says *Consumer Reports,* but their children respond to McDonald's marketing. Advertising research showed that "parents will pay 20 percent more for an advertised product with child appeal—even when the less expensive, nonadvertised product is no different," writes Stan Luxenberg in *Roadside Empires,* a book about the business of franchising (See Appendix).

So parents take their children to Hardee's for a recorded Gremlins story, and return a week later for the next in the series. If Masters of the Universe cartoons appeal to children, their images on cups will, no doubt, draw them into Burger King.

Targeting children as customers is important enough to attract millions of advertising dollars. Burger King spends millions to promote Magic Burger King, and we can safely presume that an effort of this magnitude results in increased sales.

"The popularity and success of fast food has been characterized as a marketing phenomenon rather than as a food phenomenon," then Senator George McGovern said when he convened a Senate hearing to look at fast-food labeling in 1976. He referred specifically to a 1972 survey showing that 96 percent of schoolchildren knew of Ronald McDonald. If that were true (apparently the survey was very limited), it would mean that Ronald was better known than any other figure except Santa Claus.

It probably isn't too far from the truth. After all, Santa only visits once a year, but Ronald visits every Saturday morning via television and sometimes in person—50 Ronalds travel to restaurants around the United States spreading the word about Big Macs. The executive of a competing chain called Ronald a "Pied Piper" who's brought millions of children into McDonald's.

In some outlets, a mother can arrange a birthday party for her child and at least seven others at McDonald's. The restaurant supplies each child with a "happy meal" (burger, fries, cookie, and soft drink), party hats, and favor-type toys. McDonald's hasn't forgotten the cake—not decorated with "Happy Birthday, Jennifer," but with a picture of Ronald himself and sugar-formed edible characters from McDonaldland.

For $3.50 a head "you have a place to have a party and your home isn't wrecked," said one mother. Obviously it's a plus for parents. Not surprisingly, about one fifth of McDonald's sales come from people under 15 years old, according to *Business Week*. "The company continues to pour money into its traditional Saturday morning television ads promoting Ronald McDonald," the magazine reported in 1977, "which as much as anything else explains why McDonald's dominates the children's market."

McDonald's spending leaves all other restaurants in the dust. When Wendy's first approached the children's market in 1986 with a major commitment, the company depended on in-store promotion of Gummi Bears and enough Saturday morning advertising to rival McDonald's. A Wendy's spokesperson told *Advertising Age*, "We're so outspent [in the children's market] that we couldn't get in with just a few million dollars."

Playgrounds are another attraction and so good for business that McDonald's will put them indoors, if need be, even in Manhattan where floor space is at a premium. "Restaurants with playgrounds have higher sales than restaurants without," said Joe Edwards, of the *Nation's Restaurant News*.

While the right hand sells birthday cakes, hamburgers, fries, cookies, and the image of Ronald McDonald to young children, the left hand reinforces the McDonald's logo to elementary schoolchildren—and with the blessing of school systems. McDonald's representatives developed an "Eating Right, Feeling Fit" nutrition and exercise package for schoolchildren with reproducible materials—all bearing the big M logo—and a comic book with pictures of squeaky clean Olympic gymnast, Mary Lou Retton, doing exercises with all the McDonaldland characters. McDonald's ploy of "innocence by association" spurred a nutritionist with the Chicago Heart Association to say, "Personally, I find it incongruous. McDonald's has incredible chutzpah." A food company that really cared about fitness would do something about its products that are literally oozing with fat.

These promotional techniques pervade the seemingly non-commercial and objective world of the family pediatrician and dentist, who, in cahoots with guess McWho, give out "bravery prescriptions," entitling the bearer to a free hamburger.

McDonald's is virtually the only restaurant chain with bucks big enough for these kinds of handouts, according to Scott Hume, of *Advertising Age*. But many of the restaurants now offer or plan to offer packages specially designed for children. Hardee's has an "action meal" with puzzles and games on a package containing a small burger, french fries, and a small soft drink. Arby's offers "adventure meals"—a small roast beef sandwich packaged with fries, a drink, and a prize.

Roy Rogers established the Buckaroo Club for children under ten years old. Children are issued identification cards that they flash every time they come in for a meal. The card allows them a "free small Coke or other soft drink" when they buy a sandwich, chicken, or platter.

The McDonald's "happy meal" is created with mix-and-match choices that allow some flexibility in ordering, but the cost of the total meal (including premium) is more than the sum of its food parts. Other restaurants don't always allow parents to substitute more nutritious foods. An Arby's clerk in Louisville had no problem substituting milk for a soft drink, but a Wendy's clerk in Olean, New York, refused to make a similar switch. Even if both child and restaurant agree to substitute milk, the meal is generally lacking fiber, vitamin A, vitamin C, and several B vitamins (B-6, folic acid, and pantothenic acid).

For kids a little older, McDonald's hired Menudo, a pubescent Puerto Rican rock group that appealed to the preteens in the ever-growing Hispanic market, as pitchmen for its McNuggets and Big Macs. Fast-food restaurants are an obvious choice for young teenagers who want to congregate with their friends after school. For the price of a cola and maybe some french fries, they have an afternoon of entertainment.

"Growing children shouldn't eat in fast-food restaurants more than once a week because the amount of calories is out of proportion to the amount of nutrients," Dr. Judith Anderson told *The Detroit News*. A dietician and nutrition professor at Michigan State University, Anderson cautioned that a high proportion of the calories in typical fast foods comes from fat and sugar. The average seven- to ten-year-old needs about 2,400 calories per day and should consume no more than 1,800 milligrams of sodium and 80 grams (18 teaspoons) of fat throughout the day. (See page 104, for the appropriate intakes for other age groups.) A

Whopper, onion rings, and a medium Pepsi yield 1,073 calories and 13 teaspoons of fat, plus 1,532 milligrams of sodium and 10 teaspoons of sugar.

A McNugget here and a fried pie there—pretty soon it adds up to bad nutrition. It's unfortunate that the giant restaurant chains don't use their marketing savvy to promote good eating habits while they make a buck. It would be so easy to develop special kids' packages containing fruit, juice, or milk instead of soft drinks and french fries.

BREAKFAST

Other battles are fought on the breakfast front, a relatively new territory for the fast-food industry. The morning meal is proving to be as lucrative for the restaurants as it is unhealthful for consumers.

In 1972, McDonald's put an egg, cheese, and Canadian bacon in the middle of an English muffin and began selling the product in selected markets. By 1976, Egg McMuffin was a national product and breakfast was a fast-food phenomenon.

"None of us would be serving breakfast if McDonald's hadn't spent tons of money educating the public that you could get a good breakfast at a fast-food restaurant," said Paul Mitchell, of California-based Carl's Jr. restaurant chain. Carl's now sells orange juice and its own "sunrise sandwich"—an English muffin topped with egg, meat, and cheese.

How "good" these meals are depends on your point of view. Certainly, if you have a vested interest in the fast-food business you would say they are very good. Between 1977 and 1984, restaurant breakfast traffic increased 57 percent, according to *The Wall Street Journal*. Breakfast now accounts for 15 percent of McDonald's $11 billion sales. That's a lot of muffins. Fifteen years ago, McDonald's wasn't even open in the morning.

In addition, breakfast attracts customers who don't usually eat fast foods. Traditionally, the older you get, the less fast food appeals to you. But breakfast attracts these older consumers and brings in new dollars for the companies. Ironically, some of these breakfast converts are concerned about health. "Some restaurants are attracting people who used to skip breakfast but now consider it an important part of their diet," reported *The Wall Street Journal*. While it isn't wise to skip breakfast, a look at the nutrient contribution of some fast-food breakfast choices might provoke consumers to seek more healthful choices.

Some Roy Rogers outlets offer an all-you-can-eat buffet so laden with fat you can feel your arteries stiffen as you read the choices—bacon, eggs, crescent sandwiches that provide 60 percent of their calories in the form of fat. Hardee's—whose plain biscuit contains five teaspoons of fat—tempts us with ham-, sausage-, or bacon-topped biscuits with or without eggs. Wendy's trademark is omelets, served with high-fat, salty breakfast meats. After experimenting with breakfast for six years, Burger King has abandoned biscuits and muffins in favor of croissants that, already high in fat, come topped with fatty cheese and meats.

Tests will continue, no doubt, because the breakfast market is still up for grabs. Only five percent of adults eat breakfast in fast-food restaurants, reports *The Wall Street Journal,* compared with 20 percent at lunch and 16 percent at dinner. Whether low-fat, low-sodium foods win a respectable place on breakfast menus remains to be seen. Yogurt and bran muffins seem an unlikely step for a Roy Rogers manager who told *The Wall Street Journal,* "There's only so much you can do with your menu because most people still crave the traditional American breakfast—bacon, eggs, and orange juice. If you get too cute, you're just throwing money away."

Still, there's a glimmer of hope. Atlanta-based D'Lites is testing breakfast now with low-fat bacon and sausage products, multi-grain croissants, whole-wheat pancakes, fresh fruit tables, and five kinds of muffins.

A GLIMPSE INTO THE FUTURE

As the restaurants proliferate, so do concerns about health and about diets built on fried meat, fried potatoes, and soft drinks. The representatives of many restaurant companies defend the industry by insisting that nobody encourages consumers to eat 21 meals a week at fast-food restaurants, although it's hard to imagine their objecting if consumers suddenly chose to do so. Statistics show that we eat more fast food every year, and the chain restaurants aren't spending upward of $1 billion a year suggesting that maybe you should stay home tonight and fix yourself low-fat cottage cheese with sliced fruit.

What does the future hold for fast-food restaurants and fast-food consumers? Will fast food become more nutritious or less so? Are there too many fast-food restaurants now or will the industry continue to grow? Will they deliver foods to our homes? Will they change their menus in order to compete with innovative supermarkets?

Judging from the past, the fast-food industry will become far bigger and more diverse. That means fewer independent restaurants and more empty wrappers littering our neighborhoods. While the conventional fast-food market seems as stuffed as the consumer of a triple cheeseburger, the future holds promise for a good product under good management, said one analyst. The U.S. market has room for unconventional fast-food outlets, and there is plenty of room on the highways of the Far East, Latin America, and Europe. But you can bet that some large chains will falter, fold, or be taken over by other chains.

One thing is certain. We're all getting older. As the baby boom grows up, the median age of Americans increases, and as we get older, we worry more about health and weight and care less about speedy eating.

Between competition among themselves and an audience growing more indifferent with age, fast-food companies will have to do everything short of back flips to lure us into their restaurants. Remodeled menus and restaurants augur these attempts. The future holds more.

OVERSEAS EXPANSION

Conventional restaurants—the McDonald's as we know them now—have plenty of room to expand abroad. There's only one pair of golden arches in Mexico, only one in Italy (though several thousand Romans rallied to protest the hamburger invasion, McDonald's is planning an expansion, not a retreat). Many markets outside the United States are virtually untouched and provide literally billions of potential consumers of burgers, fried chicken, franchise-style pizza, and even mass-produced doughnuts.

The "Pacific Rim" is especially attractive to these expanding chains, some of which are already well established there. As of November 1985, Kentucky Fried Chicken had 511 restaurants in Japan. McDonald's had 450 restaurants in Japan (as many as in Canada and more than a third of all holdings abroad), according to *Restaurant*

Business magazine. After touring Japan, one American restaurant executive told *Restaurant Business*, "I think the Japanese are more American than we are."

The foreign markets hold concentrated populations and promise heavy traffic, which means higher sales volume per restaurant. A McDonald's in Taiwan does twice as much business as the average U.S. restaurant. Domino's is delivering in London. Restaurants serve wine with fast food in France, beer with the burgers in Germany.

THE DINNER MARKET

In the United States, the industry talks about dinner; that is, special dinner foods with higher prices to create a new category of dining. Currently, fast foods appeal to lunch crowds with 40 percent of business typically being done between 11 A.M. and 2 P.M., said Joe Edwards, of the *Nation's Restaurant News*. A special dinner menu would have to be different enough to attract customers who have eaten a fast-food lunch and attract people who presently don't think of fast food as a real meal. "Industry insiders agree that fast-food chains' new product attention for the next few years will be focused primarily on dinner items," *Advertising Age* reported in February 1985.

Initial attempts haven't been terrifically successful. Burger King's attempts at dinner platters with vegetables failed. Wendy's can't seem to move the "dinner" idea out of test markets in Cincinnati. So far, people seem to resist paying high prices for upscale fast food. If they want to pay $6 for dinner, they can go to a full-service restaurant.

In order to convince consumers that they offer something more for dinner, the wine and beer service offered tentatively by D'Lites may become commonplace in fast-food restaurants, according to fast-food analyst Ron Paul of Technomic Consultants. Restaurants may also try table service, although California-based Carl's Jr. has already failed to carry that off.

THE NEW TV DINNERS

High technology, including VCRs and giant-screen televisions, may affect fast-food restaurants indirectly. One pizza chain executive told *Restaurant Business*, "A large part of [discretionary income] is spent on the home environment. The baby-boomer family is beginning to seek an eating experience that can be enjoyed within the luxury of the home." As a result, TV dinners may take on a whole new meaning. The next feeding boom is likely to be in frozen dinners and supermarket delis and salad bars. Supermarkets might well wage a successful counterattack on the franchised restaurants that have taken billions of dollars a year out of supermarket cash registers.

If these predictions prove accurate, pizza makers may be in better shape than many competitors. Baby boomers became familiar with delivered pizza on their college campuses, and Domino's carries the tradition into suburban neighborhoods.

Other fast-food restaurants may have trouble convincing the public to call for home-delivered chicken and burgers. Kentucky Fried Chicken has tried home delivery in Louisville without remarkable success. Wendy's subsidiary, Sister's, tried home delivery but dropped it because of high costs and bogus orders. And, according to *The Wall Street Journal*, the food at burger joints doesn't hold up on delivery. Nobody wants a limp french fry.

So they may try multiple drive-through windows, says analyst Ron Paul. Some restaurants are already testing the concept, which reduces the wait and eliminates the need for consumers to get out of their cars. Long drive-through lines are a visible deterrent for the fast-food consumer in a hurry to get home to watch TV with his or her children. Paul says it is likely that conventional fast-food restaurants will begin the phone-ahead order system that has been used for years with pizza parlors.

MORE NUTRITIOUS ALTERNATIVES?

Will the food get more nutritious? Fast-food operators discuss nutrition out of both sides of their mouths. From one side, they say the public doesn't want nutritious food. From the other side, they are touting the nutritious qualities of the foods they serve.

"Our research states that consumers will talk about nutrition, but they buy taste, convenience, and value," said Wendy's spokesperson Denny Lynch. This may mean that, in the future, fast-food companies might try a novel approach such as offering nutritious food that tastes good. "The biggest marketing challenge, fast-food operators seem to agree, is transforming the nutrition concept from a consumer turnoff into a palatable selling strategy," *Advertising Age* reported in late 1985 after a convention of fast-food operators.

New-age restaurateur Clark Heinrich seems to have met the challenge—with soybean foods, no less. His vegetarian fast-food McDharma opened in California in 1982 to offer an alternative to traditional fast food—double-decker vegetarian sandwiches, beans, and frozen yogurt. If you can sell tofu burgers at a fast-food restaurant, you should be able to sell anything. (If you want to call it McAnything, however, you might have to tangle with McDonald's in court, as Heinrich found out when he was sued over use of the "Mc" prefix.)

Though McDonald's is testing a skinless, roast-chicken dish (Chicken L.T.), in general, the traditional fast-food restaurants seem reluctant to sell nutritious foods. On the other hand, some new boys on the block are eager to earn those health-conscious dollars. It may take this type of competition, or some new blood pumping through 20-year-old promotion departments, to identify marketable products outside the fried, salted, and sweetened framework. In 1981, Atlanta-based D'Lites was opened by a former health-club owner and Wendy's franchisee. This new chain is to fast food what Miller Lite was to beer—an alternative. Besides offering a multi-grain bun and "lite" mayonnaise on its sandwiches, D'Lites offers lower-calorie versions of many traditional fish and chicken items. "In our restaurants you have a choice," a D'Lites restaurant owner told the *Fort Lauderdale News/ Sun Sentinel.* "You can certainly eat some things that people say may not be good for you. But you can also eat things extremely good for you." Some industry observers think the competition may cause enough positive changes in bigger chains to put D'Lites out of business. (Regrettably, in August 1986 D'Lites cut back from 100 outlets to 10, all in Atlanta, when financial stresses forced the chain to reorganize under bankruptcy law.)

Wendy's joined the nutrition bandwagon by combining standard menu items into a marketing tool called a "Light Menu." Started in 1985, it includes the plain baked potato, the salad bar and the side salad, diet soft drinks, and the multi-grain bun. The upgraded salad bar includes 20 items, including fresh fruits and vegetables that are rotated according to season, and four reduced-calorie dressings. While only 20 percent of sandwiches were sold on multi-grain buns in 1985, Lynch predicted that the bun sales would increase to 80 percent by 1990.

From Muncie, Indiana, comes another upstart and more competition. The hypertensive wife of a Kentucky-Fried-Chicken franchisee developed a low-fat, low-sodium chicken product that resembles fast-food fried chicken. Carolyn Duncan, who has high blood cholesterol and triglycerides in addition to her high blood pressure, said, "You can't find any place out there to go eat," if you're concerned about your health.

Saying "there's got to be a better way; there's got to be a way to [sell chicken] without the grease," Mrs. Duncan opened C. J. Carryl's in September 1985. The restaurant offers her secret chicken recipe that is cooked with hot air in a method Mrs. Duncan compares to hot-air popcorn. The fried-chicken dinner offers sides of green beans and carrots, in addition to her low-sodium mashed potatoes and gravy. She's lowered the sodium in her biscuits, offers slaw and a salad bar. She's created a fast-food restaurant with alternatives to the high-fat, high-sodium foods offered by her husband's restaurants, whose parent company requires that chicken be marinated in a high-salt mixture and then pressure-cooked in deep fat. The challenge for the Mrs. Duncans of the world, of course, is to expand from a few owner-controlled outlets into a major chain. Fresher Cooker, one outfit that tried, has had severe financial problems.

Simultaneous and independent developments indicate this hot-air technology may let us have our french fries and our nutrition, too. A new oven that circulates hot air has been used commercially by food processors like Stouffer's to reduce the fat content of food as it cooks. Originally designed to be used on board ships to avoid fires, this "Rair" oven can reduce the fat content of precut and fried potatoes by almost half. Currently, it is a slow and relatively expensive way to cook potatoes, according to one former fast-food executive, but it demonstrates that technology improves the possibility of getting more nutritious food into restaurants.

Paul Wenner, who heads Wholesome & Hearty Foods in Portland, Oregon, is an entrepreneur who has another approach to healthful fast-food eating. He has invented the Gardenburger. While it looks like a hamburger, it is made of mushrooms, onions, rolled oats, and other natural ingredients. It has one third fewer calories and less than half as much fat as a comparable hamburger. And judging from its growing popularity in dozens of restaurants, hospitals, and even local sports stadiums, the Gardenburger might spread like wildfire.

The surge of Mexican-style fast food in the early '80s foreshadows the next round of competition—Italian and Chinese fast food. Analysts say Italian fast food (other than pizza) is virgin territory, and only small inroads have been made by Chinese chains. Both of these cuisines offer many low-fat possibilities, high in complex carbohydrates, that would provide nutritious and delicious alternatives to burgers.

While food processors have shown us they can add salt and fat to just about any food, the precedent set by Quik Wok may improve standards. Burger King (a subsidiary of Pillsbury) bought the nine-restaurant chain that boasts fresh Chinese food prepared in an average of 45 seconds per order, according to *Restaurant Business*. Much of this is dinner food—the up-and-coming battleground for fast-food restaurants. Chicago cardiologist Anthony Q. Chan is also testing Oriental fast food, with his small chain of Xian restaurants. On the other hand, the Denver-based Tokyo Bowl has declared bankruptcy.

"Though food costs [at Quik Wok] are high because of the emphasis Chinese cooking places on fresh ingredients, tight operational controls maximize profitability and keep dinner prices low," *Restaurant Business* reported. Fresh food can indeed create black numbers in the company ledger.

On the other hand, restaurants that have built a reputation on selling greasy fried food might not see a need to change. A Church's Fried Chicken representative told *Advertising Age* that nutrition is not a valuable marketing tool and said he's "ignored" the trend, believing that people don't practice what they know to be nutritious eating habits.

To say the public won't eat nutritious food is like saying the public won't eat ice cream, based on the dismal sales of McDonald's Tripple Ripple, or saying the public won't eat barbecued ribs because Arby's couldn't sell them, or saying the public won't eat tuna fish because the sales at Wendy's were poor. Obviously people eat all of those things and, if surveys are to be believed, are more concerned each year about the calories, fat, sodium, and additives they consume. A 1983 Gallup survey showed that six out of ten consumers had changed their eating habits at home by eating more fruits, vegetables, and whole grains and decreasing their intake of refined sugar, animal fats, and salt. Four out of ten adults said they sustained those dietary changes when eating out. More than half of consumers interviewed considered nutrition an important aspect of fast food. Since 1983, additional data has revealed links between poor nutrition and the diseases that kill most Americans. It is not likely that the number of people watching their nutrient intake has decreased since this Gallup poll.

Fast-food restaurants have come a long way since they sold hamburgers and fries for 25 cents. For the good of the country's health and economy, they could go a lot further. The public can take an active role in changing fast food by choosing the most nutritious food offered. Highly motivated consumers might write companies with compliments and/or complaints (see Appendix for addresses) and also write their legislators to encourage passage of laws that would make ingredient and nutrition information readily accessible.

For many reasons fast food has become a way of life. But the more we eat out, the more questions we have about the quality of our diets. Many of the questions are basic. Is fast food junk food? Other questions aren't so basic. People with food allergies or other health concerns often ask specific questions about preservatives, artificial colorings, and other additives.

Zealous health advocates might declare that all fast food is poison, but those of us with jobs, children, and/or little time or enthusiasm for cooking know better. We aren't going to die from eating an occasional double cheeseburger and fries.

Still we also know that burgers and fries don't rate up there with broccoli as food of the week. And if one fifth of American adults, on a typical day, go in for "a grease job," as *Washington Post* columnist Colman McCarthy so pithily stated, it might be prudent to consider what food choices will keep us healthier, longer.

Is it possible that we can have convenience and nutrition all wrapped up in food that the kids will eat? A little nutrition knowledge goes a long way in helping us make decisions. As we shall see in the next chapter, when we know about common health problems and how food affects them, we can make wiser choices about what we eat.

THE HEALTH YOU SAVE MAY BE YOUR OWN

I f food had no more effect on our well-being than socks or wristwatches, Americans would hardly be concerned about it. But what we eat has a major impact on both our physical and mental health.

Health has long been thought of as freedom from infectious diseases or nutritional deficiencies. For most Americans, that definition is no longer relevant. Over the years, vaccines and medicines have freed us from the fear of infectious diseases like polio and tuberculosis. Federal food programs, such as school lunches, combined with higher incomes and food fortification have all but eliminated scurvy, rickets, and other "deficiency diseases" arising from inadequate diets.

Now we define health a little differently. Since infectious and deficiency diseases have been eradicated or are easily controlled, our attention turns to combating chronic, degenerative diseases. Degenerative diseases are the long-term conditions that gradually erode our health before they kill us—insidiously harmful diseases that sometimes lurk unnoticed for years, like cancer or high blood pressure, or that debilitate us, such as heart attack and stroke.

Unfortunately, drugs can't always treat these conditions. Those drugs that do treat don't cure, and many have unpleasant side effects. Diuretics, used to treat hypertension, may also increase blood cholesterol and cause sexual dysfunction, diarrhea, drowsiness, and headaches. One antihypertensive drug, Selacryn, was removed from the market after it was shown to cause liver damage and ultimately death. Even if the drugs didn't have side effects, however, a lifetime of paying for medications can cost a bundle.

The coronary-bypass operation has been a widely used method of treating heart disease, yet this incredibly expensive procedure increases life expectancy for only a small proportion of patients.

Fortunately, sophisticated research has shown that many of these diseases can be postponed for many years, or even avoided entirely, simply by taking good care of ourselves—by not smoking, by exercising, and by eating the proper foods.

Fast food, which comprises a growing portion of the national diet, is sometimes sold as "fun food," as much a toy as a source of sustenance for our bodies. The U.S. Department of Agriculture (USDA), which analyzes virtually every aspect of the nation's food system, has expressed concern about the nutritional adequacy of a diet that relies on fast foods. Karen Bunch, of USDA's Economic Research Service, contends,

> The trend toward eating more fast food reduces the variety in our diets and may increase the risk of nutritional deficiency. For example, a typical fast-food meal of a hamburger, french fries, and milk shake contains approximately half the Recommended Daily Allowances (RDA) of calories and protein for the adult male. Yet that meal gives him only one third of the RDA of vitamin C, thiamin, and niacin, and lesser amounts of iron, calcium, vitamin A, and riboflavin. The meal's large calorie count reflects a high fat level.

So, what are the proper foods? It can be difficult to tell in these days of mixed messages, when tricky advertising claims make even boxed cake mix with Jell-O stripes sound like a health food. Sometimes even health professionals seem to disagree among themselves.

 # DIETARY GUIDELINES

A look at the history of nutrition explains the confusion. Some health professionals, who may have studied nutrition several decades ago, still subscribe to the "all food is good food" concept that was popular before research showed that too much of some foods was, in fact, linked to bad health. These people learned World War II nutrition theories—when many men who enlisted in the armed forces were so malnourished that the government started a school-lunch program to make sure the next generation received at least one nutritious meal each day.

You can recognize these old-style nutritionists (some of whom aren't very old) when they insist that even empty-calorie foods, such as soft drinks, have a place in the diet, and that fat is an important source of vitamin E and calories, makes us feel full, and makes our food taste good. This philosophy comes in part from a Depression-era, food-shortage mentality. It is still appropriate today in many developing countries where starvation is more threatening than chronic disease, and where all food may indeed be good food. But overfed Americans— 34 million of whom are obese—cannot afford to live by the same rules by which Ethiopians live. Even Americans who aren't overweight still need a diet that reduces their risk of heart disease and cancer.

Degenerative diseases are difficult to study because, unlike infectious diseases, there's no one "bug" that causes them. The characteristics of an unhealthful lifestyle are linked together in a web of cause-and-effect mysteries that are difficult to isolate. Decades must pass before their ravages take hold, and reversibility is difficult to measure.

But the U.S. Departments of Agriculture and Health and Human Services recognize that a massive amount of evidence links the typical American diet to many of our most common diseases. These two government agencies have developed a new national nutrition policy known as the "Dietary Guidelines for Americans." The current guidelines, first issued in 1980, and revised slightly in 1985, are:

❑ Eat a variety of foods.

❑ Maintain desirable weight.

❑ Avoid too much fat, saturated fat, and cholesterol.

❑ Eat foods with adequate starch and fiber.

❑ Avoid too much sugar.

❑ Avoid too much sodium.

❑ If you drink alcohol, do so in moderation.

These are the modern recommendations in their mildest form. Other health organizations—including the National Cancer Institute and the American Heart Association—make somewhat stronger and more specific recommendations about the quantities of fat, cholesterol, sodium, and dietary fiber that people should consume. These rules imply that in our affluent society all food is not necessarily good food. Some foods *are* better than others. Where do fast foods fit in? Chosen with care, fast foods can be included in a healthful diet. But there is a wide world of high-fat, high-sodium, low-fiber foods available at fast-food restaurants, and it takes some expertise to pick your way through a menu for healthful choices. Advertisements don't always help. Arby's has advertised that its sandwiches give consumers "the lean advantage," although some of the sandwiches contain eight teaspoons of fat, representing as much as 55 percent of their calories.

The fast-food companies' ad writers, food technologists, and consumer psychologists devote their careers to developing ways to persuade you to buy their products. While even a Ph.D. nutritionist can be tricked by some of the industry's carefully worded claims, understanding basic nutrition principles can shift the odds in your favor when you sally forth into the fast-food restaurant jungle.

CLARIFYING THE OLD RULES

Back in the days when all food was considered good food, health professionals were guided by a basic tenet: Eating a variety of foods would provide you with all the necessary nutrients. Times changed and so did the concepts. When obesity and chronic diseases became more troublesome, health professionals added "moderation" to the concept of variety. But the health status of Americans shows that this advice wasn't nearly specific enough to clear up questions about healthful eating. Obviously, if you think that variety means choosing from among soft drinks—Coke today, 7-Up tomorrow, and so on—you won't be the healthier for it. Likewise, if you believe that moderation means limiting your dinner to one double cheeseburger, a chocolate shake, and a large order of fries, you might have a misdirected sense of nutrition. The old Basic Four could easily mean a hot dog (protein) on a white bun (grain), fries (vegetable), and ice cream (dairy).

A variety of foods in moderate portions should be chosen within a prudent nutritional framework—the diet should get no more than 25 to 30 percent of its calories from fat, should contain no more than 1,100 to 3,300 milligrams of sodium daily, and should include plenty of foods high in fiber and few high in sugar. A prudent eating pattern should contain only enough calories to maintain your weight no higher than ten percent above what is ideal for your height and body frame.

Without the help of a computer, it's difficult to monitor your diet according to these recommendations. It's only a little easier if you remember that 3,300 milligrams of sodium is found in 1½ teaspoons of salt, and 30 percent of calories from fat would be roughly 15 teaspoons per day (2,000-calorie diet). Obviously, working with these numbers is much more difficult than it is to identify and cut down on foods high in fat and sodium.

You'll probably find that such a health-promoting diet contains many foods close to their natural state. Eating a variety of fruits and vegetables, whole grains, beans, lean meats and chicken, fish, and low-fat milk products will help you attain these goals. To be healthier, Americans need to readjust the proportions of food they eat, depending less on meat, fatty rich desserts, and soft drinks, and more on high-fiber grains, beans, vegetables, and fruits. Unfortunately, fast-food restaurants do not excel in such a diet. And all too often the narrow variety of fast-food options excludes foods high in vitamins A and C and dietary fiber, while giving us foods loaded with fat.

If fast foods were a limited phenomenon, there would be little cause for alarm. But fast foods have gone beyond the drive-through window. An occasional fast-food meal no longer merely interrupts a prudent pattern of food choices. Food from over 55,000 fast-food restaurants feeds 46 million people every day. In addition, fast foods survive where meat loaf fails: In school lunchrooms and military dining rooms fast foods or their facsimiles are making money where other foods didn't. Hamburgers, pizza, and chicken nuggets—all foods from the notorious limited menus—are a way of life. Variety cannot compete with the bottom line.

"Wherever they go, young people now demand menus based on fast food," writes Stan Luxenberg in *Roadside Empires*. He recounts the story of the men aboard the U.S.S. Saratoga who suffered low morale and, when surveyed, said they wanted fast food served at meals. So the Navy redecorated the dining room in bright colors, set up a food-production method similar to a fast-food restaurant, and replaced roast beef, turkey, and tuna with cheeseburgers, fries, and shakes. "The Navy has since expanded the program to cover all its aircraft carriers," writes Luxenberg.

In their oversize burgers the fast-food restaurants dish out several portions of fatty, salty food, stick it inside a bun, and call it a sandwich. For instance, many Wendy's sell a triple cheeseburger, probably the most blatant example of excess because its 1,000-plus calories come drenched in sodium and fat. The triple cheeseburger is not the sole example, however. Some people consider a roast beef sandwich or a melted cheese sandwich with bacon two good choices for lunch. Arby's combines them into one sandwich and calls it a Bac'n Cheese Deluxe. A single fast-food sandwich like these contains half the calories an adult woman needs in a day.

QUEST FOR PROTEIN

When fast-food proponents begin to talk nutrition, protein leads the list of attributes. It's an effective selling point. Our bodies *do* need protein to build new tissues and to repair old ones. Many hormones and all enzymes consist of protein, and hair, skin, nails, blood, and bones all contain protein. Protein helps us fight disease and carries oxygen through the blood.

Millions of Americans buy the protein pitch. Perhaps because muscle is made of protein, we associate it with strength. This concept of simple protein is one that's easy to sell—it's easily grasped and unquestionably good. So affluent Americans end up preoccupied with protein. While we need less than two ounces of pure protein a day to function normally, most of us consume much more than that. One large hamburger sandwich contains more than half the protein we need in a day. And meat isn't the only food that contains protein. If we lived on nothing but beans and macaroni we'd more than meet our protein needs. Many foods, from bread to broccoli, contain protein; it isn't uncommon for Americans to eat two or three times as much as they need.

Protein requirements vary with age, sex, and ideal weight. Young children's diets should have a higher percentage of protein than those of adults (but less actual protein because children weigh less). Adults should consume about 0.36 grams of protein per pound of ideal body weight (an ideal weight is used because your body doesn't require extra protein if you add fat tissue). So if you're a woman whose ideal weight is 120 pounds, your protein requirement is $0.36 \times 120 = 43$ grams, or the amount of protein found in 5½ ounces of tuna fish.

A meal of a Burger King Whopper with Cheese, a chocolate shake, and fries contains all the protein you would need in a day, but along with it comes 1,310 calories. For some women, that's enough calories for an entire day, much less for one meal. If you opt for a diet soft drink instead of the shake you'll still be downing nearly 1,000 calories and need just seven more grams of protein to get your requirement. A meal

FAST FOODS HIGHEST IN CALORIES

COMPANY/PRODUCT	CALORIES
Dairy Queen Chocolate Malt, large, 21 fl. oz.	1060
Wendy's Triple Cheeseburger	1040
Dairy Queen Chocolate Shake, large, 21 fl. oz.	990
Burger King Double Beef Whopper with Cheese	970
Burger King Double Beef Whopper	887
Dairy Queen Triple Hamburger with Cheese	820
Carl's Jr. Super Star Hamburger	780
Dairy Queen Chocolate Malt, regular, 14 fl. oz.	760
Dairy Queen Peanut Buster Parfait	740
Jack in the Box Bacon Cheeseburger Supreme	724
Jack in the Box Scrambled Eggs Breakfast	720
Jack in the Box Supreme Nachos	718
Dairy Queen Chocolate Shake, regular, 14 fl. oz.	710
Dairy Queen Triple Hamburger	710
Burger King Whopper with Cheese	709
Burger King Specialty Chicken Sandwich	688
McDonald's McD.L.T.	680
Dairy Queen Chicken Sandwich	670
Carl's Jr. Western Bacon Cheeseburger	670
Dairy Queen Double Hamburger with Cheese	650
Arby's Baked Potato, Superstuffed, Deluxe	648
Jack in the Box Swiss & Bacon Burger	643

Fast-food restaurants are the place to go, if you want to load up on calories. For an adult who consumes 2,000 calories a day, one meal can easily provide you with half or more of your calories. Most high-calorie foods are also high in saturated fat.

of a burger, shake, and fries has lots of protein, but it's also loaded with fat and weak in other substances such as fiber and vitamins A and C.

If some protein is good, more must be better. Right? Wouldn't more protein mean more muscles, silkier hair, more attractive nails, and stronger bones? Wrong. More is not better in the case of protein, because excess protein is not stored in the body. The protein you consume each day goes to producing tissues and enzymes, and for other metabolic functions. When you don't need a protein molecule for building, the nitrogen component is removed and discarded into urine. Without nitrogen, the molecule is no longer protein, and the remaining portion is used by the body for energy (read calories). No matter where they come from, excess calories all end up in the same place— on our hips, thighs, and bellies.

Too much protein may cause other problems. Excess protein promotes calcium excretion, increasing the risk of osteoporosis (the brittle-bone disease). A few studies even suggest that a high-protein diet increases the risk of cancer, but so far it's impossible to define protein's role because people who eat high-protein diets also eat high-fat diets, and fat is clearly linked to cancer.

The most misleading aspect of the protein argument is that proponents rarely mention fat. Unless your favorite fast-food restaurant serves lentil loaf, you're most likely getting a lot of fat along with your protein. Most cuts of red meat and varieties of cheese get more calories from fat than protein. Chicken and fish are lower in fat, but not when they're batter-dipped and fried.

Obviously, protein is a valuable nutrient and no one would recommend that you try living without it. On the other hand, virtually all Americans get more than enough, so regard with skepticism any sales pitch featuring protein.

ESCHEWING THE FAT: A LOOK AT HEART DISEASE, CANCER, AND DIABETES

If any one smell characterizes a fast-food restaurant, it is the smell of grease. A fast-food restaurant without the heavy fragrance of grease is like a bicycle without wheels. Now, if all the grease did was smell up the neighborhood, that would be one thing. But medical researchers have proven that much worse than smelling too much grease, is eating too much grease. Of course, a few greasy meals won't cause anything worse than a little heartburn. However, someone who eats rich, fatty foods from childhood through adulthood stands a high risk of developing the most serious and sometimes fatal diseases.

Many an old-fashioned nutritionist will staunchly defend fat's role in the diet, saying that fat adds an essential fatty acid (linoleic), and contributes fat-soluble vitamins (A, D, E, and K). Again, this mentality may be appropriate for subsistence-level societies, where people get barely enough to eat, but not for well-fed Americans who are never more than a Big Mac away from satisfaction. Natural foods—particularly grains, seeds, and nuts—contain all the essential fatty acids we need were we never to fry the first potato. As it is, Americans eat too much fat and no one we've ever heard of in this country suffers from nutritional deficiencies because he or she eats too little fat.

Plenty of people suffer from overconsumption, however. High-fat diets complicate diabetes and are implicated in several forms of cancer. Fat in general, and saturated fat in particular, plays a significant part in heart and cardiovascular diseases, as does the fatlike substance, cholesterol.

The American Heart Association, the National Cancer Institute, the National Academy of Sciences, and many other health authorities recommend that we consume no more than 30 percent of our calories from fat. Our bodies actually need no more than about 10 percent to function properly. The typical American consumes 40 percent.

HIDDEN SOURCES OF FAT...AND CALORIES

Many of our dietary fat sources are obvious. We butter our bread, dress our salads, and fry our potatoes. Other fat sources aren't so obvious, and sometimes fat shows up where we least expect it. Red meat contributes the largest amount of fat to the American diet. Bologna, hot dogs, hamburgers, whole milk, cheese, and ice cream are major sources of fat. But there are others. Snack foods such as chips, many crackers, chocolate, and nuts are high in fat, as are sweets such as pies, doughnuts, Danish pastries, and most cakes and cookies. Even cream soups, nondairy creamers, and whipped-cream substitutes contain hidden fat.

Rather than counting every single gram of fat in your favorite foods, you will probably find it easier to identify and cut back on the major sources of fat in your diet. This allows some flexibility and doesn't force you to give up foods you "can't live without." If you can't live without your nightly bowl of ice cream, substitute fresh fruit and yogurt for your morning doughnut, or skinless chicken breast for your midday bologna.

You'll be hard pressed to find low-fat foods on fast-food menus. A glance at the charts later in this book (see Chapter Four) shows that not many fast foods get less than 30 percent of their calories from fat. Indeed, many fall into the 40- and 50-percent-fat range. Some go even higher. That's because the food that isn't high in fat to begin with gets dunked in fat before it's sold.

Fortunately, the grease and burger monopoly has been eroding. Wendy's started salad bars to draw new customers into their restaurants. Many other restaurants have followed their lead. Salad bars provide terrific low-fat alternatives, provided that the eater limits the amount of high-fat toppings such as conventional dressings, bacon, cheese, seeds, and high-cholesterol eggs. You can also get plain baked potatoes. They're nourishing, filling, and virtually fat- and sodium-free. (If you must add a topping, use a minimum of sour cream, margarine, or butter.)

Cutting down on fatty foods will have pleasant side effects for many people—it may help them lose weight without a contrived and rigorous diet. Fatty foods are generally high-calorie foods as well, because fat has more than twice as many calories per gram as do carbohydrates and protein. A plain, large baked potato weighing about eight ounces provides 250 calories while four ounces of french fries provide about 350 calories.

"Staying trim" is as basic to health as not smoking. Maintaining an ideal weight is a major defense against diabetes, hypertension, and many types of cancer. Even if we never gained a pound, however, eating too much fat is our number-one nutrition problem, playing a leading role in chronic disorders, from cancer to heart disease.

HEART DISEASE AND A HIGH FAT DIET

Coronary heart disease, stroke, and related disorders account for almost half of all deaths in this country. In 1983, heart and blood-vessel

FAST FOODS HIGHEST IN FAT

COMPANY/PRODUCT	FAT *(tsp.)*
Burger King Double Beef Whopper with Cheese	15
Wendy's Triple Cheeseburger	15
Burger King Double Beef Whopper	13
Dairy Queen Triple with Cheese	11
Carl's Jr. Super Star Hamburger	11
Burger King Whopper with Cheese	10
Jack in the Box Sausage Crescent	10
Jack in the Box Swiss & Bacon Burger	10
McDonald's McD.L.T.	10
Jack in the Box Bacon Cheeseburger Supreme	10
Dairy Queen Triple Hamburger	10
Arby's Baked Potato, Superstuffed, Deluxe	9
Roy Rogers Breakfast Crescent Sandwich with Ham	9
Roy Rogers Egg & Biscuit Platter with Sausage	9
Carl's Jr. Western Bacon Cheeseburger	9
Dairy Queen Chicken Sandwich	9
Burger King Whopper	9
Burger King Specialty Chicken Sandwich	9
Jack in the Box Supreme Nachos	9
Roy Rogers Bacon Cheeseburger	9
Roy Rogers RR Bar Burger	9
Jack in the Box Supreme Crescent	9
Jack in the Box Ham & Swiss Burger	9
McDonald's Biscuit with Sausage & Egg	9

A high fat content is the number-one problem with most diets. Adults should try to limit their fat intake to 15 teaspoons a day, active children 18 to 20. Typical fast-food meals can easily put you over the top.

diseases killed nearly a million Americans, according to the American Heart Association. One out of four Americans suffers from some form of cardiovascular disease. It costs our nation an estimated $60 billion a year to pay for medical care and for time lost from work.

Heart disease and high-fat diets are inextricably linked. When you eat foods that are high in certain fats or cholesterol, the amount of

SHORTENING USED BY RESTAURANT CHAINS

VEGETABLE OIL

Arthur Treacher's	Hot Shoppes
Burger King (everything but french fries)	Kentucky Fried Chicken
	Long John Silver's
Church's	McDonald's (everything but french fries)
D'Lites	
Denny's	Red Lobster
Friendly	Wendy's (chicken)

BEEF FAT *(mixed with a small amount of vegetable oil)*

Arby's (some outlets may use vegetable oil)	Hardee's
	Jack in the Box
Bob's Big Boy	McDonald's (french fries only)
Burger Chef	
Burger King (french fries only)	Popeyes
Carl's Jr.	Roy Rogers
Dairy Queen	Wendy's (french fries, fish)

COCONUT OIL

Taco Bell

Beef fat is a highly saturated fat and promotes heart disease. Most vegetable oils contain much less saturated fat. Coconut oil is an exception: It is a vegetable fat that is more saturated than beef fat.

cholesterol in your blood is likely to rise. The more cholesterol you have in your blood, the more likely your arteries will become clogged. And then comes the heart attack.

A LINEUP OF FATS

The fatty acids contained in fats come in three types: saturated, monounsaturated, and polyunsaturated (they are named for the type of bonds that link the atoms). Most saturated fatty acids raise blood cholesterol levels, while the monounsaturated and polyunsaturated varieties either reduce or have no effect on blood cholesterol.

Foods contain a combination of these fatty acids, but one of the three types often predominates. Animal fats, for instance, are high in saturated fatty acids. So the fat found in meat, milk, butter, cream, and lard is no friend of your arteries. In addition, two vegetable fats, coconut and palm kernel oils, are even more highly saturated. It is for a combination of reasons—cost, taste, and stability—that many fast-food restaurants use saturated animal fat or saturated vegetable fat (coconut oil) for frying potatoes and sometimes for other foods.

Dr. Daniel Levy, who heads the cardiovascular laboratory at the Framingham Heart Study in Massachusetts, told *Science Digest* magazine that he "was astonished that in this day and age, given our health consciousness, restaurants would use beef fat. . . . [If] they would change their means of preparing food to a more health-conscious one, we could save thousands if not tens of thousands of lives each year." Dr. William Castelli, director of the Framingham study, says, "One of the first steps fast-food restaurants should take is to stop frying their foods in highly saturated beef fat."

Some restaurants use natural vegetable oils for frying. Most, however, use vegetable oils whose level of cholesterol-lowering polyunsaturated fat has been reduced by processing (hydrogenation). These oils, however, still contain much less cholesterol-raising saturated fat than beef fat, palm oil, or coconut oil. In terms of heart disease, they're not a bad bargain.

THE RESEARCH

Studies of large population groups reveal that diets high in saturated fat tend to increase the risk of heart disease. The Japanese, who traditionally consume very little saturated fat, have a low incidence of heart disease (even though they smoke more cigarettes and have more high blood pressure than Americans). Japanese immigrants to Hawaii increased their fat intake three times and increased their risk of heart disease as well. Dr. Ancel Keys and his colleagues, heart researchers at the University of Minnesota, found that Americanized Japanese between 50 and 69 years old were twice as likely to have severely clogged arteries as their counterparts living in Japan.

Keys and his coworkers also found that in Scandinavian countries—where a high percentage (22 percent) of total calories comes from saturated fat—death from cardiovascular disease is much higher than in Mediterranean countries, such as Greece and Italy, where most of the fat consumed is unsaturated.

In 1984, the National Heart, Lung and Blood Institute announced the results of a landmark study on heart disease. The ten-year study, involving 3,806 men, showed that a cholesterol-lowering drug significantly reduced the risk of heart attack. For every one-percent decrease in blood cholesterol, the participants experienced a two-percent decrease in heart-attack risk. That is, a ten-percent reduction in blood cholesterol (e.g., from a count of 250 to 225) reduced the risk by 20 percent. Dr. Basil Rifkind, director of the study, said it was the "first study to demonstrate conclusively that the risk of coronary heart disease can be reduced by lowering blood cholesterol." While the study employed a drug, as well as diet, to reduce cholesterol levels, the researchers said that diet alone should have exactly the same benefit.

CHOLESTEROL

Animal-derived foods generally contain cholesterol, which, like saturated fats, can lead to higher levels of cholesterol in your blood. The cholesterol in American diets comes mostly from egg yolks, red meat, fish, and poultry. Dairy products, some baked goods, and cooking fats make up the rest.

Our bodies need cholesterol to function properly. But because our livers are dependable manufacturers of cholesterol, that substance is not a critical nutrient. Unlike vitamin C, cholesterol needn't be included in our diets.

Dr. Castelli points out that for every 100 milligrams of cholesterol you remove from your daily diet, you can decrease your blood choles-

Fast Foods Lowest in Fat

COMPANY/PRODUCT	FAT *(tsp.)*
Salad Bar Cauliflower, ½ cup	0
Salad Bar Green Peas, ½ cup	0
Hardee's Side Salad	0
Arby's Baked Potato, Plain	0
Kentucky Fried Chicken Mashed Potatoes with Gravy	1
D'Lites Soup D'Lite	1
Jack in the Box Milk, 2.0% butterfat, 8 fl. oz.	1
Long John Silver's Clam Chowder, 6.6 oz.	1
Wendy's Cottage Cheese, ½ cup	1
Wendy's Baked Potato with Chicken à la King	1
Domino's 12″ Cheese Pizza, 2 slices	1
Wendy's Pick-up Window Side Salad	1
Arby's Chicken Breast, Roasted	2
Carl's Jr. California Roast Beef Sandwich	2
D'Lites Jr. D'Lite Hamburger Sandwich	2
D'Lites Litely Breaded Chicken	2
Roy Rogers Baked Potato, Hot Topped, with Margarine	2
Wendy's Chili, 8 oz.	2
Long John Silver's Ocean Chef Salad	2
Arby's Junior Roast Beef	2
Milk or Chocolate Milk, 8 fl. oz.	2
McDonald's Vanilla or Strawberry Shake	2
Jack in the Box Club Pita	2

It is increasingly possible to get low-fat foods in a fast-food restaurant. Each of the foods in this chart contains 2 teaspoons of fat or less.

terol by five points. If Americans were to cut down from 450 milligrams to 250-300 milligrams a day, they would lower their blood cholesterol by ten points. Pair that with decreased intake of saturated fat and the changes are indeed significant. "The point is that the change comes from the diet," says Castelli.

The great body of biomedical research into the causes of heart disease has led health organizations from New Zealand to Great Britain, and from Canada to Scandinavia, to call for decreased consumption of fat and cholesterol. In the United States, the surgeon general, the American Heart Association, the Department of Health and Human Services, the Department of Agriculture, and other distinguished private and authoritative governmental agencies have all said, "Eat less fat and cholesterol." *This is the single most important dietary change that most Americans could make.*

HOW MUCH CHOLESTEROL IN YOUR BLOOD?

So, what should your blood cholesterol be? Generally speaking, the lower the better. In countries where people don't get cardiovascular disease, cholesterol levels don't go much above 200, according to Castelli. A "consensus conference" convened at the National Institutes of Health in 1984, concluded that people under the age of 30 should have blood cholesterol levels under 180. Those over 30 should aim for a cholesterol level under 200. To achieve these levels, millions of Americans will have to make major changes in their eating habits. If you haven't had your cholesterol level checked recently, get it done very soon at your doctor's office or local clinic.

It's never too early to cut back on fatty foods, because heart disease begins early in life. Autopsies of young American soldiers killed in the Korean and Vietnam wars showed significant narrowing of the arteries. By contrast, the arteries of Asian soldiers, whose diets were low in fat and cholesterol, were wide open and healthy. In Bogalusa, Louisiana, researchers discovered that children as young as seven years old had fatty streaks on the walls of their blood vessels. The higher their blood-cholesterol levels were, the more streaks they had. These streaks represent the first stage of coronary heart disease.

When children start chomping on cheeseburgers, they initiate a process that will gradually clog their arteries and increase the odds of their having heart attacks or strokes several decades later. They're also learning to love the greasy, salty food that could ultimately be the death of them. Childhood is clearly not too early a time to develop healthful eating habits.

CANCER

Cancer—long dreaded as a disease that reeled out of control with no regard for science or medicine—may in some cases be affected by the amount of fat in our diets. Population studies "have repeatedly shown an association between dietary fat and the occurrence of cancer at several parts [in the body], especially the breast, prostate, and large bowel," a special panel of the National Academy of Sciences stated in its 1982 landmark report, "Diet, Nutrition and Cancer."

A look at the same body of research convinced the government's National Cancer Institute to begin a Cancer Prevention Awareness Program that publicizes, among other things, the role of diet in cancer. The prevention project stresses three points: Americans should "keep trim, eat a variety of foods that are low in fat, and eat foods high in fiber," according to Dr. Peter Greenwald of the cancer institute. Unlike heart disease, which is promoted specifically by saturated fat, cancer incidence appears to increase when diets are high in any type of fat. The National Cancer Institute bases its dietary recommendations on the results of animal studies, population studies, and "case control studies" on humans. (A case control study compares the diet, lifestyle, and other characteristics of cancer victims with a group of healthy people having the same demographic profiles.)

Throughout the world, high-fat diets correlate with a high risk of breast cancer, which killed more than 38,000 American women in 1985 and is tied with lung cancer as the leading cause of cancer deaths in women. Consider some of the evidence:

❏ The traditional Japanese diet contains only about one fourth as much fat as the average American diet. Breast cancer is five times more common in the United States than in Japan.

❏ The rate of breast cancer among Japanese, Polish, and Italian immigrants increases when they settle in the United States and begin to consume the typical high-fat American diet.

❏ A high-fat diet increases the number of tumors in rats and mice that were simultaneously fed cancer causing material.

"If you pick countries that have half the amount of calories from fat that we do, they have half the incidence of breast cancer," said Greenwald.

In addition to eating less fat, maintaining ideal weight is another crucial step to improving your chances against breast cancer. Women who reach middle age more than ten percent heavier than their ideal weight have an increased rate of breast cancer, according to Dr. John Spratt, a cancer researcher and surgeon at the University of Louisville School of Medicine. And once overweight women get it, he said, the cancer will be "more virulent, more lethal." Because fat is such a concentrated form of energy, diets high in fat tend to be high in calories.

But the cancer-diet link doesn't stop with breast cancer. Eating less fat and more fiber can reduce the chances of a man or woman developing colon cancer—which, at about 52,000 deaths per year, is the second most common cancer killer (after lung cancer) in America. If people "increase [their] fiber intake and reduce the fat [they] eat," cancer experts predict a "30-percent reduction in colon cancer, saving 20,000 lives a year," said then Secretary of Health and Human Services Margaret Heckler in 1984. Population studies, again, show that Japanese immigrants get colon cancer at a higher rate when they settle on American soil and start eating an Americanized diet.

While stopping short of saying that a high-fat diet all by itself causes cancer, Dr. Greenwald says fat "probably acts as a promoter" and that researchers are "pretty confident" that even if you cut your fat intake late in life, you can decrease your cancer risk. Cancer experts specifically recommend that we lower our fat consumption to a maximum of 30 percent of our calorie intake (from the current average of 40 percent). That's equivalent to about 15 teaspoons of fat a day for someone on a 2,000-calorie diet.

This makes fast-food restaurants a dietary obstacle course. In terms of fat, all restaurants have good and bad choices, but often it's difficult for the average consumer to know what the best choices are. Who would guess that a stuffed, baked potato would contain between four and ten teaspoons of fat . . . or that a "lean" chicken or fish meal would provide upward of 12 teaspoons of fat? You don't have to be a genius, though, to know to avoid foods that contain fatty items piled on top of fatty items and foods that are deep-fried.

DIABETES

The common wisdom about diabetes turned out to be all wrong. Because people with diabetes have difficulty moving sugar from the blood into the cells, diabetics were encouraged to eat less sugar.

"Sugar's been looked at as the problem," says diabetes researcher Dr. James Anderson, chief of endocrinology at the Veterans Administration hospital in Lexington, Kentucky. "Sugar's not the big problem. Fat's the big problem. The major problem with fast foods is that they are high in fat. They are so packed with calories from fat that they should be a cause of concern for anybody with a metabolic disorder. People need to cut down on all fat."

There are two types of diabetes: In Type I (commonly known as childhood diabetes), the pancreas fails to produce insulin. Insulin is the hormone that blood sugar must hook up with in order to enter the cells where it is used for energy. The Type-I diabetic is insulin-dependent—since he or she produces no insulin and must inject some at every meal. The amount of insulin one needs depends a great deal on the amount of fat in the diet.

Type-II diabetics (who usually develop the condition as adults) actually produce plenty of insulin, but the cells either have too few insulin receptor sites or else the receptor sites don't function properly. Type-II diabetics often take insulin or other medications, but if they change their diet or lose weight, they may not need any at all.

Being overweight is a major factor in Type-II diabetes. Eight out of ten Type-II diabetics are obese. But most obese people are not diabetics. Only one in four obese people becomes diabetic because of his or her faulty insulin receptors. It appears that the functioning of the receptors is linked to genetics, to the diabetic's weight, and to the fat content of the diet—the more overweight a diabetic is, and the higher the fat content of his or her diet, the less efficiently the receptor sites function.

But even Type-I diabetics, who do need some insulin, may be able to use lower doses with a low-fat diet. That's a benefit because the infamous side effects of diabetes—blindness, kidney failure, nerve damage in the feet and legs, and clogged arteries—may be heightened by the amount of insulin injected. "The general consensus is the less [injected] insulin the better," says Janet Tietyen, a dietitian working with Anderson.

Insulin aside, however, diabetics should avoid high-fat diets because they come with lots of calories. Excess calories lead to obesity, and obesity can exacerbate diabetes. Also, diets high in saturated fat tend to raise blood cholesterol, which is linked to heart disease and stroke. Heart disease is the number-one cause of death for diabetics.

DIETARY FIBER

Dietary fiber is a type of carbohydrate that passes through the body largely undigested and unabsorbed. Nutrition lessons used to dismiss fiber as a nonnutrient. Teachers called it "bulk" or "roughage," and said the only thing it was good for was proper bowel movement. These days, the lessons have changed. It may just be that fiber is one of the best things to be discovered since penicillin.

It seems that for every ill that you can attribute to fat, you can attribute good to fiber. Dr. Denis Burkitt is the English physician-researcher who has waged a worldwide publicity campaign to popularize the benefits of high-fiber diets. Burkitt believes there is ample evidence that such diets can help us avoid such troublesome, though rarely fatal, diseases as diverticulosis, hemorrhoids, hiatus hernia, appendicitis, varicose veins, and gallstones.

Recalling his earliest thoughts on fiber, Burkitt told one interviewer that he became "acutely conscious that a high proportion of the beds in any Western hospital are filled with patients suffering from diseases which are rare or unknown in the rest of the world." These diseases, he thought, might well come from the Western diet—a diet high in refined foods from which fiber is removed and fat and sodium added. "When you take out the fiber," Burkitt told a medical conference, "you pass small stools and you need big hospitals." By trading some of these high-fat, high-sodium foods for high-fiber foods, we can make inroads in conquering common degenerative diseases. Burkitt's observations provoked a great deal of research, and his theories are being borne out. It seems that high-fiber diets help protect against diabetes, cancer, and heart disease.

The term *dietary fiber* includes a large family of substances that occurs in foods of plant origin, but never of animal origin. Beans, bran, fruits, and vegetables are among the best sources of dietary fiber.

Researchers are now trying to identify the benefits of different types of fiber. They have identified at least two general categories of fiber—soluble and insoluble. Within these two categories are numerous fibers that seem to affect specific diseases. For example, whole wheat is rich in insoluble forms of fiber that seem to protect against colon cancer, diverticulosis, and constipation. Oat bran, on the other hand, contains soluble forms of fiber that help decrease the chances of heart disease.

FIBER AND CANCER

In the pamphlet, "Good News: Better News: Best News"; the National Cancer Institute explains that "every day you can do something to help protect yourself from cancer." Eating a high-fiber diet is one of those things.

High-fiber diets appear to decrease the risk of colon (large intestine) cancer, which Burkitt calls a "deficiency disease of Western civilization." The way in which a high-fiber diet protects against colon cancer is not absolutely clear, but researchers think that it goes something like this: Bile acids are secreted into the intestines to help digest fat. The fattier the diet, the more bile acids in the gut. A high concentration of bile acids in the feces is associated with an increased risk of colon cancer. High-fiber diets increase the size and water content of stools as they are forming in the large intestine, thereby diluting the bile acids and reducing the risk of cancer.

Recent studies on fiber and cancer should encourage consumers to head for the salad bar and whole-wheat bread.

❑ People in Finland consume high-fat, high-fiber diets. When compared with people in the United States, whose diets are high in fat and low in fiber, the Finns showed half the incidence of colon cancer.

❑ In northern India where colon cancer is relatively rare, diets are rich in roughage and vegetable fibers. People in southern India, whose diets are nearly devoid of these things, suffer a higher incidence of colon cancer.

❑ In 1982, scientists from the International Agency for Cancer Research performed a carefully controlled study on 30 randomly selected residents from each of four populations: low-risk Parikkala, Finland; intermediate-risk Helsinki, Finland; intermediate-risk Them,

Denmark; and high-risk Copenhagen, Denmark. For each group of 30, the higher the cancer rate in the population they represented, the lower the group's fiber intake and the higher the concentration of bile acids in their feces.

Finally, high-fiber diets help control weight. At least two studies show that people eating high-fiber diets absorb fat less efficiently than when on a low-fiber diet. And keeping yourself near ideal weight seems to help reduce the risks of certain cancers.

FIBER AND HEART DISEASE

High-fiber diets help prevent heart disease in several ways. First, if you eat foods high in fiber—such as fruits, vegetables, grains, and beans—chances are, you will simultaneously eat fewer fatty foods, because you have less room for them. That alone will help prevent heart disease.

In addition, specific types of fiber lower blood-cholesterol levels, thereby lowering the risk of heart attack. The soluble fiber in oat bran (and to a lesser extent, oatmeal), and that in prunes, peas, corn, black-eyed peas, and many types of beans lowers blood cholesterol. After adding three ounces of oat bran a day to the regular diet of men aged 35 to 62, Anderson found that blood cholesterol levels dropped by about 15 percent.

FIBER AND DIABETES

A high-fiber diet helps prevent the onset of, and helps curb the symptoms of, diabetes. First, it can help people maintain suitable weight, which reduces the risk of diabetes. Second, dietary fiber seems to improve the way we use other carbohydrates. "Starches and sugars are more slowly absorbed when they are eaten as part of a high-fiber diet," according to Anderson. Therefore, blood sugar does not rise as much after a high-fiber meal as it would after a low-fiber meal, and does not require a rush of insulin to empty sugar from the blood.

A 1972 study showed that Africans who eat large quantities of fiber-rich foods had lower fasting blood glucose and insulin levels than their European employers. In another study a year later, the researchers speculated that the high proportion of unrefined carbohydrates in the diet might explain the relative rarity of Type-II (noninsulin dependent) diabetes in Africans.

DIETARY FIBER CONTENT OF COMMON FOODS

FOOD	SERVING SIZE	FIBER *(gr.)*
100% Bran	1 oz.	8.5*
Whole-wheat or Rye Bread	2 slices	5.4*
Peas	½ cup, cooked	5.2*
Apple	1 large	4.9*
Kidney beans	½ cup, cooked	4.5*
Bran Chex	1 oz.	4.4*
Orange	1	3.8
Baked potato	1 medium	3.8
Spinach, corn	½ cup, cooked	3.2*
Raisin Bran	1 oz.	3.0*
Carrot	1 raw	3.0
Broccoli	½ cup, cooked	2.9
Shredded Wheat	1 oz.	2.6*
Zucchini	½ cup, cooked	2.5
Green pepper	1 raw	2.4*
Tomato	1 small, raw	2.0
Popcorn, plain	2 cups	1.9
White bread	2 slices	1.6
Strawberries	½ cup	1.6
Green beans	½ cup, cooked	1.6
Brown rice	½ cup, cooked	1.3
Peach/plum	1 medium	1.3

No recommended daily allowance has been set for dietary fiber, but a reasonable target to shoot for would be 25 to 35 grams per day.

*A single serving of these foods contains at least two grams of insoluble fiber, the type of fiber that increases stool bulk and is most likely to protect against cancer.

Other studies support the trends seen in population groups. By increasing the fiber in their diets, Anderson reduced the insulin needs of Type-II diabetics. "We have been able to discontinue insulin therapy in more than half of the patients who have followed [a high-fiber, low-fat] program." Overall, hospital studies involving more than 1,000 patients have shown that a low-fat, high-fiber, high-carbohydrate diet allowed insulin doses to be lowered by an average of 70 percent and insulin was discontinued in two thirds of lean adults. Blood cholesterol levels dropped by an average of 30 percent. Among outpatients, insulin doses decreased by 72 percent and blood cholesterol levels dropped by 11 percent over four years.

High-fiber diets are a double benefit to diabetics, who run twice the risk of heart disease as the nondiabetic population. Because a high-fiber, low-fat diet not only alleviates the symptoms of diabetes, but also can lower blood cholesterol by about 30 percent, such diets reduce a diabetic's risk of heart disease and stroke.

GETTING ENOUGH FIBER

How much dietary fiber is enough? Right now, Americans consume an average of about 15 grams per day. The National Cancer Institute recommends that we consume twice that much. Back-to-basics nutrition that includes more fresh fruits, vegetables, whole grains, and beans should provide adequate fiber. These unrefined plant foods not only contain lots of fiber and little fat, but they generally contribute more vitamins and minerals to the diet. A baked potato has more vitamin C than french fries; whole grains have more vitamins and minerals than refined grains. By including more high-fiber foods in your diet, you will naturally include a better balance of nutrients in a lower-calorie package.

While a bowl of bran cereal—which has not yet appeared on the fast-food scene—in the morning gets you off to a good fiber-rich start, it doesn't mean you can forget about fiber for the rest of the day. Bran cereal contains large amounts of one type of insoluble fiber. As we have seen, it takes a variety of fibers—found in a variety of foods—to promote optimal health.

Beans are one of our best sources of fiber. Unfortunately, with the exception of a few fried chicken restaurants that offer baked beans; Wendy's, which serves chili with beans; and the Mexican restaurants that serve refried beans, legumes are not easy to find.

Since the late '70s high-fiber foods have been showing up at salad bars, especially those bolstered with kidney or garbanzo beans and fruit. Also, baked potatoes eaten with their skins are a good source of fiber: Ordering them plain (and perhaps adding a pat of sour cream or margarine) helps you avoid excess salt and fat. (While baked potato skins are an excellent fiber source, ordering skins only is a risky proposition—they are usually deep-fat fried and often come with salty, fatty toppings.)

Whole grains, another good source of fiber, have made a tentative appearance in multigrain buns at Wendy's and in some regional restaurant chains such as D'Lites. However, Wendy's multigrain bun contains only ten-percent whole grain. D'Lites executives won't divulge their company's bun formula. In many "wheat" bread products, caramel coloring is used to make them look dark, as if they were rich in whole grains. Until fast foods are fully labeled, consumers won't know how much better multigrain buns are than their processed white counterparts. The nutrition brochures that many companies offer do not now list dietary fiber.

SODIUM

Salty and greasy are probably the two primary taste sensations associated with fast foods. They are simple tastes, inexpensive ones to include in foods, and, unfortunately, linked to serious health problems.

Most of the salt in fast foods (and in other processed foods) comes from salt, good old sodium chloride. Like protein and fat, sodium is essential to a properly functioning body. It keeps cells from bursting with excess fluid and helps transmit electrical messages from nerves to muscles. But like protein and fat, a little dab'll do ya. The body requires slightly more than 200 milligrams—the amount found in $1/10$ teaspoon of salt—each day to function properly. "Our body's physiology is designed to hold on to sodium," says Dr. Norman Kaplan, of the University of Texas Health Science Center in Dallas. Therefore, our daily need is small. Knowing that it is virtually impossible to eat so little, experts recommend that we shoot for a range of 1,100 to 3,300 milligrams a day, or $1/2$ to $1 1/2$ teaspoons of salt. Teenagers should aim for 900 to 2,700 milligrams, while children seven to ten should shoot for 600 to 1,800 milligrams. Unfortunately, American sodium consumption goes beyond the pale, averaging 4,000 to 6,000 milligrams per day (some estimates are even higher). These high levels have been linked to high blood pressure.

SODIUM AND HYPERTENSION

An estimated 60 million Americans—one out of three adults—have high blood pressure (hypertension). Among people over 65, half have high blood pressure. Blacks have significantly higher rates than whites.

Hypertension is a silent disease that has no outward symptoms, but can be easily detected by means of a simple, painless procedure. Compared to people with normal blood pressure, people with high blood pressure have eight times the risk of having strokes, three times the risk of having heart atttacks, and five times the risk of having congestive heart failure.

No one can predict exactly who will develop the disease. Family history and obesity certainly influence the onset of hypertension, but they aren't the only risk factors. A diet high in sodium is the crucial factor in many cases.

A great deal of research supports the connection between high-sodium diets and hypertension. In animal experiments, researchers raised the blood pressure of rats, dogs, pigs, chickens, and monkeys by feeding them high levels of salt. In other studies, rats bred to be especially prone to hypertension did not develop high blood pressure when fed a diet low in sodium; blood pressure rose only when dietary sodium did.

The Japanese, largely protected from heart attacks and from many cancers by their traditionally low-fat diets, do suffer high rates of hypertension and stroke. Their diet, high in pickled and fermented foods, and high in soy sauce and other high-sodium foods, makes their sodium consumption and their incidence of high blood pressure greater than ours. Moreover, populations in northern Japan who eat particularly large amounts of sodium (more than 20,000 milligrams a day) have a higher incidence of high blood pressure than their southern neighbors.

An important study done in 1982 in England showed quite clearly the effect of sodium on blood pressure. In this study, the participants

FAST FOODS HIGHEST IN SODIUM

COMPANY/PRODUCT	SODIUM (mg.)
Roy Rogers Roast Beef with Cheese, large	1953
Wendy's Triple Cheeseburger	1848
Roy Rogers RR Bar Burger	1826
Jack in the Box Supreme Nachos	1782
Roy Rogers Roast Beef Sandwich with Cheese	1694
Jack in the Box Jumbo Jack with Cheese	1665
Arby's Hot Ham'n Cheese Sandwich	1655
Dairy Queen Super Hot Dog with Cheese	1605
Dairy Queen Super Hot Dog with Chili	1595
Hardee's Ham & Egg Biscuit	1585
Jack in the Box Chicken Supreme	1582
Jack in the Box Pasta Seafood Salad	1570
Roy Rogers Bacon Cheeseburger	1536
Burger King Specialty Ham & Cheese Sandwich	1534
Arby's Beef'n Cheddar	1520
Jack in the Box Taco Salad	1436
Burger King Specialty Chicken Sandwich	1423
Roy Rogers Cheeseburger	1404
Arby's Bac'n Cheddar Deluxe Roast Beef	1385
Carl's Jr. Charbroiler Chicken Sandwich	1380
Dairy Queen Super Hot Dog	1365
Jack in the Box Swiss & Bacon Burger	1354

Salt is a cheap seasoning and abundant in fast foods. One teaspoon of salt contains 2,000 milligrams of sodium. Each of the foods listed contains ⅔ teaspoon of salt or more. Reasonable targets are 2,200 milligrams a day for adults and 1,200 milligrams for children.

were put on a diet containing 1,900 milligrams of sodium, as compared to their customary intake of 4,400 milligrams of sodium per day. Their blood pressure dropped significantly. Then, the participants were given placebo pills containing no active ingredient. Their blood pressure remained stable. Finally, they were given time-release sodium tablets to bring their sodium intake back to their normal levels. The higher-sodium diet returned their blood pressure to what it had been at the start of the study. Not only did these experiments show that blood pressure is affected by sodium, but also they showed that even mild sodium restriction can often lower blood pressure.

A few skeptics still maintain that scientists can't prove that sodium raises blood pressure and that the link between hypertension and sodium is indirect. "Perhaps," says University of Texas' Kaplan, but "the circumstantial evidence is strong." So strong, in fact, that he and thousands of other physicians confidently place hypertensive patients on low-sodium diets, and strong enough for other scientific and government authorities to advise limits on sodium intake. The U.S. surgeon general, the Food and Drug Administration (FDA), the U.S. Department of Agriculture (USDA), and the National Academy of Sciences all advocate lower sodium diets.

In 1972, hypertension was so rampant, disabling, and life-threatening that the National Institutes of Health began a massive project to educate both the public and physicians about the hazards of the disease. The two slogans associated with the program were "See Your Doctor" and "Treat it for Life." Partly as a result of the program, death from stroke has been cut in half, and heart-disease rates dropped by one third between 1968 and 1985.

But the program had at least one drawback: It implied that drugs were the primary answer to the problem. Drugs are certainly useful, but they are not necessarily the best answer. The drugs that are used to treat hypertension have side effects ranging from headaches and insomnia to depression and sexual dysfunction—not a pleasant prospect for 60 million Americans. And the cost of putting one third of American adults on drugs for life was estimated at $30 billion.

Dr. Robert Levy, then director of the National Heart, Lung and Blood Institute that organized the education project, recommended in 1979, that the 35 million "borderline hypertensives" deal with their condition by reducing their weight and their dietary salt. Drugs are necessary for many of the remaining 25 million "definite" hypertensives. (Both borderline and definite hypertensives have an increased risk of heart attack and stroke.)

SALT, SALT, EVERYWHERE

Most of our dietary sodium comes from table salt (sodium chloride). Though all foods contain some naturally occurring sodium, 90 percent of the sodium we eat comes from salt, but not necessarily from the saltshaker. Estimates differ, but it's clear that much of the salt we eat is added during manufacturing. Natural cheddar cheese, for instance, contains less than 200 milligrams of sodium per ounce, while processed cheese contains more than twice that. Two ounces of broiled pork contain 40 milligrams of sodium, but the same amount of bologna contains over 500 milligrams.

Since excess sodium adversely affects such a large proportion of the population, the FDA requires sodium labeling on about half of all processed food and has asked all other processors to label voluntarily the sodium content of their products. Fast-food purveyors do not label their products, but many will provide a pamphlet providing sodium information.

Nearly all fast food is riddled with salt. A Roy Rogers cheeseburger contains 1,404 milligrams of sodium—almost half of the maximum recommended daily level. Long John Silver's Fish & More dinner contains over 2,000 milligrams—equivalent to a whole teaspoon of salt. One bright spot on the sodium front is that McDonald's reduced levels in its products by an average of 15 percent between 1984 and 1985. It is to be hoped that other companies will make as large or larger reductions.

It's difficult to know by tasting just how much sodium is in a food—processed cheese doesn't seem to taste saltier than natural cheese and we probably don't think of biscuits as being saltier than English muffins. Without lists like the ones in this book (see Chapter Four), it's difficult (if not impossible) to cope with fast foods as an informed consumer.

Surprisingly, french fries tend to be one of the lowest-sodium foods offered. The salt that is sprinkled on before they are served is all on the outside of the product, making them taste particularly salty. Ask the clerk to hold the salt and you'll save yourself a couple of hundred milligrams. Other safe bets, as usual, are the baked potato and salad bar (without added bacon, cheese, croutons, and Chinese noodles).

SUGAR

The alluring sweetness of sugar tempts us so predictably that food processors put it in all manner of foods they make, from shakes and colas to ketchup and peanut butter. Many foods that don't contain sucrose (table sugar made from sugar cane or sugar beets) contain other caloric sweeteners—principally those from corn, which are increasingly popular as the cost of table sugar rises. Corn syrup is often used to sweeten soft drinks, for instance.

Like food processors, executives of fast-food companies know their food will sell better if they add sugar for taste or appearance. The french fries, for instance, have a sugar coating that browns when it hits the hot grease. The batter coatings on many foods contain sugar. Colas and shakes contain a great deal of sugar. Unfortunately, most fast-food (and other) companies do not reveal how much sugar their foods contain. Instead, their charts show the total amount of carbohydrates, which includes sugar, starch, and fiber. For foods such as malts, sundaes and pastries there is no way to determine an accurate sugar value without knowing the recipes. The figures in this book represent our best estimates and calculations.

With sugar being added to so many processed foods, it's no wonder that our consumption of it has climbed steadily. In 1951, average sugar consumption was 110 pounds per person. By 1984, consumption had climbed to 126.5 pounds per person. In 1870, the figure was only about 40 pounds. Yet refined sugar is not a required dietary nutrient and there is no Recommended Daily Allowance for it.

The single greatest contributor of sugar to our diet is soft drinks. Each year our consumption climbs, aided no doubt by our more frequent trips to fast-food restaurants. In 1950, the average person drank the equivalent of 106 twelve-ounce cans of soft drinks a year. By 1984, that figure had climbed to 469, or almost 1⅓ per day. A twelve-ounce soft drink contains from eight to ten teaspoons of sugar. Compare the nutritional contribution of soft drinks (calories) with that of orange juice (vitamin C, potassium, folic acid, and thiamin) or milk (protein, calcium, riboflavin, and vitamins A and D) and you may order

FAST FOODS HIGHEST IN SUGAR

COMPANY/PRODUCT	SUGAR *(tsp.)*
Dairy Queen Chocolate Shake, large, 21 fl. oz.	29
Dairy Queen Chocolate Malt, large, 21 fl. oz.	25
Dairy Queen Chocolate Shake, regular, 14 fl. oz.	21
Dairy Queen Mr. Misty Freeze, 14 fl. oz.	20
Dairy Queen Peanut Buster Parfait	20
Dairy Queen Float	19
Dairy Queen Mr. Misty Float	17
Dairy Queen Mr. Misty, regular, 11 fl. oz.	16
Carl's Jr. Carbonated Beverages, regular	15
Carl's Jr. Shakes, regular	14
Dairy Queen Chocolate Sundae, large, 8.4 fl. oz.	14
Dairy Queen Dipped Chocolate Cone, large	13
Arby's Jamocha Shake	12
Dairy Queen Chocolate Malt, small, 10 fl. oz.	12
Dairy Queen Mr. Misty, small, 8.4 fl. oz.	12
Dairy Queen Hot Fudge Brownie Delight	11
McDonald's Orange Drink, 12 fl. oz.	11
Arby's Chocolate Shake	11
Dairy Queen Cone, large	11
Hardee's Milk Shake	11
Jack in the Box Pancake Breakfast with Syrup & Bacon	11
McDonald's Chocolate Shake	11

Dairy Queen, with its variety of desserts and beverages, is king of the high-sugar foods. Cutting back on the sugary desserts is a simple way of cutting back on calories.

FAST-FOOD THIRST QUENCHERS

NUTRIENTS	COCA-COLA 12 oz.	ORANGE JUICE 6 fl. oz.	2% MILK 8 oz.	VANILLA SHAKE 10 oz.
Calories	144	85	121	352
Added sugar (tsp.)	9	0	0	10
Vitamin A (% U.S. RDA)	0	8	10	7
Vitamin C (% U.S. RDA)	0	140	4	5
Calcium (% U.S. RDA)	0	0	44	33
Fat (tsp.)	0	0	1	2
Protein (gm.)	0	1	8	9

something other than a soft drink the next time you eat out. Fast-food shakes, while containing the healthful nutrients of milk, contain more than twice the calories of whole milk, and nearly three times the calories of two-percent (low-fat) milk.

Sugar can have one of two effects on a diet. It either adds extra calories, contributing to obesity, or it replaces more nutritious foods. The first problem is obvious; the second needs some explaining. Refined sugar can easily constitute 20 to 25 percent of a diet. That means the eater must obtain 100 percent of the necessary nutrients from only 75 to 80 percent of the food. While theoretically possible, government statistics reveal that the typical sugary diet is not making it in the vitamin and mineral department. Many people, especially women and children, get less than 70 percent of their daily requirements for vitamins A and C. Even more people get too little calcium and vitamin B-6.

Also, one shouldn't ignore sugar's common companion—fat. There's a whole realm of food we call "dessert" where sugar is cooked up with fat. A batch of homemade sugar cookies, for instance, gets 800 calories from fat, only 240 from sugar. One eighth of a double-crust apple pie gets 130 calories from fat, only 30 from sugar. Many doughnut recipes call for a minimum of sugar, but deep-frying gives them many calories from fat. Fruit pies and turnovers, like the rest of their genre, taste sweet but get as many as half their calories from fat. Arby's cherry turnover, to cite one sugary example, gets 56 percent of its calories from fat.

Of course, regardless of calories, sugar promotes tooth decay. It does this by providing food for oral bacteria that, in turn, produce the acid that decays teeth. In 1973, Dr. Abraham Nizel, associate professor of oral health services at Tufts University, told a Senate nutrition committee that he and his students had "never found a single patient whose [cavity] problem could not, in part, be traced to the patient's inordinate consumption of sugar."

Though they may not be quite the villains they're sometimes made out to be, sugary foods can easily take over too large a part of our diets. They replace nutrient-laden foods in our diet, rot our teeth, and make such high-fat foods as pies and cookies taste so delicious we'll eat them even if it kills us. For these reasons, the U.S. Department of Health and Human Services and the U.S. Department of Agriculture (USDA) recommend that Americans cut back on sugar.

VITAMINS AND MINERALS

Although we need them in much smaller amounts, vitamins and minerals are no less vital to our health than are protein, fat, and carbohydrates. And while there is no lack of protein, fat, and carbohydrate in the American diet, the same is not necessarily the case for vitamins and minerals.

Our old-fashioned ideas of health relate severe deficiencies of nutrients to such diseases as scurvy, beriberi, and rickets. "Good nutrition" traditionally meant freedom from these diseases. But a modern evaluation of vitamins and minerals shows us that their health benefits are more far-reaching. A growing volume of evidence indicates that the consumption of adequate quantities of vitamins and minerals helps fend off chronic diseases including cancer.

Numerous surveys have found that millions of Americans are not consuming adequate amounts of vitamins A and C, calcium, and iron. While no nutrient is more important than the others, these are among those commonly deficient in American diets. They also happen to be included in many fast-food companies' nutrition information.

VITAMIN A

Vitamin A is well-known for its role in the light-detection mechanism in the retina of the eye. It also plays a part in the formation of teeth, bones, and the mucous membranes. Lack of vitamin A can result in reproductive problems and dry scaly skin—even blindness when deficiencies are severe. Furthermore, vitamin A and beta-carotene (a yellow-orange pigment—found in carrots and other foods—that the body converts to vitamin A) may help prevent cancer.

Studies on human populations indicate that vitamin A enables the body to ward off lung cancer. In one study of 2,000 men, the 488 who reported eating diets lowest in beta-carotene had seven times the rate of lung cancer as the 488 who reported eating the highest amounts of beta-carotene. Promising studies on animals suggest that various forms of vitamin A may help prevent cancers of the skin, breast, and urinary bladder as well. These and other findings prompted the National Academy of Sciences' Committee on Diet, Nutrition, and Cancer to recommend in its 1982 report that people eat more foods (especially fruits and vegetables) high in vitamin A and beta-carotene.

Liver contains large amounts of vitamin A, while eggs and dairy products contain modest amounts. Since vitamin A is fat soluble, and therefore removed from milk when the fat is, skim and low-fat milk are fortified with the vitamin. Beta-carotene, the plant form of vitamin A, can be found in abundance in dark green leafy vegetables, such as collards, broccoli, and spinach, and in bright orange fruits and vegetables such as carrots, sweet potatoes, winter squash, cantaloupes, and peaches. The salad bar is the best place to load up on vitamin A, though several chicken restaurants have begun offering fried liver, a vitamin-packed but fatty food. At McDonald's a hamburger, cola, and apple pie yields less than 2 percent of the Recommended Daily Allowance (U.S.RDA) for vitamin A. That means 98 percent of the allowance must come at other meals.

Although it is possible to get too much vitamin A, it is unlikely you will do so from dietary sources alone. Prompted by stories that vitamin A could diminish acne, some teenagers began taking massive doses of the vitamin and, as a result, suffered abdominal discomfort, fatigue, headaches, and painful areas over bones. The recommended daily allowance of vitamin A is 5,000 International Units (I.U.); overdoses usually fall in the 50,000 to 100,000 I.U. range taken for many months, even years. Overdoses of beta-carotene, while possible in carrot lovers, result only in harmless yellowing of the skin.

VITAMIN C

Vitamin C made its reputation more than 200 years ago when the British doctor James Lind identified a factor in certain foods that could control symptoms of scurvy. This deadly disease was rampant among sailors who went to sea for long periods. Ship captains had fought scurvy by carrying citrus fruits, including limes, to sea long before Lind's controlled experiment proved the benefit of the fruit, and before the vitamin itself was isolated.

Vitamin C is a sensitive vitamin—heat and exposure to air (oxidation) can destroy it. Since it is water soluble, it tends to leach out of foods and into cooking water. Steaming, therefore, is the best way to cook vegetables. Stir-frying also minimizes losses since it is done quickly and no broth is discarded.

Vitamin C hit the big time in 1970 when two-time Nobel laureate Linus Pauling claimed that massive doses could prevent the common cold or diminish its symptoms. Subsequent scientific studies did not substantiate Pauling's sweeping theories, but did indicate that high doses of vitamin C could sometimes shorten the duration of colds.

Beyond scurvy, beyond the common cold, vitamin C may play an important role in maintaining health, including reducing the risk of cancer. Several epidemiological studies link low stomach-cancer rates to diets rich in high vitamin-C foods. Animal studies demonstrate that vitamin C can inhibit the formation of cancer-causing nitrosamines, and sometimes reduce the number of cancers caused by nitrosamines as well. As a result, both the National Academy of Sciences' Committee on Diet, Nutrition, and Cancer and the American Cancer Society have recommended that people increase their consumption of foods rich in vitamin C.

Good sources include all citrus fruits—oranges, grapefruits, limes, lemons, and tangerines, for example. But other sources shouldn't be overlooked—baked potatoes, red and green peppers, strawberries, tomatoes, dark leafy greens, papaya, Brussels sprouts, and broccoli all contain generous amounts of vitamin C. The U.S. RDA of vitamin C is 60 milligrams, an amount found in four ounces of orange juice.

Orange juice is one of the most common vitamin C-rich foods

served in fast-food restaurants. The oversize baked potatoes contain more than half of the daily vitamin C allowance—even more if the potato is topped with broccoli. Otherwise, vitamin C-rich foods are found primarily at the salad bar, discounting the sliver of tomato that might garnish your hamburger.

CALCIUM

If vitamin C is the most famous vitamin, then calcium probably holds top honors in the mineral category. And its prominence has recently been boosted by large advertising campaigns from both the dairy and the nutrient-supplement industries. Our bones and teeth, of course, contain large amounts of calcium. In addition, calcium is necessary for muscle contraction, for blood coagulation, and for the "cement" that holds cells together. Recent research at the Oregon Health Sciences University indicates that calcium may help lower high blood pressure in some individuals.

American diets are frequently deficient in calcium. Kids don't do too badly, despite their voluminous consumption of soft drinks, because most of them also down two or three glasses of milk a day. But adults tend to just drink coffee, soft drinks, or booze. According to a major USDA dietary survey in 1978, 40 percent of the population consumed less than two thirds the recommended intake of calcium which, for adults, was 800 milligrams a day (a glass of milk contains about 300 milligrams of calcium). But in 1984, a Consensus Panel of the National Institutes of Health (NIH) urged women to consume even more calcium—1,000 milligrams daily for premenopausal women and 1,500 milligrams for postmenopausal women. If food-consumption surveys were measured against the higher standard, many more women would report a deficiency.

Health officials are recommending higher calcium intakes primarily to combat osteoporosis, a condition of porous, brittle bones that is common in older Americans, usually women. It shows up most often in the form of broken hips and wrists. "Osteoporosis is a common condition affecting as many as 15 to 20 million persons in the United States," according to a 1984 report from NIH. When the diet is deficent in calcium, the body will steal a little from the bones for muscles, such as the heart, to keep contracting properly. Sustained deficiency could result in osteoporosis, which results in approximately

FAST FOODS HIGHEST IN CALCIUM

COMPANY/PRODUCT	CALCIUM % U.S. RDA
Dairy Queen Chocolate Shake, large, 20 fl. oz.	70
Carl's Jr. Shakes, large	60
Hardee's Milkshake, 11 fl. oz.	45
Arby's Baked Potato, Superstuffed, Taco	45
Jack in the Box Supreme Nachos	41
Domino's 16" Cheese Pizza, 2 slices	40
Domino's 16" Pepperoni Pizza, 2 slices	40
Jack in the Box Cheese Nachos	37
Jack in the Box Shake (any flavor), 10.8 fl. oz.	35
Wendy's Baked Potato with Cheese	35
Wendy's Triple Cheeseburger	35
Dairy Queen Triple Hamburger with Cheese	35
D'Lites Baked Potato with Bacon & Cheddar	35
Dairy Queen Double Hamburger with Cheese	35
Dairy Queen Chocolate Shake, small, 10 fl. oz.	35
Roy Rogers Bacon Cheeseburger	34
Roy Rogers RR Bar Burger	34
Roy Rogers Cheeseburger	34
Roy Rogers Roast Beef with Cheese, large	34
Roy Rogers Roast Beef Sandwich with Cheese	34
McDonald's Vanilla Shake, 10 fl. oz.	33

Calcium is a vital nutrient, especially for women and children. Each of the foods shown provides one third or more of the U.S. RDA for adults. But note that many of the foods are loaded with sugar, calories, or fat. Skim milk or yogurt made from skim milk, which are unlikely menu items at fast-food restaurants, are among the best sources of calcium.

1.3 million fractures and costs Americans $3.8 billion annually, according to the NIH report.

In the land where the soft drink is king, sustained deficiency is a distinct possibility. Milk and milk products are the most concentrated sources of calcium, yet milk consumption has been on a steady decline, while consumption of soft drinks keeps increasing. Milkophobes are at high risk of calcium deficiency unless they obtain calcium from other foods, such as green vegetables, salmon bones and sardine bones, cheese, yogurt, and cottage cheese. (In 1986, soft-drink companies began adding a little calcium to some of their otherwise worthless products. Obviously, there are better sources of calcium, but many soft-drink addicts will certainly benefit from the fortification.)

Fast-food restaurants make a handsome profit off soft drinks and show no signs of promoting milk instead, even in their "kids' meals." Virtually all high-calcium products in fast-food restaurants are also high in fat and/or calories. As a starter, it's difficult, if not impossible, to get skim or 1 percent-butterfat milk at major chains. The "shakes" contain about one third of the adult U.S. RDA of calcium, but the price tag is between 300 and 400 calories—three times higher than in low-fat milk. The processed cheese slapped onto burgers or melted onto potatoes is a good source of calcium, but it is also high in saturated fat, sodium, and calories. Cottage cheese may be found at the salad bar, but it is only a fair source of calcium.

IRON

Iron is one vital nutrient that abounds in meat-oriented fast-food restaurants. A typical roast beef or large hamburger sandwich contains about 25 percent of the U.S. RDA.

Blood loss is the one major way the body loses significant amounts of iron, so adequate intake is especially important for women between puberty and menopause. Since iron is essential for growth, an adequate intake is imperative for children and pregnant or nursing women. Yet these are the very groups who often don't eat enough iron-rich foods to maintain their iron stores.

Because iron helps carry oxygen from our lungs to other parts of our body, adults low in iron are likely to feel tired and "run down." Children with iron deficiencies may suffer decreased attention spans and, if severely deficient, may have learning disabilities. An iron

FAST FOODS HIGHEST IN IRON

COMPANY/PRODUCT	IRON % U.S. RDA
Wendy's Triple Cheeseburger	60
Dairy Queen Triple Hamburger	50
Burger King Double Beef Whopper	41
D'Lites Double D'Lite Burger	40
Jack in the Box Jumbo Jack	39
Dairy Queen Double Hamburger	35
McDonald's McD.L.T.	35
Wendy's Double Hamburger, White Bun	35
Arby's Roast Beef Deluxe	35
Carl's Jr. Super Star Hamburger	35
Jack in the Box Ham & Swiss Burger	34
Jack in the Box Pasta Seafood Salad	33
Hardee's Steak & Egg Biscuit	32
Carl's Jr. Old Time Star Hamburger	30
Arby's Beef 'n Cheddar	30
Domino's 16" Cheese Pizza, 2 slices	30
Carl's Jr. California Roast Beef Sandwich	30
D'Lites Mexican Potato	30
Dairy Queen Chocolate Malt, large	30
Jack in the Box Mushroom Burger	30
Hardee's Chicken Fillet Sandwich	27
Jack in the Box Bacon Cheeseburger Supreme	27
McDonald's Big Mac	27

Women, especially, need iron. Be careful, though, most of the iron-rich foods are also high in fat and calories.

supplement quickly cures the problem.

The exact amount of iron absorbed from food depends on the form of the iron in the food, the overall makeup of the meal, and whether the person is iron deficient. Iron is absorbed much better from meat, poultry, and fish than from eggs, beans, grains, and green vegetables. However, if these latter foods are eaten along with meat, poultry, fish, or with a good source of vitamin C, more iron becomes available. Because of the body's wondrous adaptive mechanisms, someone with adequate iron stores may absorb only ten percent of the iron in his or her diet while someone who needs iron will absorb up to 20 percent.

A large hamburger patty contains about one fifth of the 18 milligrams of iron recommended daily for women and children (adult men require only 10 milligrams). Hardee's Big Roast Beef Sandwich provides 45 percent of a woman's daily iron quota. High-vitamin-C fast foods that enhance iron absorption include citrus juices, baked potatoes, and tomatoes. You'll find additional iron at the salad bar in garbanzo beans, broccoli, cauliflower, and spinach.

ADDING IT ALL UP

Evaluating the nutritional value of a food, as you have probably concluded, is a complicated process. A certain food might be low in fat, but high in sodium. Or it might be high in vitamins and minerals, but literally oozing with fat. How does one weigh all these different factors and decide whether to buy or not buy?

To give you a little help, we have devised the Gloom Factor. This number, which we calculated with the aid of a computer for hundreds of fast-food products, rates the overall nutritional value of foods. Excesses of fat, sodium, and sugar are the biggest dietary bugaboos for most Americans, so our formula gives the most weight to them. The Gloom Factor also considers the calorie, vitamin A, vitamin C, iron, and calcium content of a food. (A more detailed explanation of the Gloom Factor is provided in Chapter Four.)

The more fat, sodium, refined sugar, and calories a certain food contains, the greater the Gloom score. A high content of vitamins A and C and the minerals iron and calcium, on the other hand, will lower the Gloom rating. For instance, Arby's plain baked potato has a Gloom

FAST FOODS WITH HIGHEST GLOOM FACTORS

COMPANY/PRODUCT	GLOOM
Wendy's Triple Cheeseburger	85
Burger King Double Beef Whopper with Cheese	76
Burger King Double Beef Whopper	66
Dairy Queen Triple Hamburger with Cheese	59
Carl's Jr. Super Star Hamburger	59
Jack in the Box Supreme Nachos	59
Jack in the Box Bacon Cheeseburger Supreme	59
Burger King Specialty Chicken Sandwich	58
Jack in the Box Swiss & Bacon Burger	57
Roy Rogers RR Bar Burger	57
Burger King Whopper with Cheese	56
McDonald's Biscuit with Sausage & Egg	56
Roy Rogers Breakfast Crescent Sandwich with Ham	56
Jack in the Box Scrambled Eggs Breakfast	56
Jack in the Box Sausage Crescent	55
Carl's Jr. Western Bacon Cheeseburger	54
Roys Rogers Bacon Cheeseburger	54
McDonald's McD.L.T.	54
Roy Rogers Egg and Biscuit Platter with Sausage	53
Dairy Queen Chicken Sandwich	53
Dairy Queen Super Hot Dog with Cheese	53
Jack in the Box Supreme Crescent	52
Jack in the Box Jumbo Jack with Cheese	52

An excellent diet for adults should contain no more than 75 to 105 Gloom points a day. Active teenage boys could handle up to 120 points and teenage girls 95 points. Most of the highest Gloom foods are loaded with fat.

rating of 1. But Arby's baked potato stuffed with a mushroom-and-cheese concoction has a rating of 29.

You can add up the Gloom ratings of individual foods to get a Gloom rating of a meal or even a whole day's diet. To place the Gloom scale in context, an excellent diet for adults would rate 75 to 105 points on the Gloom scale. Reasonable targets for teenage boys would be 120 points, for teenage girls 95 points. Children 6–11 should aim for 85 points.

CHEMICAL CUISINE:
COLORINGS, PRESERVATIVES, AND OTHER ADDITIVES

Like other manufactured foods, many fast foods contain a wide variety of chemical additives. The additives preserve, extend, emulsify, color, and otherwise "enhance" the products to ensure uniformity, taste, and profitability. However, many of the chains refuse to disclose what additives are in which foods. This secrecy makes it impossible to discuss the potential consequences of all the additives in fast foods. The profiles on individual companies (see Chapter Four) include as much specific information about additives as we have been able to learn.

A few additives deserve special attention. Aspartame (NutraSweet or Equal) or saccharin, for instance, is used in most diet products, particularly soft drinks. Nitrite is a preservative, coloring, and flavoring in hot dogs, bacon, ham, and cured sausage. Monosodium glutamate (MSG) shows up as a flavor enhancer. These and others may pose health risks to the consumer and for that reason their presence in food should be minimized.

As you read about the hazardous additives, don't forget that the fat, cholesterol, sodium, or sugar content of a food generally poses a greater health risk than the additives. Additives may contribute to several thousands of deaths a year. But fat, sodium, and cholesterol excesses, and fiber deficiencies, contribute to hundreds of thousands.

ARTIFICIAL COLORINGS
A rainbow of food dyes accounts for pink strawberry shakes, green

and purple candy, and lemon-yellow soft drinks. For decades dyes have been suspected of being toxic or carcinogenic, and many have been banned. Safety questions swirl around the few that remain.

Yellow Dye Number 5, America's second most popular food color (behind Red Number 40), is associated with allergic reactions in some people. The dye causes hives, runny or stuffy noses, and occasionally severe breathing difficulties. For some reason, most of those who have been found to be sensitive to the dye are also sensitive to aspirin. The Food and Drug Administration (FDA) estimates that between 47,000 and 94,000 Americans are sensitive to the dye.

The FDA requires food manufacturers to list specifically the presence of Yellow Dye Number 5 on ingredient labels rather than putting it under the general heading, "artificial coloring." Once these manufactured foods make it to the fast-food restaurant, however, the consumer is cast back into ignorance—not many would presume that an apparently white "shake" contains a yellow food dye. McDonald's, long a prime user of Yellow Dye Number 5, recently removed the dye from shakes, hotcakes, and sundae toppings in anticipation of ingredient disclosure requirements.

ASPARTAME

This sugar substitute, sold commercially as NutraSweet and Equal, was hailed as the savior of dieters who for decades had put up with saccharin's nasty aftertaste. Aspartame would save the tastebuds of diet-cola drinkers, sweet-iced-tea fans, and waist watchers across the country. It tasted like sugar and was made primarily of two apparently harmless amino acids, the building blocks of protein. Proponents touted it as the closest you could come to natural without the calories. Discovered in 1965, aspartame was approved for limited use in 1981. In 1983, the FDA approved its use in soft drinks. While food manufacturers readily add it to presweetened cereals and drink mixes, aspartame is not suitable for use in foods that are cooked or baked for any length of time because it breaks down into chemicals that are no longer sweet.

As loudly as it was hailed by the industry, aspartame was assailed in other quarters. The first problem is phenylketonuria (PKU). One out of 20,000 babies is born without the ability to metabolize phenylalanine, one of the two amino acids that make up aspartame (and also found in many proteins). Toxic levels of this substance in their blood can result in mental retardation. As a result, the FDA requires all packaged goods that contain aspartame to bear a warning notice for the benefit of people with PKU. Foods served at restaurants or cafeterias are not covered by this regulation.

Some scientists believe that high aspartame intakes could pose some risk to the fetuses of pregnant women who carry the trait for PKU but who do not themselves have the disease. If such women consume large amounts of aspartame—more than a few artificially sweetened foods a day—those scientists say, their babies could be born mentally retarded. The FDA disputes this claim. With regard to these women, the American Academy of Pediatrics' Committee on Genetics and Environmental Hazards wrote in a 1984 report that "insufficient information is available to indicate whether a high, but nonabuse level, intake [of aspartame] by certain individuals is likely to cause harm."

Beyond PKU, aspartame safety has been bedeviled by other questions. Several scientists are concerned that aspartame might cause altered brain function, brain tumors, and behavior changes in consumers. And, in fact, many people (though still a minuscule fraction of those who have consumed the additive) have reported dizziness, headaches, epileptic-like seizures, and menstrual problems after ingesting aspartame. While FDA panels and boards of inquiry have continued to insist on aspartame's safety for all but a few sensitive individuals, *Common Cause* magazine published an exposé of faulty procedures used to approve the additive, and law suits were filed to block its use. The courts, however, upheld FDA's approval process.

Aspartame should be considered of questionable safety, especially for pregnant women, infants, people who think they experience side effects from using aspartame, and those suffering from PKU.

BHA, BHT

These two closely related chemicals are added to oil-containing foods to prevent oxidation and to retard rancidity.

Until recently, BHA (butylated hydroxyanisole) was firmly ensconced on the FDA's list of additives that are Generally Recognized As Safe (GRAS). But in 1982, a Japanese researcher found that BHA induced tumors in the forestomachs of rats. While humans don't have forestomachs, any kind of animal tumor is cause for concern. The Japanese government proposed a ban on BHA, but American trade associations and the FDA persuaded the Japanese to wait until the data could be analyzed. A review committee, assembled in 1983 with scientists from Japan, Canada, Britain, and the United States, concluded that the experiment was well conducted, but when it came to banning BHA, the committee balked and, with only the Japanese dissenting, recommended that BHA be used until further studies were done. Americans continue to eat BHA in processed foods such as potato chips, presweetened cereals, and bouillon cubes. It is often added to the frying oils in fast-food restaurants (see Chapter Four for further details).

BHT (butylated hydroxytoluene) has been the subject of numerous tests that have yielded divergent, sometimes bizarre, results. A 1959 study showed that large doses of BHT caused rats' hair to fall out, increased cholesterol in the rats' blood, and caused birth defects. This study prompted a new wave of studies, none of which could duplicate the 1959 results. Other studies, though, showed that high-BHT diets caused the livers of lab animals to enlarge and develop inappropriately high levels of certain enzymes, provoking at least one researcher to recommend that the government ban BHT.

BHT's cancer-inducing ability is also the subject of conflicting reports. Some studies show reduced incidence of tumors with the addition of BHT; some show increased incidence. The laboratory evidence on whether BHT causes, prevents, or has no effect on cancer in mice and rats is mixed, but because of the possibility that it might increase the risk of cancer, BHT should be phased out of our food supply, including fast-food frying oils. The occasional person who is allergic to BHT would also be helped by such a ban. In the meantime, it should certainly be listed on labels.

CAFFEINE

Caffeine is a stimulant occurring naturally in tea, coffee, cocoa, and kola nuts. It is used in no small measure by truck drivers, office workers, students, and others who want to increase alertness and productive time. But a stimulant drug, even if natural, is usually not without its adverse side effects. As caffeine fights fatigue, it also promotes gastric acid secretion (possibly increasing symptoms of peptic ulcers), temporarily raises blood pressure, and dilates some blood vessels while constricting others.

Excess caffeine intake results in a condition called "caffeinism." Its symptoms include nervousness, anxiety, irritability, jitteriness, muscle twitching, and insomnia, according to Dr. John F. Greden, a psychiatrist at the University of Michigan. And while those who habitually consume caffeine may be unaffected by caffeine-containing foods, occasional consumers may be greatly affected. A study at the National Institute of Mental Health showed that 8- to 13-year-old boys who normally did not consume caffeine experienced restlessness, nervousness, nausea, and insomnia after consuming the caffeine equivalent of either two or seven cans of soft drinks. Because of differences in body weight, the amount of caffeine in a 12-ounce soft drink has about the same impact on a child as the caffeine in a six-ounce cup of coffee has on an adult.

Pregnant women should be aware that caffeine may affect their developing baby. Experiments with laboratory animals link caffeine to birth defects such as cleft palates, missing fingers and toes, and skull malformations. Some of these problems result after hefty intakes of 20 or more cups of coffee per day, but one study showed that the equivalent of three cups per day delayed bone growth. In addition, caffeine consumption seemed to enhance the ability of other ingested chemicals to cause birth defects. Missing fingers and toes have been seen in several babies whose mothers consumed about ten cups of coffee a day. The Food and Drug Administration (FDA) has advised pregnant women to avoid caffeine.

Caffeine is also linked to fibrocystic breast disease (benign breast lumps). Breast lumps are sometimes painful and can be dangerous, because they could hide more serious, malignant lumps. Several studies have found greater caffeine consumption in women with fibrocystic disease. Many women claim that a caffeine-free diet causes lumps to diminish or disappear. For those who experience regular discomfort from lumps they know to be benign, it's certainly worth avoiding caffeine for a few months to see if the lumps disappear.

While small amounts of caffeine do not pose a problem for everyone, many people, including children, pregnant women, and those inclined to develop benign breast lumps, may be adversely affected. These people should certainly consider cutting down on or cutting out caffeine-containing drinks, such as tea, coffee, and many soft drinks. At fast-food restaurants, water, juice, or milk are the alternatives.

MONOSODIUM GLUTAMATE (MSG)

Early in this century, a Japanese chemist identified monosodium glutamate (MSG) as the substance in certain seasonings that enhanced the flavor of protein-containing foods. Soon Japanese firms produced it commercially, and people around the world enhanced the flavor of everything from soup to nuts with a dash of MSG.

Unfortunately, a heavy hand with the flavor enhancer can lead to headaches, a tightness in the chest, and a burning sensation in the forearms and the back of the neck. These symptoms, also referred to as "Chinese Restaurant Syndrome," were identified in 1968 and linked to soup served in Chinese restaurants. Soup is a particular problem, because it often contains a large dose of MSG and is often consumed on an empty stomach, which means MSG will be readily absorbed into the blood.

In 1969, studies involving laboratory animals showed that injections of MSG resulted in damage to nerves and brain cells; feeding studies turned up eye problems in infant animals. While not all studies showed the same results, baby-food manufacturers responded to public pressure by removing the MSG from their products. They acknowledged that the chemical was added only to make the product more appealing to mothers. MSG is an ingredient of several fast foods (see Chapter Four).

NITRITE AND NITRATE

Sodium nitrite and sodium nitrate are two closely related chemicals that have been used for centuries to preserve meat. They maintain a red color, contribute to the flavor, and prevent the growth of potentially dangerous bacteria. While nitrate is harmless, it eventually breaks down to form nitrite. When nitrite combines with compounds called "secondary amines," it forms "nitrosamines," extremely powerful cancer-causing molecules. The chemical reaction occurs most readily at the high temperatures of frying.

Over the past decade, meat processors have gradually reduced the amount of nitrite in food, and have almost totally dropped nitrate, but low levels of nitrosamine contamination still persist, especially in bacon. Regardless of the presence of nitrite or nitrosamines, the high-fat, high-sodium content of most processed meats should be enough to discourage health-conscious people from eating these foods.

Unfortunately, the breakfast menus at many fast-food restaurants rely heavily on sausage, bacon, and ham, and more and more hamburger sandwiches are being made with bacon.

SACCHARIN

A classic combination of the bitter and the sweet, this sugar substitute has been used for nearly a century as a noncaloric sweetener whose one drawback was its unpleasant, bitter aftertaste. But the taste got more bitter when studies associated saccharin with cancer in laboratory animals. In the early '70s several studies linking saccharin with bladder cancer in animals provoked the federal government to remove saccharin from the list of chemicals that are Generally Regarded As Safe (GRAS). Further studies resulted in a 1977 decision by the FDA to ban saccharin. Predictably, public reaction was immense—consumers wanted calorie control and sweet taste too. Industry saw profits going down the drain—saccharin is cheaper than sugar; often more money can be made from artificially sweetened products.

The resounding objection to the ban caused Congress to intercede and pass a law exempting saccharin from normal food-safety laws. By 1986, the exemption had been extended several times and saccharin has assumed a comfortable place in our dietary habits, despite the warnings on sweetener packets and cans of saccharin-containing diet beverages, and despite the studies linking the sugar substitute to cancer. For better or for worse, though, aspartame is rapidly replacing saccharin in many foods.

SULFITES

Sulfites are a class of chemicals famous among restaurateurs for keeping produce looking fresh far beyond the time it actually is fresh. While fresh-cut lettuce, avocado, potatoes, and other foods will soon turn brown, sulfite treatment allows them to retain a fresh appearance. Sulfites also prevent discoloration in apricots, raisins, and other dried fruits; control "black spot" in freshly caught shrimp; and prevent discoloration, bacterial growth, and fermentation of wine.

Though sulfites have been used for centuries, only in the past decade have doctors discovered that this preservative can cause allergic reactions in many asthmatics and occasionally non-asthmatics—reactions severe enough to have killed at least half a dozen people between 1982 and 1986. Most of these people unwittingly ate sulfite-treated food in restaurants. In the early 1980s, while the FDA was paralyzed by regulatory inertia, the National Restaurant Association urged its members to abandon the use of sulfiting agents. Subsequently, several local and state governments banned the use of sulfites by restaurants, themselves, though these laws do not stop restaurants from using foods that processors have treated with sulfites. In July 1986, the federal government finally banned sulfites in most fresh fruits and vegetables. The ban did not cover potatoes and other foods so individuals who are sulfite-sensitive must continue to be careful when eating out. None of the large fast-food chains adds sulfites at its outlets (however, certain potato products at Arby's and Kentucky Fried Chicken may still contain small amounts of sulfite previously added by processors).

Now that you're fortified with all this information about the health impact of fast-food ingredients, we bet you're going to run down to the nearest outlet and decipher the information on the wrappers.

Slow down. Before you rush out, please take a few moments to read the next chapter and learn why most restaurant chains long considered ingredient information to be a deep, dark secret.

WHAT'S IN THIS STUFF, ANYWAY?

A t the grocery store, we can wheel our carts down the aisle and when little Billy grabs a flexible carton of "hula punch" we can look at the label and see that it contains sugar, artificial coloring, and other substances we don't think Billy ought to have and that it lacks the vitamins we *do* think Billy ought to have. We can read the labels of similar-looking packages until we run across a natural fruit juice he likes just as well and satisfies our quest for good nutrition. Even if we don't take the time to compare products at the supermarket, we can study the label at the kitchen table and, if necessary, vow "never again."

Unfortunately, when you bring Billy into a fast-food restaurant and he wants a hamburger, it's been difficult to evaluate his requests, because ingredient or nutrition information may be completely unavailable. And you know from comparing the labels of purple punch and purple grape juice that looks can be deceiving.

Still, you assume that chicken is better for him because it's lower in calories and fat, and you encourage him to choose the nuggets. You might choose the fish for the same reason. But in a fast-food restaurant, these products very often aren't better for you. In fact, they may be a worse choice than beef, because many chicken and fish products contain more fat than a hamburger or roast beef sandwich. Sometimes, the chicken and fish are even fried in beef fat.

The makers of fruit punch and fruit juice are required to put a list of ingredients on the container to comply with federal laws governing packaged foods. Also, if a company adds vitamins or minerals to its foods, or makes a nutritional claim on the label, it is required to print nutrition information on that label. (Nutrition labeling reports on vitamins, minerals, protein, fat, carbohydrates, and calories, and is essential for people on low-fat, low-sodium, or high-calcium diets.)

Fast-food companies—though they sell food in boxes, pouches, and other standardized packages—have not been required to comply with this law and not one has complied voluntarily. Supermarket shoppers can read the label of frozen french fries to find out what oil and preservatives they contain, but there's nothing in a Hardee's restaurant that will divulge the ingredients of those french fries; no wrapper on a Burger King Whaler that discloses the ingredients in the batter; no way to tell how many calories are lurking in a Dairy Queen shake.

INGREDIENT LABELING

Traditional restaurants have never been required to reveal what's in their food, principally because ingredients could change daily and there is really no place for a label, as such, to appear. It's difficult to imagine Emil and Flora down at the Koffee Kup Café figuring out ingredient labeling for Thursday's bean soup when they don't know yet how much ham is going to be left over from Wednesday's blue-plate special.

Fast-food restaurants are a whole different ball game, however, one that federal regulators knew little about when they came up with their labeling rules in 1938. Fast-food restaurants can be compared to mini food factories, but instead of turning out cans of chicken and tomato soup, they are producing boxes of cheeseburgers and pouches of fries. Instead of selling via supermarkets, they sell directly to consumers. Most, if not all, of these foods come in wrappers or containers that could accommodate ingredient labeling.

Government agencies acknowledged in the late 1970s that the restaurant industry was changing. At that time the Food and Drug Administration (FDA), the U.S. Department of Agriculture (USDA), and the Federal Trade Commission (FTC) were studying food labeling and wrote, " . . . in the growing number of fast-food restaurants, food is generally served in individually-wrapped portions, such as foil-encompassed sandwiches, potatoes in bags, and pies in boxes. In these circumstances, the application of labels, and therefore the requirement of ingredient listing, is a realistic possibility."

As fast foods have become an important part of our lives, numerous health and other problems associated with the ingredients in fast food make it important for consumers to know what they are getting when they order chicken nuggets and a shake. Many people concerned about heart disease would want to know that the nuggets may be fried in saturated beef fat. People sensitive to Yellow Dye Number 5 need to know when to avoid the shakes, and those with dietary and religious concerns would like to know how to avoid beef, pork, or dairy products.

Indicative of the consumer viewpoint on labeling was an informal opinion survey conducted by the *Detroit Free Press:* 89 percent were in favor; only 11 percent opposed. Readers said such things as, "We've a right to know what they're selling our children" and "If we did, they'd lose all their sales."

BENEFITS OF INGREDIENT LABELING

By reading labels, consumers who are allergic to specific ingredients can find out instantly if they should avoid a certain product. The National Institute for Allergy and Infectious Diseases says that reading labels may be the most effective way to identify substances that cause allergic reactions. The FDA acknowledged this in 1979 when it published the Food Labeling Background Papers. The FDA stated, "sufferers of allergies and persons following special diets would benefit from ingredient labeling of restaurant foods." Today, however, millions of allergy-prone Americans must either take chances or avoid fast foods altogether because the ingredients are often kept secret.

Most consumers don't know the trauma of food allergy. Sulfites, corn, soybeans, and milk cause reactions in only a small percentage of the population. But chronic diseases have reached epidemic proportions—heart disease, hypertension, diabetes, and cancer touch all of our lives and often are related to the food we eat. As a result, many people choose to avoid foods that promote these diseases. Labels disclosing the ingredients of foods, including the fats in which they are fried, would benefit millions of people.

In addition, consumers might not want to pay for what they consider inferior products. If a restaurant selling nuggets made of processed chicken meat, skin, and a bunch of additives sits next to a restaurant selling nuggets made from chunks of chicken breast, consumers might opt for the latter. Systematic labeling is a more reliable source of this information than occasional reports in the media.

THE RESTAURANT INDUSTRY SAYS NO

The National Restaurant Association (NRA) vehemently opposes the labeling of fast foods. Mandatory labeling is not in the public's interest, NRA president Ted Balestreri wrote in *USA Today*, because consumers can't understand the chemical terms that create "confusion and the specter of fear without any reason for it." The NRA has told the government that labeling is useless because it's after-the-fact information—the consumer has already bought the product so reading labels won't help. This is ridiculous, since chronic disease (unlike allergic response) comes about after repeated and long-term ingestion. Consumers can muse over the meaning of the hamburger ingredients much as they did with this morning's cereal. Next time, they might make another choice, or, if they like what they read, they might make the same choice. However, in addition to on-package labeling, restaurants could also offer brochures or display posters listing ingredients.

The NRA says that "self-initiated customer inquiry is the most direct and accurate method of determining ingredient content." In other words, they want you to ask the employees what's in the food. This reasoning sounds terrific in theory. But if you've ever asked the 17-year-old at the counter of a fast-food restaurant if the salad ingredients are preserved with sulfites, this discussion need go no further. Just to try it out, though, we asked the assistant manager of a Newhall, California, Jack in the Box what kind of lettuce was in the taco salad and she didn't know. The manager of a Roy Rogers in Washington, D.C. erroneously told us their foods were fried in vegetable oil. When we insisted that he check the label he discovered that beef fat was the main shortening. The truth is that asking the employees if milk shakes contain yellow dye or if the french fries are coated with corn sugar is likely to get, at best, a blank stare and some stammering.

In addition, the fast pace of the fast-food restaurant is not an atmosphere conducive to long discourses by counter clerks over the fine points of food preparation. Inquiring into the composition of the food is like taking 43 items through the express-checkout line at the supermarket. The five anxious people in the line behind you are not likely to be thrilled by the delay.

Next, try calling the corporate headquarters. Some chains will tell you that you must put your request in writing. Let's say you do. If you're lucky, the restaurant will answer. After two letters, Arby's sent the Center for Science in the Public Interest (CSPI) a list of ingredients contained in the foods they sell, but failed to mention that sulfites were used as a preservative in the potato cakes. Only after a third letter did Arby's report that their potato cakes contain sulfites previously added by processors. Sulphites are an additive to which many people are allergic. But—according to the Arby's spokesperson—after cooking, the amount of sulfite is miniscule and unlikely to pose a problem. Despite the one omission, we applaud Arby's for being the first company to disclose ingredients to us.

More often we got a partial response or no response at all. Long John Silver's failed to respond to requests until many telephone calls were made and ultimately their response was "no comment." Several restaurants told us that they offered too many items to begin revealing the ingredients. "Due to the enormous amount of time that would be required to list the numerous ingredients for each of our products, we regret that we cannot provide you with this information," said our Jack in the Box correspondent. When we called requesting specific information about the shortening they used, they asked us to put the request in writing. When we wrote the company, the question went unanswered. Taco Bell admitted the use of dyes and preservatives, but wouldn't say which ones were used in which foods. So much for eating at Taco Bell.

A woman in Coralville, Iowa, wrote McDonald's concerning the contents of their shakes. The company told her that these products contain 1¼ glasses whole milk, 1 teaspoon nonfat milk powder, 1½ tablespoons sugar, 1 teaspoon corn sugar, a dash of stabilizer (used to control ice crystal size), and an ounce of flavor. When CSPI pressed McDonald's for further details, the company acknowledged that the shakes actually contained whole milk, sucrose, cream, nonfat milk solids, corn syrup solids, mono- and diglycerides, cellulose gum, polysorbate 80, guar gum, carrageenan, artificial flavor, and Yellow Dye Numbers 5 and 6 (Yellow Dye Number 5 is no longer used, however Yellow Dye Number 6 may still be used).

According to spokesperson Christopher Garrity, McDonald's sends the type of letter received in Iowa as a matter of course when somebody requests information about the shakes. (Yes! McDonald's shakes do, in fact, contain milk. Wouldn't labeling be reassuring?!) For many of us, however, the hazards of the world are great enough without public-relations people reading our minds to see what it is we "really" want when we request information. Had the woman from Iowa been allergic to yellow dye, the initial incomplete response could have caused a great deal of trouble and maybe even a lawsuit.

So, assuming that, like CSPI, a consumer goes to the trouble of asking a clerk or writing a letter, the chance of getting a quick, complete, and accurate response is pretty slim. We have found that even company-generated pamphlets are likely to be indecipherable, out-of-date, or inaccurate. This fairly dismal record further establishes the case for laws requiring accurate information. When a federal watchdog is looking over their shoulders, companies are likely to pay as much attention to the quality of their consumer information as they do to their financial reports.

HIGHLY SECRET INFORMATION

Some restaurants oppose mandatory labeling on the grounds that they don't want to reveal their ingredients to the competition, which will snatch their secrets, recreate competitive products, and steal business. Does that mean knowing the words to "Eleanor Rigby" will make you as rich and famous as the Beatles? Probably not. It doesn't take a mental giant to figure out the recipe for Egg McMuffin, but Burger King tried muffin sales and they didn't work.

It is ridiculous to think that restaurants can hide the recipes from each other, or to think that they don't already know what the other is cooking. Many of them buy from the same suppliers, and top executives frequently switch from one company to another.

No, indeed. They have wanted to hide the information from consumers. Failing to reveal ingredients leaves all consumers completely in the dark to the fact that foods might be fried in beef fat, might contain artificial flavorings, or might have sugar coatings to make them brown better. "Patrons who order a chicken sandwich to avoid cholesterol may instead get fat and cholesterol equal to 11 pats of butter," said a *New York Times* editorial favoring labeling. "Fast-food patrons are also exposed to artificial preservatives and some suspect food colorings. Small wonder the major fast-food chains prefer not to disclose their recipes."

The industry also insists that labeling is impractical, because the same packages are used for numerous foods, and because ingredients are always changing. "Colas, sugarless colas, iced tea, shakes, fruit juices, and other beverages are all served in the same-size container," wrote the restaurant association's president Ted Balestreri in *The New York Times*. Actually, different cups are generally used for different beverages, and in any case there's plenty of room on the side of a cup for the ingredients of several different flavors of soft drinks or shakes.

For fast-food restaurants to imply that the food isn't standardized is disingenuous and misleading. McDonald's uses preshaped frozen patties. Ketchup dispensers squeeze out the right amount of ketchup, and cheese is regulation size. These storefront food factories know as much about what goes into a hamburger sandwich as Nabisco knows about Oreos. In fact, the bulk containers in which the foods are shipped to restaurants all list ingredients.

Finally, industry representatives claim ingredient labeling is not cost-effective—that consumers don't want to pay higher food prices. Frankly, some consumers aren't crazy about footing a $1-billion television advertising bill, either. In reality, the cost of listing ingredients on the label is trivial and would have an insignificant effect on the price of the foods. If the companies were truly concerned about cutting costs they would spare us a few million dollars' worth of commercials.

))) PETITIONING FOR BETTER LABELING

Unconvinced by industry's arguments, the New York State Consumer Protection Board and the Food Allergy Committee of the American College of Allergists joined with CSPI to petition the FDA and the USDA to adopt regulations regarding fast-food labeling. (USDA regulates the labeling of meat- and poultry-containing foods. FDA regulates all other foods.) The June 1985 petition, which would apply only to chains of ten or more units, was later supported by over one hundred eminent biomedical researchers, including former directors of the National Cancer Institute and the National Heart, Lung and Blood Institute. The American Heart Association and the American Dietetic Association also said labeling was long overdue. The petition explained the many reasons why ingredient labeling is necessary and reminded the FDA and USDA that they had at one time recognized that the 1938 law regarding ingredient disclosure of packaged foods also applied to fast foods. "Present legal authority would be adequate to extend ingredient labeling to those restaurant foods that come in 'containers' or that have 'wrappers'," stated the government's food-labeling background papers issued in 1979.

USDA SAYS NO

Even though unlabeled packaged foods violate the requirements of the law, the government is reluctant to order the fast-food industry into compliance. In December 1985, the USDA rejected the consumer and health groups' petition; the FDA took a little longer, but in September 1986 it too rejected the petition.

U.S. Representative Stephen J. Solarz (Democrat, NY) believes the law requires labeling on fast-food packaging and supported the petition. In a February 1986, letter addressed to then Secretary of Agriculture John Block, Solarz said, "I am troubled by the USDA's denial of the petition. Not only does fast-food ingredient labeling make eminent good sense from a public health standpoint, but it appears to be required by the very statutes Congress has entrusted the Department to enforce." Solarz sent a similar message of support for the petition to the FDA.

WE'VE GOT OUR REASONS

USDA officials, in rejecting ingredient labeling, conjured up a kaleidoscope of reasons for doing so. First was their image of food products as fairly amorphous combinations of ingredients that change swiftly and therefore cannot be regulated. The very thought of a clerk placing a pickle on a hamburger sends them into a regulatory tizzy— how can they possibly account for the possibility of changing ingredients? Just the way it's done in supermarkets: a list of ingredients for the basic food and then a list of other possibilities: pickle, mayonnaise, ketchup, mustard, and so on. Not so tough.

After all, one entrepreneur came up with a way "to keep the hot, hot and the cold, cold" for the incredible marketing success of McDonald's McD.L.T. With that in mind, a *Washington Post* editorial supporting ingredient disclosure said, "Any industry that can exercise such ingenuity in quality control over what goes on our hamburgers can surely find a way, somehow, to let us know what goes into them."

The cost of checking up on fast-food establishments would be prohibitive, according to the USDA, which in these days of deregulation finds both inspecting restaurants and spending money distasteful. But the FDA, with only 500 field scientists and 700 investigators, manages to watch over food and drug manufacturing and labeling nationwide. Obviously, they aren't checking every pharmaceutical factory every day of the year; they don't make daily appearances at all food-processing plants. They manage with a small staff by making intermittent inspections, by keeping their eyes on habitual offenders, and by depending on competitors and consumers to keep them informed. Presumably, fast-food restaurants could be regulated in much the same way.

USDA regulators, who now approve all labels on meat and poultry-containing foods, wring their hands over additional label approval. "To regulate and enforce labeling requirements for ingredients in products prepared in approximately 55,000 fast-food restaurants . . . would require a significant reallocation of inspection resources," wrote then Assistant Secretary of Agriculture Raymond D. Lett. Indeed, were they to inspect the labels used by each of the thousands of McDonald's restaurants it would prove cumbersome. But fast-food chains number in the dozens, not the thousands, and they would only have to approve one label per product for the entire chain.

From a legal standpoint, the USDA's most important statement on labeling was made in response to Representative Solarz's inquiry. USDA Acting Assistant Secretary Alan T. Tracy acknowledged that the USDA did, in fact, have the legal authority to require fast-food restaurants to list ingredients on wrappers, but would not now invoke that authority.

Notwithstanding the USDA's opposition to ingredient labeling, President Reagan appears to favor it, at least in principle. In a proclamation issued in December 1985, in honor of National Consumers Week, Reagan said:

> To make responsible decisions in our dynamic and abundant economy, consumers need both information and education if they are to reap the full benefits of the marketplace. They need information, the facts about goods and services: they need to be educated so they can analyze those facts

before making a purchase. This will enable them to make wise choices whether they are shopping for food, shelter, clothing, transportation, recreation, health care, entertainment, and so on. Prudent, informed, discriminating consumers put pressure on suppliers to keep improving products and services while devising production efficiencies that will permit them to keep their prices competitive.

THE NEED FOR NUTRITION LABELING

Labeling would be even more useful if it included information about calories and specific nutrients, such as protein, fat, and vitamins. Many people would be surprised to learn that the stuffed baked potato they ordered contained a whopping 500 calories, the shake 600, and the burger 700. Wouldn't it be nice to have a big, bold calorie listing on every package as a reminder? The American Medical Association recently encouraged fast-food restaurants to have nutrition information about their food items immediately available to customers upon request.

The fast-food answer to nutrition information is pamphlets that many of the companies send out in response to consumer inquiries. Some chains are now providing the pamphlets at their outlets. These pamphlets do include much useful nutrition information concerning many of their products. But there are problems with the pamphlet approach. The first problem, of course, is that few pamphlets ever get into the hands of consumers. Furthermore, much of the companies' information is out-of-date. The brochure that Kentucky Fried Chicken was distributing in mid-1986 contained 1981 nutrition information. It did not contain information on the new biscuit, the chicken nuggets, or other items developed in recent years. A consumer writing for nutrition information, as the restaurant association suggests we do, would have to write more than once—with additional delays possibly extending over years—to try to obtain information on these "new" products.

The restaurant may also supply inaccurate information. We found several of the companies' information sheets to be so riddled with inaccuracies as to be almost completely unreliable. In a couple of cases, restaurant officials agreed that their data were erroneous. If restaurant executives treated their account books the way they treat their nutrition data, Wall Street would have written their pink slips long ago. It seems that without the worry of a government agency verifying that the numbers are accurate, companies don't have a great incentive to keep the materials accurate and up-to-date.

 # LABELING BREAKTHROUGHS

Despite apathy (or worse) at the FDA and USDA, and resistance to labeling from most restaurant chains, a flurry of legislative proposals and pressure from state attorneys general are breaking the logjam of corporate secrecy. In late 1985, Joliet, Illinois, located just 35 miles southwest of McDonald's headquarters, became the first community to require restaurants to disclose the types of fat they use for frying. This action came at the initiative of Mayor John Bourg, who, after undergoing heart-bypass surgery, learned the importance of cutting back on saturated fat. The Joliet law applies to all restaurants, not just the fast-food variety. Restaurateurs found that the signs stimulated great interest among patrons. In August 1986 San Francisco became the first city to require fast-food restaurants to disclose both ingredients and nutrients.

Ingredient disclosure laws have been proposed in the states of New York, New Jersey, Washington, and California. Most of the bills call for listing ingredients on either packages or posters or in brochures. The California bill, though, like Joliet's, would require disclosure only of the types of frying fats used.

A *New York Times,* editorial in April 1986, in support of the New York State bill, said, "Forcing disclosure would stimulate the chains to compete on the basis of content as well as taste. . . . The costs would be minimal, the benefits substantial."

At the federal level, Representative Solarz and Senator John H. Chafee (Republican, RI) have introduced legislation that would order the FDA and USDA to apply the ingredient labeling laws to fast-food restaurants. Representative Solarz said, "If the public knew what was in their food, we might find sayings like 'Hold the pickle; hold the lettuce,' become 'Hold the MSG; hold the Yellow Dye Number 5.' " Senator Chafee believes that ingredient labeling "would be a tremendous boon to the public health. It would allow consumers to vote with their fast-food dollars, prompting fast-food chains to compete on the basis of nutrition. Imagine how our diets would improve if the full force of the fast-food giants were put behind a race to offer the most wholesome food!"

THE PRESSURE GETS TO BIG MAC

The first big breakthrough came on April 30, 1986, and ironically enough, it came from McDonald's. That chain had long been almost totally unwilling to disclose ingredients. In fact, just a few weeks earlier McDonald's president Michael Quinlan had sneered at ingredient labeling, telling a group of Wall Street money managers, "I couldn't care less."

But McDonald's became the first chain to consent to a government agency's request to make ingredient and nutrition information available to patrons in its outlets, at least in company-owned ones (about half of all McDonald's) in New York State. What happened was that, at CSPI's request, New York State Attorney General Robert Abrams was investigating the accuracy of a television ad that implied that Chicken McNuggets were made from pure chicken. Negotiations between New York and McDonald's evolved from an examination of the specific ad to the more general problem of consumer information about products. The outcome of the negotiations was that McDonald's agreed to initiate a one-year experiment in which outlets in New York would provide consumers with a pamphlet listing both nutrients and ingredients. The experiment began in July 1986. While the pamphlet contains all kinds of malarkey about the great nutrition at McDonald's, careful readers can find the ingredient listings that the restaurant industry had long maintained could never be revealed.

The New York-McDonald's agreement had three immediate benefits for consumers. First, consumers in New York would be able to avoid or to choose foods based on the ingredients. Second, the mere fact of knowing that its ingredients would be widely publicized contributed to a corporate decision to reformulate some of its products, including frying fewer foods in beef fat and removing Yellow Dye Number 5 from all its products. Third, Wendy's and Burger King said that they would go McDonald's one better by reiterating an earlier vow to provide ingredient and nutrition pamphlets in their (company-owned) outlets nationwide.

In July 1986, the attorneys general of Texas and California got into the act and reached additional agreements with fast-food companies. Their pressure spurred McDonald's to expand their information program nationally, and they also got Jack in the Box and Kentucky Fried Chicken to publish ingredient information. While Taco Bell refused to cooperate, it is clear that the days of arrogant secrecy are drawing to a close. But the agreements reached to date do suffer from important limitations. Due to anti-trust laws, fast-food companies cannot require franchised outlets (as opposed to company-owned outlets) to offer the pamphlets. Also, what happens when the first batch of pamphlets runs out? McDonald's, for instance, gave each of its stores only 100 pamphlets; additional copies will have to be purchased from headquarters. We still need legislation to ensure that ingredient information is printed on each and every fast-food wrapper.

Letters of praise from consumers to the presidents of companies that do disclose ingredient and nutrition information would certainly be in order, as would letters of criticism to the heads of companies that maintain secrecy (see Appendix for the list of addresses).

FILLING THE INFORMATION GAP

Until all fast-food providers are required, systematically, to reveal ingredients and nutrients in their foods, restaurant patrons will be unable to act as President Reagan hoped consumers could act—making intelligent purchasing decisions based on information. With that in mind, CSPI has collected as much information as possible and has paired it with tools to help you make educated decisions in the fast-food setting. Because many of the restaurants are reluctant to part with the information that will help you make prudent choices, the listings in this book are incomplete. Also, be aware that companies may modify their products from time to time.

Now, let's take a closer look at major companies' products and figure out how to make the best of an oftentimes grim situation.

CHOOSING A FAST-FOOD MEAL

S hopping for healthful fast food isn't as easy as shopping for groceries. In a supermarket, virtually all processed foods have labels revealing their contents (in descending order by weight). In addition, many labels will tell you how much fat, sodium, protein, and other nutrients the food contains.

On the other hand, fast-food purveyors have not been required to reveal the details of food preparation. Most people don't realize that some companies' french fries get their flavor from beef fat. Tasty as they may be, if you were concerned about heart disease, you might not order them.

Ingredients aren't the only information missing from fast food. Nutrients—protein, fat, minerals, and all the rest—are also important. Without nutrition labeling, there's no way to know that each Wendy's Bacon & Cheese Hot Stuffed Baked Potato is loaded with more than 1,100 milligrams of sodium and nearly seven teaspoons of fat.

Until fast-food restaurants disclose the ingredients and nutrients in their food at the point of purchase or, less likely, stop selling junky, greasy products, we must rely on various other means in order to pick our way healthfully through a fast-food menu.

COPING IN THE FAST-FOOD JUNGLE

Before we examine the products offered by the major fast-food companies, we should fortify ourselves with some basic principles of selecting foods.

Eating out, for some reason, allows us to abandon our nutrition principles and to throw caution to the wind. Disregarding for a time what we know to be good for us, we often eat differently from the way we do at home. Our tongue plays a dirty trick on the rest of our body.

People see eating out as "an episode and not as a continuous pattern," says Doris Derelian, a consulting dietitian in Santa Monica. When people go into a restaurant they tend to abandon their usual rules for eating. "It's like a birthday party or Thanksgiving dinner," she says—a special event when we excuse ourselves for eating something that isn't good for us. But since fast foods have become such an integral part of our lives, it's crucial that people who want to stay healthy use all the meal-planning techniques in these restaurants that they do at home.

To help you fight your way through the fast-food jungle, we have devised the Gloom rating. Gloom ratings emphasize the fat, sodium, and sugar content of foods, three of the biggest problems in the American diet. The higher the Gloom rating, the worse the food. For example, a regular McDonald's hamburger, which contains 506 milligrams of sodium and 11.3 grams of fat, rates 16. The larger McD.L.T., which dishes up 1,030 milligrams of sodium and 44 grams of fat, hits 54 on the Gloom scale. (See page 111 for details on how Gloom scores are calculated.)

Men should aim for about 100 Gloom points per day or less. For

DAILY DIETARY GOALS FOR HEALTHFUL EATING

	CALORIES	FAT (tsp.)	SODIUM (mg.)	GLOOM QUOTA
CHILDREN				
6–11	2400	18	1200	85
FEMALES				
12–17	2100	16	2000	93
18–44	2000	13	2000	83
45 and over	1800	11	2000	77
MALES				
12–17	2600	21	2000	120
18–54	2700	17	2000	104
55 and over	2400	15	2000	95

women and young children, the target is 75–85 points. Big-eating teens can go up to 120. In general, the worse your diet, the more Gloom points it will provide.

The tables in this book will help guide you through specific menus. But a few general rules apply everywhere. Until fast-food restaurants label their foods with nutrition data or ingredient information, use these rules to avoid unwanted fat, sodium, and calories.

CUT DOWN ON FAT; HOLD THE SALT; GO FOR THE FIBER

To avoid fat, forgo sauces such as mayonnaise and tartar sauce on your food. Ordering fish without tartar sauce at Long John Silver's saves more that 120 calories (choose the seafood sauce instead, to get 35 calories and no fat); getting a Whopper without mayonnaise saves about 150 calories. Also, set aside cheeseburgers, because they add extra fat; one slice of cheese adds more than 100 calories to McDonald's Quarter Pounder. As a rule, toppings add fat to potatoes, so it is wise to order them plain or with vegetables only. Dressing adds fat to salads, 140 per ounce in the case of Thousand Island, 160 for blue cheese. Choose a low-fat substitute now available on many salad bars or use vinegar with just a little oil.

One dollop of sauce on a bun can contribute unwanted fat and sodium to your diet. Arby's Horsey Sauce gets nearly half its calories from fat; a one-ounce serving yields 120 calories. An ounce of McDonald's Barbeque Sauce contains more than 300 milligrams of sodium, almost three times as much as in a regular order of fries.

Processed meats are usually high in fat, so avoid bacon on your burger, pepperoni on your pizza, sausage on your biscuit.

Deep-fried foods tend to be fattier than grilled or broiled foods. And since many restaurants use saturated fats for frying, the fish and the chicken may be no better for you than a hamburger. When you do order deep-fried foods, discard the breading and batter and avoid the "extra crispy" versions.

To cut your salt intake, hold the pickles, mustard, ketchup, and special sauce. Do without cheese and avoid ordering processed meats such as bacon, ham, sausage, and hot dogs. Order pizza without sausage, pepperoni, salami, ham, anchovies, or olives. Stick with green pepper, mushroom, and onion toppings. And to really cut down on fat and sodium, try a cheese-less or half-cheese pizza topped with tomato sauce and vegetables. It sounds spartan, but is really delicious, and you won't leave the restaurant feeling bloated. (Tell the clerk you're allergic to cheese, if you want to avoid discussions of cholesterol and atherosclerosis.)

To get fiber, choose from the salad bar. Fresh fruits and fruits canned in their own juice, not in syrup, are good sources of fiber without added calories. Load up on vegetables, at least the ones not coated with added mayonnaise, sour cream, and other dressings. Kidney, garbanzo, and green beans are other good salad-bar choices.

BREAKFAST

Probably more than any other meal, breakfast at a fast-food restaurant is fraught with sodium and fat. Biscuits, croissants, bacon, ham, sausage—there's very little to choose from that's good for you.

The sausage-and-egg croissant at Arby's contains 645 milligrams of cholesterol—more than twice the total daily dose recommended by the American Heart Association. An Egg McMuffin at McDonald's contains four teaspoonsful of fat, plus 885 milligrams of sodium (almost half a teaspoon). Even scrambled eggs get scrambled up with so much grease they tend to have a higher percentage of fat than dinner's hamburger and roast beef sandwiches. A Scrambled Eggs Breakfast at Jack in the Box is eased down your throat by ten teaspoons of fat and 260 milligrams of cholesterol. More than half of this loser's 720 calories come from fat.

Visit restaurants that serve low-fat milk, fruit juices, and English muffins or plain toast. Pancakes without butter are a good low-fat option, too. A McDonald's breakfast of orange juice, English muffin with butter, and low-fat milk scores a decent 14 on the Gloom scale. Add an order of scrambled eggs and you're still at only 28 points. On the other hand, a Hardee's Sausage & Egg Biscuit and glass of whole milk saddles you with fat (ten teaspoons), sodium (1,158 milligrams), and calories (671) that add up to 56 Gloom points.

KIDS' MEALS

Beware of the special kids' meal packs. You often pay extra for the fancy packaging that will end up in the trash bin in 15 minutes—or, even worse, will come home with you and remind your child to pester you to return to the restaurant again and again.

Making nutrition-oriented modifications in kids' meals is certainly worth a try. Patronize restaurants that allow you to swap milk for the soft drink in package deals. Soft drinks have nothing but calories or artificial sweeteners and a flock of additives. Although whole milk has fat, it also has lots of calcium, protein, and B vitamins. Ask for low-fat milk, but don't have any great expectation of getting it.

BURGERS TO ROAST BEEF TO BACON BITS

If you're thinking beef, think roast beef, not hamburger. The fattiest roast beef is leaner than the leanest hamburger meat. Roy

FAT AND PROTEIN CONTENT OF ROAST BEEF AND HAMBURGER MEAT

COMPANY/PRODUCT	% FAT	% PROTEIN
Roy Rogers Roast Beef, 3.4 oz.	2	22
Arby's Roast Beef, 2.8 oz.	13	19
Hardee's Roast Beef, 2.9 oz.	14	19
D'Lite ¼ lb. Burger, 2.5 oz.	17	25
Burger King Whopper, 2.7 oz.	20	23
McDonald's Quarter Pounder, 2.8 oz.	20	23
Wendy's ¼ lb. Hamburger, 2.6 oz.	21	24
Roy Rogers Hamburger, 2.5 oz.	21	24
Hardee's Hamburger, 2.4 oz.	22	22
Denny's Dennyburger, 3.3 oz.	22	22
Jack in the Box Jumbo Jack, 2.3 oz.	23	23
Carl's Jr. Famous Star Hamburger, 2.5 oz.	24	22

These results are from a test conducted by Lancaster Laboratories on samples obtained March-April 1986. The study was sponsored by the Center for Science in the Public Interest.

Rogers offers by far the leanest roast beef. In fact, it is the leanest meat product we have found in any fast-food restaurant. If you're going for a burger, though, D'Lites' meat is the leanest we found. (See the chart on page 114.)

Avoid anything that sounds big—"deluxe," "whopper," "double-decker," and "super" all add up to at least twice the calories of the more modest versions and nearly always come with a 100-calorie wallop of special fat-based sauce. A Burger King Double Beef Whopper contains more than three times as many calories (887) as a regular hamburger (275).

Small burgers are not only the best calorie bargains, they're the most nutritious and economical too. The money saved will allow you to pay the extra dime or so for fresh vegetables (lettuce, tomatoes, and onions), which add a bit of fiber and probably some vitamins to boot. Order a side salad or a baked potato (if you have calories to spare) and you have a reasonably nutritious meal. Drinking a glass of milk rather than a shake saves about 200 calories.

In pizza and Mexican restaurants, "deep-dish" and "grande" usually promise more fat and calories. Opt for thin crusts and taco offerings. Get beans instead of cheese where there's a choice, and if you're trying to decide about extras at pizza parlors, get vegetable toppings rather than more cheese or meat.

For the dieter venturing into a fast-food restaurant, salad bars are a godsend. Low-fat, high-fiber, and vitamin-rich choices include vegetables, fruits, and garbanzo and kidney beans. Dress the salad with vinegar, lemon juice, or low-calorie dressings. Avoid coleslaw, potato salads, and pasta salads that are bound with mayonnaise, which is virtually pure fat. To avoid fat, sodium, and cholesterol, skip bacon, cheese, and egg toppings.

FISH AND CHICKEN

You have to take special care to escape with your health at one of the 11,000 chicken or several thousand seafood restaurants, because the menus are loaded with deep-fried foods. You can strike a major blow for nutrition, if you have the willpower, by removing and discarding the skin from your chicken or fish. Stay away from "extra crispy" coatings—they generally contain more fat and salt. Skip sweet sauces. And fill out your meal with corn on the cob, baked potato, mashed potatoes, or salad. Biscuits, which often come with chicken, get their flakiness from layers of fat and rise with the aid of sodium-rich leavening.

Arby's, Arthur Treacher's, D'Lites, and several other chains have baked or broiled chicken and fish items—these offer substantial fat and calorie savings. Avoid tartar sauce in favor of the less fattening ketchup or cocktail sauce. Even better, try a squeeze of lemon or a shake of vinegar. When possible, order multigrain buns or rolls, even though they are made with little whole-grain flour.

The Gloom ratings tell it all. Lightly Breaded Chicken at D'Lites has a Gloom score of 11. A small order of chicken nuggets at McDonald's or Kentucky Fried Chicken scores 27. A Burger King Specialty Chicken Sandwich, with its nine teaspoons of fat, has a Gloom rating of 58.

If you like chicken "nuggets" made from processed chicken, possibly with added skin, go to McDonald's, Kentucky Fried Chicken, or Church's. If you prefer whole pieces of chicken, visit Burger King or Popeyes.

OTHER TACTICS

The drive-in window can be a friend to the nutrition-conscious. Order the basics from the window and take them home to serve with skim milk, fruit, and fresh vegetables.

If you feel assertive and want to do your bit for society, ask the personnel (preferably the manager) for items you want but don't see listed on the menu. Ask for skim milk even if you know whole milk is all they serve. Ask if they have bran muffins at breakfast and whole-grain buns for your burgers. While the person at the counter will inevitably say "no," the companies want to make money. If they thought there was a demand for bran muffins, they just might try them.

Of course, one obvious way of coping is to avoid the restaurants altogether since it actually takes less time to wash an apple and grab a carton of yogurt than it does to go out for fast food. Even if it weren't more convenient, food from home can be more healthful and cheaper.

If convenience is the key factor in your lunch choice, think about shopping at the supermarket for products that make for low-hassle brown bagging. Small cans and boxes of fruit juices, cups of yogurt, low-fat presliced meats, whole-grain bread, whole fruits, small boxes of raisins, or bags of nuts and seeds are just some of the foods that make taking your lunch easy and nutritious. And more and more grocery stores are installing salad bars to regain customers captured by fast-food and other restaurants.

If your office has a microwave oven, you might want to carry a raw (or precooked) potato to work with you. It doesn't drip or spill and requires no special container. Just stick a washed potato in your briefcase or purse and heat it up at lunchtime. Even better, choose a sweet potato, which is rich in vitamins A and C. Microwaves also offer more exotic options for people who cook. Studies show that many foods have less "leftover" flavor when reheated in a microwave. This bodes well for extras from last night's dinner—including your own homemade, healthful pizza, fish, chicken, and hamburgers.

If you are traveling with children, packing a picnic lunch not only saves money, but also sets a good example. If you pack tuna-fish sandwiches on whole-grain bread, and plums and bananas and crunchy carrots, kids will learn to enjoy healthful foods and are likely to develop good eating habits.

But knowing that we'll sometimes want to head for fast-food-land, let's take a closer look at the fare offered by the major companies.

The following lists reveal all the information that is now available regarding key fast-food nutrients: calories, fat, sodium, sugar, cholesterol, vitamins A and C, iron, calcium, protein, and carbohydrates (includes added sugar, when present.) The percentage of calories from fat is another key indicator of nutritional values. We also show the Gloom score, a capsule indication of a food's (or a meal's) overall nutritional rating. The greater the Gloom score, the more you should avoid the product. Also provided is all available information on ingredients. Even these charts are incomplete, however, as test markets come and go, and products are modified. With each restaurant we point out some of the best choices available, though for some restaurants the "best" is not particularly good. "Best" choices, designated by a ✔ generally have no more than 350 calories, three teaspoons of fat, 800 milligrams of sodium, and 25 Gloom points.

Popeyes and Taco Bell do not offer any nutrition information. Church's and Long John Silver's have not analyzed the vitamin and mineral content of their products.

AN EXPLANATION OF THE GLOOM RATING

The Gloom rating is designed to give a quick summary of a food's or a meal's overall nutritional value. This rating emphasizes the fat, sodium, and added sugar content. These three substances are overabundant in most American diets, contributing to heart disease, high blood pressure, diabetes, tooth decay, and certain cancers. The Gloom rating also reflects the "nutrient density" of a food. A food has a high nutrient density if it is rich in vitamins, minerals, and protein compared to calorie content, and a low nutrient density if it is relatively poor in vitamins, minerals, and protein for a given calorie count. In general, the lower the Gloom rating of a food or meal, the better it is for your health, because of a low fat, sodium, and sugar content, and a high nutrient density.

The formula for the Gloom rating first adds 1 point per gram of fat in a serving of food, 1 point for every 100 milligrams of sodium, and 1 point for every 10 grams of refined sugar. This sum is then multiplied by a number ranging from 0.75 to 1.25 depending on the food's nutrient density (based on protein, calcium, iron, vitamin A, and vitamin C). The multiplier would be 1 if the average nutrient density of the five nutrients is 1. The higher the nutrient density, the lower the multiplier. The Gloom rating will be on the low side when figures for fat, sodium, or sugar are missing. It will be slightly higher than it should be when figures for vitamins, minerals, or protein are missing.

FAST FOOD: FRENCH FRIES

COMPANY/PRODUCT	CALORIES	FAT (tsp)	SODIUM (mg.)	GLOOM
Arby's French Fries	211	2	30	9
Dairy Queen Fries, regular	200	2	115	11
McDonald's Fries, regular	220	3	109	13
D'Lites French Fries, regular	260	3	100	14
Long John Silver's Fryes	247	3	6	14
Kentucky Fried Chicken Kentucky Fries	268	3	81	15
Church's French Fries	256	3	—	15
Jack in the Box French Fries, regular	221	3	164	15
Arthur Treacher's Chips	276	3	39	15
Hardee's French Fries, regular	239	3	180	15
Wendy's French Fries, regular	280	3	95	16
Roy Rogers French Fries	268	3	165	16
D'Lites French Fries, large	320	3	120	17
Burger King French Fries, regular	227	3	160	17
Dairy Queen French Fries, large	320	4	185	21
Carl's Jr. French Fries, regular	250	3	460	21
Roy Rogers French Fries, large	357	4	221	22
Hardee's French Fries, large	406	5	306	27

Though they're deep-fried and salted, french fries are not quite as bad as their reputation would have them. A small serving should be more than enough, and ask the clerk to hold the salt. Kudos to Long John Silver's for making salt-free "Fryes" its standard.

FAST FOOD: SHAKES, MALTS

COMPANY/PRODUCT	CALORIES	FAT (tsp.)	SODIUM (mg.)	SUGAR (tsp.)	GLOOM
Jack in the Box Strawberry Shake, 11 fl. oz.	320	2	240	9	**13**
McDonald's Vanilla Shake, 10.2 fl. oz	352	2	201	10	**15**
McDonald's Strawberry Shake, 10.2 fl. oz.	362	2	207	10	**15**
Arby's Vanilla Shake, 8.8 fl. oz.	295	2	245	8	**16**
Burger King Vanilla Shake, 10 fl. oz.	321	2	205	9	**16**
Roy Rogers Vanilla Shake, 10.8 fl. oz.	306	2	282	9	**17**
Hardee's Milkshake, 11 fl. oz.	391	2	241	11	**17**
Carl's Jr. Shakes, large	490	2	350	14	**17**
McDonald's Chocolate Shake, 10.2 fl. oz.	383	2	300	11	**17**
Burger King Chocolate Shake, 10 fl. oz.	374	3	225	9	**18**
Dairy Queen Chocolate Malt, small, 10 fl. oz.	520	3	180	12	**21**
Dairy Queen Chocolate Malt, regular, 14 fl. oz.	760	4	260	18	**29**
Dairy Queen Chocolate Shake, large, 20 fl. oz.	990	6	360	29	**43**

Typical shakes contain about as much sugar as a can of cola, as much fat as a glass of milk, and as many calories as a cola and milk combined. They are good sources of calcium. Not a bad choice for a combined beverage and dessert, you can also make it better by sharing one with a friend (or, in the case of Carl's Jr. and Dairy Queen's large shakes and malts, two or three friends).

FAST FOOD: HAMBURGERS, CHEESEBURGERS

COMPANY/PRODUCT	CALORIES	FAT (tsp.)	SODIUM (mg.)	GLOOM
D'Lites Jr. D'Lite	200	2	210	9
Wendy's Kid's Meal Hamburger	200	2	265	11
D'Lites ¼ lb. D'Lite Burger	280	3	240	14
McDonald's Hamburger	263	3	506	16
Burger King Hamburger	275	3	509	17
Wendy's Hamburger, Multi-Grain Bun	340	4	290	20
Wendy's Hamburger, White Bun	350	4	410	22
Hardee's Hamburger	276	3	589	22
Jack in the Box Cheeseburger	323	3	749	22
Burger King Whopper Jr.	322	4	486	22
McDonald's Cheeseburger	318	4	743	23
D'Lites Double D'Lite	450	5	290	24
Carl's Jr. Old Time Star	450	5	625	26
Dairy Queen Single with Cheese	410	5	790	28
McDonald's Quarter Pounder	427	5	718	31
Roy Rogers Hamburger	456	6	495	34
Burger King Double Cheeseburger	478	6	827	35
Jack in the Box Mushroom Burger	477	6	906	36
Hardee's Big Deluxe	503	7	903	38
Burger King Bacon Double Cheeseburger	510	7	728	38
Carl's Jr. Famous Star	530	7	705	40
Wendy's Double Hamburger, White Bun	560	8	575	40

COMPANY/PRODUCT	CALORIES	FAT (tsp.)	SODIUM (mg.)	GLOOM
Hardee's Bacon Cheeseburger	556	7	888	42
McDonald's Quarter Pounder with Cheese	525	7	1220	43
McDonald's Big Mac	570	8	979	45
Dairy Queen Double with Cheese	650	8	980	46
Burger King Whopper	626	9	842	47
Wendy's Double Cheeseburger, White Bun	630	9	835	48
Jack in the Box Ham & Swiss Burger	638	9	1330	51
Dairy Queen Triple Hamburger	710	10	690	51
Jack in the Box Jumbo Jack with Cheese	630	8	1665	52
McDonald's McD.L.T.	680	10	1030	54
Burger King Whopper with Cheese	709	10	1126	56
Roy Rogers RR Bar Burger	611	9	1826	57
Jack in the Box Bacon Cheeseburger Supreme	724	10	1307	59
Carl's Jr. Super Star	780	11	785	59
Burger King Double Beef Whopper	887	13	922	66
Burger King Double Beef Whopper with Cheese	970	15	1206	76
Wendy's Triple Cheeseburger	1040	15	1848	85

Befriend your arteries by choosing small burgers and skipping the "special sauces." Cheeseburgers provide some calcium, but skim milk, yogurt, and green vegetables are much better, lower-calorie sources.

FAST FOOD: CHICKEN

COMPANY/PRODUCT	CALORIES	FAT (tsp.)	SODIUM (mg.)	GLOOM
Roy Rogers Chicken Leg	117	2	162	8
Kentucky Fried Chicken Original Recipe Drumstick	147	2	269	11
D'Lites Litely Breaded Chicken Filet	170	2	430	11
Church's Fried Chicken Leg	147	2	286	12
Roy Rogers Chicken Wing	142	2	266	13
Long John Silver's Chicken Plank, 1 piece	152	2	515	14
Kentucky Fried Chicken Extra Crispy Drumstick	173	3	346	15
Wendy's Chicken Sandwich, Multi-Grain Bun	320	2	500	15
Arby's Chicken Breast, roasted	254	2	930	15
Burger King Chicken Tenders, 6 pieces	204	2	636	16
D'Lites Chicken Filet Sandwich	280	3	760	19
Kentucky Fried Chicken Original Recipe Side Breast	276	4	654	24
Roy Rogers Chicken Breast	324	4	601	24
Church's Fried Chicken Breast	278	4	560	24
Arby's Turkey Deluxe	375	4	850	25
Roy Rogers Chicken Thigh	282	4	505	25
McDonald's Chicken McNuggets	323	5	512	26
Arby's Chicken Salad Sandwich	386	5	630	27
Kentucky Fried Chicken Kentucky Nuggets, 6 pieces	276	4	840	27
Church's Fried Chicken Wing	303	4	583	27

COMPANY/PRODUCT	CALORIES	FAT (tsp.)	SODIUM (mg.)	GLOOM
Arthur Treacher's Chicken	369	5	495	27
Arthur Treacher's Chicken Sandwich	413	4	708	28
Church's Fried Chicken Thigh	305	5	448	28
Carl's Jr. Charbroiler Chicken Sandwich	450	3	1380	28
Kentucky Fried Chicken Extra Crispy Thigh	343	5	549	30
Roy Rogers Chicken Thigh & Leg	399	6	667	33
Kentucky Fried Chicken, Extra Crispy Side Breast	354	5	797	34
Hardee's Turkey Club	426	5	1185	34
Roy Rogers Chicken Breast & Wing	466	6	867	37
Hardee's Chicken Fillet	510	6	1307	38
Arby's Chicken Breast Sandwich	592	6	1340	42
Arby's Chicken Club Sandwich	621	7	1300	46
Jack in the Box Chicken Supreme	601	8	1582	52
Dairy Queen Chicken Sandwich, fried	670	9	870	53
Burger King Specialty Chicken Sandwich	688	9	1423	58

Chicken starts out lean and wholesome, but once it is battered, breaded, fried, and smothered with a mayonnaise sauce, it will be loaded with fat and calories. Look for baked or broiled chicken, hold the sauces, and discard the grease-soaked breading.

FAST FOOD: FISH

COMPANY/PRODUCT	CALORIES	FAT *(tsp.)*	SODIUM *(mg.)*	GLOOM
D'Lites Litely Breaded Fish Filet	190	2	95	11
Arthur Treacher's Broiled Fish, 5 oz.	245	3	144	16
Church's Catfish, 3 pieces	201	3	453	18
Long John Silver's Ocean Chef Salad	229	2	986	18
Long John Silver's Batter-Fried Fish, 1 piece	202	3	673	20
Arthur Treacher's Fried Fish	355	5	450	26
Dairy Queen Fish Sandwich	400	4	875	27
¼ lb. D'Lites Fish Filet Sandwich	390	5	520	27
Hardee's Fisherman's Filet	469	5	1013	31
Jack in the Box Moby Jack	444	6	820	34
Arthur Treacher's Fish Sandwich	440	5	836	34
Burger King Whaler Sandwich	488	6	592	35
McDonald's Filet-O-Fish	435	6	799	35
Carl's Jr. Filet of Fish Sandwich	570	6	790	36
Burger King Whaler Sandwich with Cheese	530	7	734	39
Long John Silver's Seafood Salad	426	7	1086	45
Long John Silver's Seafood Platter	976	13	2161	91

Most fish is low in fat and quite healthful. But most fast food is deep-fried and as fatty as many hamburgers. Seek broiled or baked fish, and season with lemon juice instead of butter and tartar sauce.

FAST FOOD: ROAST BEEF

COMPANY/PRODUCT	CALORIES	FAT (tsp.)	SODIUM (mg.)	GLOOM
Carl's Jr. California Roast Beef Sandwich	300	2	505	11
Arby's Junior Roast Beef	218	2	345	12
Roy Rogers Roast Beef, regular	317	2	785	17
Hardee's Roast Beef Sandwich	312	3	826	20
Arby's Regular Roast Beef	353	3	590	21
Roy Rogers Roast Beef, large	360	3	1044	21
Arby's French Dip	386	3	1111	23
Arby's King Roast Beef	467	4	765	27
Arby's Super Roast Beef	501	5	800	29
Roy Rogers Roast Beef with Cheese, regular	424	4	1694	34
Arby's Roast Beef Deluxe	486	5	1288	36
Arby's Beef 'n Cheddar	490	5	1520	37
Roy Rogers Roast Beef, with Cheese, large	467	5	1953	38
Arby's Bac 'n Cheddar Deluxe Roast Beef	561	8	1385	50

Plain roast beef is lower in fat than hamburger meat, and the beef used by Roy Rogers and Carl's Jr. is extremely low in fat. But the final sandwich may be a different story, once it is topped with bacon, cheese, and sauces. No roast beef sandwich is anywhere near as fatty as a McD.L.T. or Whopper, let alone a double or triple cheeseburger.

ARBY'S

Over 20 years ago, Arby's put Sunday dinner's roast beef on a Kaiser roll and introduced an upscale sandwich—fancier than the hamburger and just as portable. While the chain has introduced its own hamburgers, a salad bar (in half the outlets), deep-fried chicken, and stuffed potatoes, its sliced-beef sandwiches account for an estimated 40 percent of sales, according to *Advertising Age* magazine. This sandwich clearly sets Arby's apart from the rest of the hamburger specialists.

Founded in 1964 by the Raffel Brothers (it's the initials R. B. that yield Arby's name), Arby's started with one store in Boardman, Ohio, that sold roast beef sandwiches and potato chips. Now owned by Royal Crown Companies, Arby's is the eleventh largest fast-food franchiser in the world, according to *Restaurants & Institutions* magazine, with over 1,500 outlets in 50 states, as well as Canada, the Philippines, and Japan. Arby's expansion rate will probably pick up, because it worked out an agreement with a motel chain, Day's Inns, to install restaurants in many of the motels.

Making a uniform, predictable, sliced-meat product is facilitated by judicious processing, resulting in a lot more than straight roast beef. In the Arby's process, lean chunks of beef are ground up and combined with water, salt, and sodium phosphate. In the absence of nutrition labeling, consumers remain unaware of the product's high sodium content. A regular Roast Beef Sandwich, according to the company, contains about 590 milligrams of sodium. It's not clear how much comes from the beef and how much from the bun.

Arby's set aside $25 million for 1986 to advertise that "Arby's roast beef sandwiches are lean enough for customers to consume them frequently without feeling guilty," according to *Restaurant Business* magazine. The beef itself is certainly leaner than hamburgers, but Arby's beef is significantly fattier than Roy Rogers'. According to tests sponsored by CSPI, Arby's roast beef is 13-percent fat compared to 1.7-percent at Roy Rogers.

But roast beef at a fast-food restaurant is not eaten by itself, but as part of a sandwich. The regular Arby's Roast Beef Sandwich gets 38 percent of its calories from fat. Arby's high-calorie Beef'n Cheddar (39 percent of calories from fat) and Bac'n Cheddar Deluxe Roast Beef (55 percent of calories from fat) sandwiches can hardly be considered lean. Magazine ads touting Arby's "lean advantage" included nutrition information on calories, fat, cholesterol, and sodium. But the nutritional values—in grams and milligrams—didn't enable the average person to realize that one sandwich contained eight teaspoons of fat, while another contained three quarters of a teaspoon of sodium. Even if the numbers were clearer, they wouldn't justify the misleading "lean advantage" claim.

Top that with cheese, or bacon and cheese, and you really rack up the Gloom points. High levels of both sodium and fat contribute to the Bac'n Cheddar Deluxe Roast Beef's 50-point Gloom rating. By nobody's definition is 55-percent fat calories a "lean dish." Whoever invented the "lean" campaign should be enrolled in Nutrition 101.

Arby's says it will be phasing out croissant sandwiches in favor of biscuits. Currently, though, the Chicken Salad Croissant weighs in at 460 calories, more than 70 percent of which come from fat, and the Sausage & Egg Croissant contains 499 calories, almost 60 percent of which come from fat. The Ham & Swiss and the Mushroom & Swiss are better choices. (Nutrition information on the new biscuits was not available when we went to press.)

Watch out for so-called diet foods. In the last few years most of us have come to think of potatoes as a hot, satisfying, low-calorie choice in a dietetic wasteland of carrot sticks and cottage cheese. And a plain baked potato is a dynamite food, high in vitamin C and dietary fiber. But Arby's loads its Deluxe Superstuffed Baked Potatoes with enough sour cream, butter, bacon, cheese, and chives to yield 648 calories (more than half of which are fat calories)—making it more caloric than anything else on the menu! Its Gloom rating is 44, compared to 1 for an unadorned potato. The Taco Superstuffed Potato is right behind with 619 calories and six teaspoons of fat (36 Gloom points).

You might have trouble finding the more healthful menu items at your local Arby's. Some outlets, for instance, do not carry baked potatoes. Some restaurants offer a nice salad bar complete with cucumbers, carrots, mushrooms, and low-calorie dressings, but others do not.

If roasted Chicken Breast is available in your area, by all means choose it when you're at Arby's for lunch or dinner. Even with more than 900 milligrams of sodium, this item is one of the few in the fast-food world that is both low in fat (24 percent of calories) and low in calories (254). As a result, its Gloom rating is a mere 15. Otherwise, the chicken at Arby's manages to dispel the bird's low-calorie, low-fat image. The chicken sandwiches rate in the mid-40s for Gloom and contain six to eight teaspoons of fat. The Chicken Breast and Chicken Club sandwiches contain upward of 1,300 milligrams of sodium. You could order a roast beef sandwich and fries for less fat than you'd get in a chicken breast sandwich; and since many Arby's outlets fry in beef fat, there's no health advantage in ordering this deep-fried chicken. At the very least, ask the "chef" to hold the two big plops of mayonnaise that turns the sandwich into a soggy mess. The Chicken Club sandwich contains 621 calories, nearly half of which are fat calories.

Try the French Dip Sandwich, which is relatively low in fat, if your Arby's serves it, or follow the fast-food rule of thumb by ordering the children's portion. The French Dip unfortunately racks up 1,111 milligrams of sodium; the Arby's Junior Roast Beef contains 345. (Remember, your body needs just a few hundred milligrams each day; 2,000 in a day is a reasonable maximum.)

Sodium is always difficult to avoid at fast-food restaurants— virtually all prepared foods contain an overabundance. But the Arby's Hot Ham'n Cheese goes overboard with 1,655 milligrams in one sandwich—over three fourths of a teaspoon.

Arby's children's meal package (Mr. Men and Little Miss Adventure meals) includes a small roast beef sandwich, french fries, a drink, and a toy. The drink choices include whole milk, a much better choice than a soft drink and one that makes this meal a comparatively good bet for children, though still woefully deficient in vitamins A and C.

For breakfast we suggest you eat elsewhere. The pickin's are thin at Arby's.

Following the nutrition data is a comprehensive list of ingredients.

ARBY'S INGREDIENTS

Main Items

Ham: varies with supplier used; contains sodium nitrite, salt.

Roast beef: beef, water, salt, sodium phosphates.

Turkey: turkey, turkey broth, salt, dextrose, sodium phosphates.

Side Dishes

Buns: flour (enriched), sugar, lard or vegetable fat, salt, yeast, optional milk, emulsifiers, dough conditioner, mold inhibitors, wheat gluten, yeast nutrients, sesame seeds.

Cheese, pasteurized processed

American: American cheese, water, sodium phosphate, sodium citrate, enzyme-modified cheese, cream, salt, lactic acid, acetic acid, lecithin, artificial color.

Cheese, pasteurized processed Swiss: Swiss cheese, water, cream, sodium citrate, sodium phosphate, enzyme-modified cheese, salt, lactic acid, acetic acid, sorbic acid, lecithin.

Shoestring fries and potato cakes: potatoes parfried (partly fried) in shortening (very small amount of sulfite used in potato cakes).

Fats

Buttering agent (for buns): partially saturated soybean oil, lecithin, artificial flavoring, artificial coloring, BHA, BHT, dimethylpolysiloxane antifoaming agent.

Frying oil: partially saturated soybean oil, TBHQ (preservative), citric acid, dimethylpolysiloxane antifoaming agent.

Shortening: caustic refined bleached beef fat, antioxidant.

Desserts

Apple turnover: apples, flour, vegetable shortening, sugar, hazelnuts, raisins, chemically modified food starch, salt, dextrin, citric acid, cinnamon, water.

Blueberry turnover: flour, blueberries, vegetable shortening, sugar, chemically modified food starch, dried apples, salt, dextrin, citric acid, water.

Cheesecake: water, cottage cheese, sugar, vegetable and animal shortening (contains one or more of partially saturated palm kernel, coconut, cottonseed, palm or soy oils, beef fat, or lard), flour, Neufchatel cheese, graham flour, blend of whey, skim milk and buttermilk solids, corn sweetener, chemically modified tapioca starch, gelatin, molasses, salt, sodium caseinate, xanthan gum, honey, sodium bicarbonate, artificial flavor, lecithin, hydroxypropyl methylcellulose, polysorbate 60, glyceryl-lacto esters of fatty acids, natural flavoring, artificial color.

Cherry turnover: cherries, enriched flour, vegetable shortening, water, sugar, chemically modified food starch, corn syrup, salt, dextrin.

Beverages

Chocolate (shake base): corn syrup, water, cocoa powder, saturated coconut oil, salt, sodium bicarbonate, carrageenan, vanillin (artificial flavor), sodium phosphate.

Jamocha syrup (shake base): corn syrup, water, instant coffee, cocoa powder, saturated coconut oil, salt, potassium sorbate, carrageenan, tetrasodium pyrophosphate, vanillin (artificial flavor).

Condiments

Arby's sauce: water, tomato paste, corn syrup, vinegar, salt, corn starch, spices, karaya, spice extractives, flavorings, sodium benzoate.

Bacon bits: bacon, hickory smoked flavor, water, salt, sugar, sodium phosphate, sodium ascorbate or sodium erythorbate, sodium nitrite.

Blue cheese dressing: soybean oil, vinegar, blue cheese, water, eggs, sugar, corn syrup, salt, xanthan gum, sour cream solids, spice, garlic powder.

Cheddar cheese sauce: water, aged cheddar cheese, partially saturated soybean oil, modified whey solids, chemically modified food starch, sodium phosphate, salt, sodium caseinate, natural flavors, yeast extracts, artificial colors, monosodium glutamate, Yellow Dye Number 5.

Coleslaw dressing: soybean oil, sugar, vinegar, eggs, corn syrup, water, salt, spice.

Creamy cucumber dressing: soybean oil, cucumber juice, water, dehydrated sour cream, corn syrup, nonfat dry milk, vinegar, onion, salt, polysorbate 60, spice, xanthan gum.

Creamy Italian dressing: soybean oil, vinegar, water, salt, sugar, lemon juice, garlic, onion, xanthan gum, propylene glycol alginate, red bell peppers, spice, calcium disodium EDTA, carotenal coloring.

Croutons: unbleached enriched flour (wheat flour, malted barley flour, niacin, iron, thiamin mononitrate, riboflavin), vegetable shortening (partially saturated soy and/or cottonseed oil), corn syrup, dried whey, salt, yeast, corn starch, nonfat dry milk, soy flour, romano cheese, spices, vinegar, garlic powder, monosodium glutamate, sodium phosphate, deactivated enzymes.

Dressing for turkey and club sandwiches: soybean oil, corn syrup, water, distilled vinegar, whole eggs, salt, onion powder, xanthan gum, black pepper extractives, parsley flakes, garlic powder, disodium EDTA.

Horsey sauce: soybean oil, water, corn syrup, distilled vinegar, chemically modified food starch, egg yolks, salt, horseradish powder, mustard flour, imitation oil of horseradish and mustard, disodium EDTA.

Ham and cheese sauce: water, sugar, apricot purée, vinegar, corn starch, spices, karaya, potassium sorbate, food coloring.

Imitation shredded cheddar cheese: water, sodium, and calcium caseinates (milk protein derivatives), partially saturated soybean, coconut and/or cottonseed oils, cheddar cheese, whey, sodium and calcium phosphates, salt, sodium citrate, adipic acid, sorbic acid, artificial coloring, artificial flavorings, vitamin A palmitate, riboflavin.

Low-calorie Italian dressing: white vinegar, salt, sugar, soybean oil, garlic, xanthan gum, spices, onion, red bell peppers, calcium disodium EDTA, artificial colors.

ARBY'S

COMPLETE NUTRITIONAL VALUES[1]

	WEIGHT* (gm.)	CALORIES	PROTEIN (gm.)
Apple Turnover	85	310	2
Arby's Sub (no dressing)	269	484	20
Bac 'n Cheddar Deluxe Roast Beef	225	561	28
Bacon & Egg Croissant	128	420	16
✓ Baked Potato, Plain	312	290	8
Baked Potato, Superstuffed, Broccoli & Cheddar	340	541	13
Baked Potato, Superstuffed, Deluxe	312	648	18
Baked Potato, Superstuffed, Mushroom & Cheese	300	506	16
Baked Potato, Superstuffed, Taco	425	619	23
Beef 'n Cheddar	190	490	24
Blueberry Turnover	85	340	3
Butter Croissant	57	220	5
Cherry Turnover	85	320	2
Chicken Breast Sandwich	210	592	28
✓ Chicken Breast, roasted	143	254	43
Chicken Club Sandwich	200	621	26

"Q" sauce: water, tomato paste, corn syrup, vinegar, salt, corn starch, spices, karaya, spice extractives, flavorings, sodium benzoate.

Ranch dressing for Super Roast Beef and Beef 'n Cheddar sandwiches: soybean oil, corn syrup, sugar, vinegars, water, tomato paste, salt, spices, xanthan gum, onion, garlic, beet powder.

Red French dressing: soybean oil, vinegars, sugar, water, tomato paste, salt, onion, xanthan gum, garlic, soy sauce, spices, corn syrup, beet powder, mustard, hot sauce, propylene glycol alginate, spice extractives.

Russian (Thousand Island) dressing: soybean oil, water, vinegar, relish, sugar, corn syrup, tomato paste, eggs, chemically modified food starch, salt, artificial flavors, sodium benzoate, onion, paprika, spice.

Sweet and sour dressing: soybean oil, sugar, vinegar, corn syrup, water, salt, onion, xanthan gum, celery seed, lemon juice, calcium disodium EDTA, spice extractives, artificial flavor, artificial colors.

CARBOHYDRATES (gm.)	ADDED SUGAR[3] (gm.)	FAT[4] (gm.)	FAT % CALORIES	SATURATED FAT (gm.)	CHOLESTEROL (mg.)	SODIUM (mg.)	VITAMIN A (% U.S.RDA)	VITAMIN C (% U.S.RDA)	IRON (% U.S.RDA)	CALCIUM (% U.S.RDA)	GLOOM
30	22	21	61	—	0	240	0	0	4	2	30
37	0	16	30	—	58	1354	4	4	25	20	30
36	0	34	55	—	78	1385	0	6	15	10	50
32	0	25	54	—	440	550	15	0	10	6	32
66	0	1	2	—	0	12	0	105	10	2	1
72	0	22	37	—	24	475	10	6	15	15	28
59	0	38	53	—	72	475	20	4	15	30	44
61	0	22	39	—	21	635	15	4	15	30	29
73	0	27	39	—	145	1065	60	8	20	45	36
51	0	21	39	—	51	1520	0	0	30	8	37
30	24	20	53	—	0	255	2	2	2	0	29
28	0	10	41	—	50	225	6	0	6	4	13
32	22	20	56	—	0	254	0	2	4	2	29
56	0	27	41	—	57	1340	0	0	20	10	42
2	0	7	24	—	196	930	0	0	8	4	15
57	0	32	46	—	108	1300	20	4	15	15	46

ARBY'S

COMPLETE NUTRITIONAL VALUES[1] CONTINUED

	WEIGHT[2] (gm.)	CALORIES	PROTEIN (gm.)	
Chicken Salad Croissant	142	460	22	
Chicken Salad Sandwich	150	386	18	
Chocolate Shake, 10.6 fl. oz.	300	384	9	
Coke, small, 12 fl. oz.	355	96	0	
Coke, medium, 16 fl. oz.	474	128	0	
Coke, large, 20 fl. oz.	592	160	0	
Coke, one-liter, 33.5 fl. oz.	992	268	0	
French Dip Roast Beef Sandwich	156	386	23	
French Fries	71	211	2	
Ham & Swiss Croissant	114	330	15	
Horsey Sauce, 1 oz.	28	120	1	
Hot Ham 'n Cheese Sandwich	161	353	26	
Jamocha Shake, 10.8 fl. oz.	305	424	8	
✓ Junior Roast Beef	86	218	12	
King Roast Beef	192	467	27	
Mushroom & Swiss Croissant	114	340	11	
Potato Cakes	85	201	2	
✓ Regular Roast Beef	147	353	22	
Roast Beef Deluxe	234	486	26	
Sausage & Egg Croissant	156	499	23	
Super Roast Beef	234	501	25	
Turkey Deluxe	197	375	24	
Vanilla Shake, 8.8 fl. oz.	250	295	8	

1. *A dash means that data not available.*
2. *To convert grams to ounces (weight), divide by 28.35; to convert grams to fluid ounces (volume), divide by 29.6.*

CARBOHYDRATES (gm.)	ADDED SUGAR[3] (gm.)	FAT[4] (gm.)	FAT % CALORIES	SATURATED FAT (gm.)	CHOLESTEROL (mg.)	SODIUM (mg.)	VITAMIN A (% U.S.RDA)	VITAMIN C (% U.S.RDA)	IRON (% U.S.RDA)	CALCIUM (% U.S.RDA)	GLOOM
16	0	36	70	—	111	725	4	2	10	5	45
33	0	20	47	—	30	630	0	4	15	6	27
62	42	11	26	—	32	300	8	4	6	30	19
24	24	0	0	0	0	—	0	0	0	0	3
32	32	0	0	0	0	—	0	0	0	0	4
40	40	0	0	0	0	—	0	0	0	0	5
67	67	0	0	0	0	—	0	0	0	0	9
47	0	12	28	—	55	1111	0	0	25	6	23
33	0	8	34	—	6	30	0	10	6	0	9
33	0	15	41	—	70	995	10	20	8	15	24
3	—	6	41	—	0	0	0	0	0	0	7
33	0	13	33	—	50	1655	4	40	10	20	28
76	47	10	21	—	31	280	6	0	6	30	18
22	0	8	33	—	20	345	0	0	10	4	12
44	0	19	37	—	49	765	2	4	25	10	27
34	0	18	48	—	60	630	15	0	6	20	25
22	0	14	63	—	13	425	0	6	4	0	21
32	0	15	38	—	39	590	0	2	20	8	21
43	0	23	43	—	59	1288	0	0	35	10	36
31	0	33	59	—	645	705	10	0	15	6	41
50	0	22	40	—	40	800	15	60	25	10	29
32	0	17	41	—	39	850	6	8	15	8	25
44	32	10	31	—	30	245	8	4	4	30	16

3. *To convert grams of sugar to teaspoons of sugar, divide by 4.0.*
4. *To convert grams of fat to teaspoons of fat, divide by 4.4.*

ARTHUR TREACHER'S

Arthur Treacher's, based in Youngstown, Ohio, is on its way back from a series of economic misfortunes. Founded in 1969, the number of restaurants dwindled from an all-time high of nearly 800 in 1979 to only 215 in northeastern Ohio and the Washington, D.C., area in 1986.

After regrouping and reorganizing, the fish-and-chips chain was opening about one store a month. Until recently, the menu pickin's have been extremely slim. If you don't want to eat batter-dipped, deep-fried foods, you'd find it difficult to eat at Arthur Treacher's. Granted, there has always been coleslaw and clam chowder, but the bulk of the menu is deep-fried chicken, fish, hush puppies, and thick-cut English-style french fried potatoes.

Recently, the folks at Arthur Treacher's realized that all this talk about health wasn't just a fad. Redecorating to entice family dining would do no good without more food options, so they expanded the menu to include a salad bar, broiled fish, chicken (as of spring 1986), and plain baked potatoes. Complete nutrition information is not yet available on these items, but it appears that you can order a dinner as nutritious as you'd make yourself. Some of the restaurants serve two-percent low-fat milk, and that's the milk that goes into the chowder. The restaurants are not open for breakfast.

The deep-fried options, of course, come nowhere near the healthful goal of 20 to 30 percent of calories a day from fat. The Fish

ARTHUR TREACHER'S
COMPLETE NUTRITIONAL VALUES[1]

	WEIGHT[2] (gm.)	CALORIES	PROTEIN (gm.)
Baked Potato, plain	— no data —		
Chicken, fried	136	369	27
Chicken Sandwich	156	413	16
Chips (french fries)	113	276	4
Chowder	170	112	5

Sandwich is 49 percent, and the Chicken Sandwich is 42 percent.

Arthur Treacher's is one of the few big chains that sells hot dogs. In this case, they are specially designed batter-dipped, deep-fried hot dogs that the restaurant calls Krunch Pups. Even though they're on the fatty side, they have the virtue of being small. One Pup contains slightly more fat than a Burger King hamburger, but only one third as much protein.

A spokesperson for Arthur Treacher's said that the type of fish used is cod (two ounces for batter-dipped, five ounces for broiled), but other ingredient information is a "trade secret." Although CSPI did not test Arthur Treacher's products, the company claims to use unsaturated peanut oil for all its deep frying. While this oil is low in saturated fat, it still seems to clog arteries. Finally, we tip our hat to Arthur Treacher's for providing information on the levels of saturated fat.

ARTHUR TREACHER'S INGREDIENTS

Main Items

Fish (cod): (breading ingredients not revealed)

Hot dog: beef, water, salt, corn syrup, dextrose, flavoring, sodium phosphate, paprika, sodium ascorbate, sodium nitrite.

Fats

Frying oil: peanut oil.

Beverages

Lemon juice (from concentrate): water, lemon juice concentrate, lemon oil, with less than 0.1-percent sodium benzoate and sodium bisulfite added as preservatives.

Condiments

Tartar sauce: soybean oil, water, corn syrup, vinegar, pickles, egg yolks, chemically modified food starch, salt, sugar, dried onion, spices including paprika and turmeric, dried garlic, preservatives (potassium sorbate, sodium benzoate, calcium disodium EDTA), natural flavors.

CARBOHYDRATES (gm.)	ADDED SUGAR [3] (gm.)	FAT [4] (gm.)	FAT % CALORIES	SATURATED FAT (gm.)	CHOLESTEROL (mg.)	SODIUM (mg.)	VITAMIN A (% U.S.RDA)	VITAMIN C (% U.S.RDA)	IRON (% U.S.RDA)	CALCIUM (% U.S.RDA)	GLOOM
— no data —											
17	—	22	53	4	65	495	2	3	4	1	27
44	0	19	42	3	3	708	2	3	9	6	28
35	0	13	43	2	1	39	2	10	3	1	15
11	0	5	43	2	9	835	7	3	1	6	14

ARTHUR TREACHER'S

COMPLETE NUTRITIONAL VALUES¹ CONTINUED	WEIGHT² (gm.)	CALORIES	PROTEIN (gm.)	
Coke, small, 12 fl. oz.	355	96	0	
Coke, medium, 16 fl. oz.	474	128	0	
Coke, large, 20 fl. oz.	592	160	0	
Coke, one-liter, 33.5 fl. oz.	992	268	0	
✓ Cole Slaw	85	123	1	
✓ Fish, broiled, 5 oz.	142	245	20	
Fish, fried, 2 pieces	147	355	19	
Fish Sandwich	156	440	16	
Krunch Pup (batter-fried hot dog)	57	203	5	
Lemon Luv (fried pie)	85	276	3	
✓ Salad Bar	—			
Shrimp, fried	115	381	13	

1. A dash means that data not available.
2. To convert grams to ounces (weight), divide by 28.35; to convert grams to fluid ounces (volume), divide by 29.6.

BURGER KING

With 4,600 restaurants worldwide, Pillsbury-owned Burger King has been playing a valiant, but apparently futile, game of catch-up with McDonald's. Fortunately for fast-food consumers, Burger King adds some competition to the marketplace and bases part of its marketing effort on improved nutrition. From time to time in its advertising, Burger King takes a slap at McDonald's.

Burger King built its reputation on flame-broiled and custom-made hamburgers. What does flame broiling do for a burger? It adds a unique flavor not found in those from other restaurants. However, our tests found that the meat in Burger King's and McDonald's hamburgers contained virtually identical levels of fat—just over 20 percent (though

CARBOHYDRATES (gm.)	ADDED SUGAR[3] (gm.)	FAT[4] (gm.)	FAT % CALORIES	SATURATED FAT (gm.)	CHOLESTEROL (mg.)	SODIUM (mg.)	VITAMIN A (% U.S.RDA)	VITAMIN C (% U.S.RDA)	IRON (% U.S.RDA)	CALCIUM (% U.S.RDA)	GLOOM
24	24	0	0	0	0	—	0	0	0	0	3
32	32	0	0	0	0	—	0	0	0	0	4
40	40	0	0	0	0	—	0	0	0	0	5
67	67	0	0	0	0	—	0	0	0	0	9
11	0	8	60	1	7	266	3	99	1	2	9
10	0	14	—	—	—	144	—	—	—	—	16
25	0	20	50	3	56	450	2	3	3	2	26
39	0	24	49	4	42	836	2	3	8	9	34
12	0	15	66	4	25	446	1	6	3	1	21
35	12	14	45	2	1	314	1	2	5	1	21
depends on ingredients											
27	0	24	57	3	93	538	2	2	4	6	32

3. *To convert grams of sugar to teaspoons of sugar, divide by 4.0.*
4. *To convert grams of fat to teaspoons of fat, divide by 4.4.*

Burger King's own data indicate that the meat is somewhat fattier than McDonald's).

Breakfast at Burger King is grease city. People who want to avoid calories, fat, and/or cholesterol should avoid Croissan'wiches—the soggy bulwark of the Burger King breakfast menu. All the breakfast croissants come with cheese, and the meat choices are all traditional, salty, breakfast meats—ham, bacon, and sausage. Unfortunately, there is no way to turn croissants into a prudent breakfast choice; adding salty meats and fatty cheese only increases their Gloom rating. As far as taste and texture are concerned, a Croissan'wich is to a real croissant as a piece of Wonder Bread is to a chewy, fresh-baked bagel. To expand its variety of greasy choices, Burger King is now testing the "A.M. Express," four different meals based on deep-fried or otherwise fat-laden french toast.

For many years, information about breakfast nutrients was unavailable, so consumers could only guess as to the most healthful choice among croissants, egg platters with hash browns, and french toast. Even though Burger King has served breakfast for six years and croissants for three, the company never provided nutrition information. In July 1986, Burger King was preparing an up-to-date pamphlet containing the ingredient and nutritional content of all its foods. Ask for it, if you eat at one of their outlets, or write to Burger King's headquarters (see the Appendix for the address).

The Whopper was changed recently, but not for the better—it has more beef, more fat, and less bun. The Double Beef Whopper with cheese is near the top of the list of bad choices for dinner. The Gloom rating of 76 tips us off to its almost thousand calories, high sodium content (about 1,200 milligrams), and 15 teaspoons of fat. This is the fast-food industry's second fattiest food.

Burger King's Specialty Chicken Sandwich is the second fattiest chicken product made by fast-food chains, with nine teaspoons of fat. You can chop the fat in half by asking the clerk not to dump the mayonnaise on your sandwich.

After the all-American choice of a plain hamburger (Gloom = 17), the best you can choose at Burger King is the Whaler Sandwich, where 50 percent of the 488 calories come from fat. For years the company had used a highly saturated beef-vegetable fat blend to deep-fry its products, making the chicken and fish choices no more prudent than the flame-broiled beef. But in March 1986, the company began switching to a less saturated fat (80-percent soy, 20-percent peanut) for all deep-fried products except french fries. This change results in a product that, while just as high in fat and calories, contains significantly less saturated fat and cholesterol.

The switch to vegetable oil by such a huge company is a boon to Americans' arteries. Burger King's move elicited a most unusual and perhaps unprecedented form of praise. The nonprofit National Heart Savers Association, based in Omaha, Nebraska, ran small ads in 175 newspapers saying, "Thank you, Burger King! for introducing . . . low-cholesterol, low-saturated-fat 'Chicken Tenders'." It is to be hoped that some of the other chains will try to get similar compliments in the future.

Burger King promoted its new Chicken Tenders product partly on the basis of their being fried in vegetable oil and made from whole pieces of chicken—both digs at McDonald's McNuggets—and sales went through the roof. In fact, Burger King had to halt its advertising, because it could obtain only 1.4 million pounds of chicken a week, while it needed 1.8 million pounds to supply all of its restaurants. Incidentally, some industry observers suggested that Burger King went to the market prematurely with the chicken, because its $40 million "Where's Herb?" campaign was a dismal failure. Partly because of Burger King's ads, McDonald's moved McNuggets from fryers filled with beef fat to ones loaded with vegetable oil.

Chicken Tenders beat the breading off McDonald's Chicken McNuggets. Tenders contain one-third fewer calories and half the fat. The Tenders' Gloom rating of 16 is about half that of McNuggets (27). Only in the sodium department are the McNuggets a little better.

Burger King's salad bar offers healthful choices including fresh vegetables and low-fat dressing. Burger King, in fact, probably manages more salad bars than any other company in the world. The salad bar is your best shot at getting a fine meal, and it's certainly a good reason to patronize this chain. Perhaps some day Burger King will offer skim or low-fat milk, fresh fruits, yogurt, and whole-grain buns at all of its outlets, too.

Wall Street investors certainly cannot accuse Burger King of ignoring the lucrative children's market. Much of its advertising is geared toward children, and it has packaged children's meals for several years. The Burger King character was an early attempt to win young customers away from Ronald McDonald. Other promotions draw on movies and cartoons with child-appeal. In 1985, the Masters of the Universe cartoon theme was used in a comic strip on the outside of the meal box. Inside were puzzles and a cardboard crown in addition to a sandwich, fries, and a drink. Soft drinks came in a sturdy plastic cup with comic-book characters around the outside. This lavish packaging makes one wonder just the teensiest bit about the validity of complaints that ingredient labeling is too expensive.

The 1986 attempt for kids' loyalty included the "Burger Book." A bag unfolds from the middle of the child-oriented magazine. When dinner's over, a child can tear the bag away, saving the 12-page pamphlet and its puzzles, games, stickers, and Burger King logos.

BURGER KING INGREDIENTS

Main Items

Chicken Specialty: chicken, marinade (water, salt, sodium phosphate, monosodium glutamate, food starch), batter and breading [bleached wheat flour, salt, spices, partially saturated vegetable oil (soybean, cottonseed, and/or palm) whey, monosodium glutamate, yeast, sweet peppers, onion powder, garlic powder, dextrose, leavening (monocalcium phosphate, sodium acid pyrophosphate, sodium bicarbonate), corn starch, oat flour, natural flavoring]. Fried in 100-percent vegetable shortening (soybean and peanut oil).

Chicken Tenders: white chicken breast meat, marinade (water, salt, sodium phosphate, chemically modified food starch, flavoring), batter and breading (bleached wheat flour, corn flour, salt, spices, dextrose, garlic powder, monosodium glutamate, monocalcium phosphate, buttermilk, natural flavors). Fried in 100-percent vegetable shortening (soybean and peanut oil).

Egg mix: Grade A fresh eggs mixed with whole milk and salt, grilled in vegetable shortening.

Whaler fish fillet: skinless and boneless cod fillets breaded and battered in bleached wheat flour, chemically modified corn starch, corn flour, water, salt, whey, natural spices, carrageenan, soybean oil, cellulose gum, malt syrup, dried yeast, nonfat milk, dextrose, leavening (sodium acid pyrophosphate, sodium bicarbonate, monocalcium phosphate), calcium propionate. Fried in 100-percent vegetable shortening.

Whopper patty/burger patty: 100-percent ground beef (broiled).

Side Dishes

Bacon: bacon cured with water, salt, hickory-smoked flavor, sugar, dextrose, sodium erythorbate, sodium nitrite, BHA and BHT added as antioxidant preservatives.

French toast: Egg Bread: (wheat flour, bleached flour, malted barley, water, sugar, vegetable shortening (palm and soybean) yeast, salt, wheat gluten, corn flour, dextrose, egg yolk, dough conditioners (mono- and diglycerides, sodium stearoyl lactylate, calcium stearoyl lacty-late), calcium propionate, lecithin, turmeric, paprika, natural flavors, yeast nutrients (monocalcium phosphate, calcium sulfate, ammonium sulfate, ammonium chloride), beta carotene, potassium bromate, enriched with ferrous sulfate, niacin, thiamin hydrochloride and riboflavin; eggs, water, soybean oil, enriched wheat flour, soy flour, artificial flavors, sodium bicarbonate, dextrose. Fried in 100-percent vegetable shortening.

Bun for Whopper, Burger, and Specialty: enriched wheat flour, water, sugar (sucrose or high fructose corn syrup), sesame seeds, shortening (animal and/or vegetable), salt, wheat gluten, yeast, yeast food, mono-and diglycerides, sodium and/or calcium stearoyl lactylate, ammonium sulfate, calcium stearoyl lactylate, ammonium sulfate, calcium propionate, calcium peroxide, potassium bromate, azodicarbonamide, potassium sorbate, protease enzyme, potassium iodate, calcium sulfate, monocalcium phosphate.

Cheese: pasteurized American cheese (cultured milk, salt, enzymes, annato color), cream, water, enzyme-modified cheese, sodium citrate, salt, sodium aluminum phosphate, sodium phosphate, sorbic acid (preservative), acetic acid, phosphoric acid, lecithin, carotenal color.

Croissant: wheat flour, vegetable shortening (soybean and cottonseed), water, sugar, milk, yeast, whole eggs, salt, mono- and diglycerides, annatto extract, calcium propionate, sodium phosphate, lecithin, carrageenan, spice oils (turmeric and paprika).

French fries: potatoes, shortenings (animal and vegetable), dextrose, pyrophosphate (sodium acid or disodium dihydrogen). Fried in combination beef fat/vegetable shortening.

Ham: smoked ham cured with water, salt, dextrose, corn syrup, sodium phosphate, sodium erythorbate, sodium nitrite.

Hash browns: potatoes, vegetable shortenings, salt, natural flavor, dehydrated onion and/or onion flavoring, dextrose, pyrophosphate (sodium acid or disodium dihydrogen). Fried in 100-percent vegetable shortening.

Onion rings: rehydrated onion, vegetable shortening, bleached wheat flour, wheat flour, gelatinized wheat starch, water, sugar, yellow corn flour, sodium alginate, soy flour, dextrose, carbohydrate gum, calcium chloride, salt, garlic powder, natural flavoring, leavening (monocalcium phosphate, sodium bicarbonate), dried whey, polysorbate 80, silicon dioxide, onion extractives, BHA. Fried in 100-percent vegetable shortening.

Sausage: pork sausage patty with spices added (salt, spices, sugar, pepper, monosodium glutamate, hydrolyzed vegetable protein).

Fats

For fries: beef tallow, cottonseed oil, monoglyceride citrate, BHT, BHA, propyl gallate, propylene glycol.

For other foods: partially hydrogenated soybean oil, peanut oil, TBHQ, citric acid, dimethylpolysiloxane.

Desserts

Apple pie: apples, flour, vegetable shortening, corn sweetener, sugar, water, chemically modified food starch, salt, potassium sorbate, cinnamon, casein, lecithin, sodium phosphate, carrageenan, extract of turmeric and paprika.

Cherry pie: cherries, flour, sugar, partially saturated vegetable shortening (soybean, cottonseed, and/or palm oils), water, chemically modified food starch, corn sugar, salt, potassium sorbate, casein, lecithin, sodium phosphate, carrageenan, extract of turmeric and paprika.

Cinnamon raisin danish: enriched flour (malted barley flour, niacin, iron, thiamin mononitrate, riboflavin), corn syrup, sugar, partially saturated vegetable shortening (soybean and cottonseed oils), fresh whole eggs, water, raisins, skim milk, mono- and diglycerides, yeast, salt, chemically modified food starch, cinnamon, fresh egg whites, baking powder (sodium acid pyrophosphate, baking soda, corn starch, monocalcium phosphate, calcium sulfate), casein, agar, gelatin, annatto extract.

Pecan pie: corn sweetener, flour, pecans, whole eggs, water, vegetable margarine (soybean oil, water, salt, skim milk, lecithin, mono- and diglycerides, sodium benzoate, citric acid, artificial flavor, beta carotene, vitamin A palmitate), salt, potassium sorbate.

Beverages

Chocolate shake: milk, sugar, water, corn sweetener, cream, whey, partially delactosed nonfat milk, mono- and diglycerides, cellulose gum, guar gum, karaya gum, cocoa processed with alkali, dipotassium phosphate, sodium citrate, carrageenan, salt, sodium carbonate, sodium phosphate. *Note:* In some areas, the following syrup may be added: corn sweeteners, water, sugar, cocoa, caramel color, salt, artificial flavors, potassium sorbate, artificial colors (Blue Dye Number 1 and Red Dye Number 3), sodium alginate.

Diet Pepsi: carbonated water, caramel, phosphoric acid, potassium benzoate, calcium saccharin, citric acid, aspartame, caffeine, natural flavorings, dimethylpolysiloxane.

Dr. Pepper: carbonated water, sugar, corn syrup, caramel, artificial and natural flavoring, phosphoric acid, caffeine, sodium benzoate, monosodium phosphate, lactic acid.

Hot chocolate: sugar and/or corn sweeteners, water, vegetable shortening, skim milk, cocoa (processed with alkalai), whey solids, salt, disodium phosphate, chocolate liquor, soy lecithin, artificial flavors, cream.

Mountain Dew: carbonated water, corn sweetener and/or sugar, orange juice and other natural flavors, citric acid, sodium benzoate, caffeine, sodium citrate, gum arabic, erythorbic acid, EDTA, brominated vegetable oil, Yellow Dye Number 5 artificial coloring.

Pepsi Cola: carbonated water, corn sweetener and/or sugar, caramel, phosphoric acid, caffeine, citric acid, natural flavorings.

7 Up: carbonated water, sugar and/or corn sweetener, citric acid, sodium benzoate, sodium citrate, natural lemon and lime flavorings.

Strawberry shake: same base as Vanilla Shake. The following syrup is added: corn sweeteners, water, citric acid, artificial flavor, artificial colors (Yellow Dye Number 5 and Red Dye Number 40), sodium benzoate.

Vanilla shake: milk, sugar, water, corn sweetener, cream, whey, partially delactosed nonfat milk, mono- and diglycerides, artificial flavor, cellulose gum, guar gum, karaya gum, dipotassium phosphate, sodium citrate, carrageenan, salt, sodium carbonate, annatto, caramel colors. *Note:* In some areas, the following syrup may be added: corn sweeteners, water, artificial flavor, sodium benzoate, citric acid, caramel color.

Condiments

Barbecue sauce: water, sugar, distilled vinegar, tomato paste, salt, food starch, liquid brown sugar, hickory-smoked flavor, soybean oil, xanthan gum, sodium benzoate, spices.

Blue cheese dressing: soybean oil, water, blue cheese, distilled vinegar, egg yolk, sugar, salt, garlic powder, black pepper, potassium sorbate, sodium benzoate, rehydrated cultured buttermilk, white pepper, xanthan gum.

Creamy Italian dressing: water, soybean oil, vinegar, sugar, salt, garlic, xanthan gum, onion spice, polysorbate 60, propylene glycol alginate, red bell pepper, lemon juice concentrate, calcium disodium EDTA, natural flavor.

French dressing: soybean oil, sugar, water, tomato paste, vinegar, salt, dehydrated onion, xanthan gum, dehydrated garlic, calcium disodium EDTA.

Golden Italian dressing: soybean oil, water, vinegar, sugar, salt, garlic, xanthan gum, onion, mustard flour, citric acid, red bell pepper, spice, natural flavor, calcium disodium EDTA, oleoresin paprika, Yellow Dye Number 5.

Horseradish sauce: soybean oil, water, horseradish, sugar, salt, egg yolks, distilled vinegar, mustard flour, xanthan gum, horseradish flavor, spices, calcium disodium EDTA, lemon juice, dehydrated garlic, dehydrated onion.

BURGER KING

COMPLETE NUTRITIONAL VALUES[1]

	WEIGHT[2] (gm.)	CALORIES	PROTEIN (gm.)
Apple Pie	125	305	3
Bacon Double Cheeseburger	159	510	33
Bacon, Egg, & Cheese Croissan'wich	120	355	14
✓ Cheeseburger	120	317	17
✓ Chicken Tenders, 6 pieces	95	204	20
Chocolate Shake, 10 fl. oz.	284	374	8
Diet Pepsi, medium	366	1	0
Double Beef Whopper	350	887	51
Double Beef Whopper with Cheese	373	970	56
Double Cheeseburger	170	478	29
Double Hamburger	148	394	25
French Fries, regular	74	227	3

House dressing: soybean oil, water, corn syrup, cultured buttermilk, egg yolks, salt, vinegar, sugar, monosodium glutamate, lactic acid, garlic, onion, citric acid, natural flavor, sodium benzoate, potassium sorbate, calcium disodium EDTA, spice, xanthan gum, parsley, buttermilk.

Ketchup: tomatoes, sugar and/or corn sweetener, water, distilled vinegar, salt, onion powder, spices and natural flavors.

Mayonnaise: soybean oil, water, egg yolk, corn sweetener, distilled vinegar, spices, salt, disodium EDTA.

Mustard: water, vinegar, mustard seed, salt, turmeric, paprika.

Reduced calorie Italian dressing: water, vinegar, sugar, salt, soybean oil, garlic, xanthan gum, onion, spice, red bell pepper, natural flavor, calcium disodium EDTA, artificial colors (Yellow Dye Numbers 5 and 6).

Sweet & sour sauce: water, light brown sugar, distilled vinegar, pineapple concentrate, crushed pineapple, food starch, Worcestershire base, xanthan gum, soybean oil, sodium benzoate, white pepper, allspice, garlic powder.

Tartar sauce: soybean oil, water, dill relish with onions (cucumber, vinegar, onions, salt, natural flavors, alum), corn sweetener, distilled vinegar, egg yolk, spices, salt, sodium benzoate, xanthan gum, EDTA.

Thousand Island dressing: soybean oil, water, sugar, vinegar, chopped pickle, tomato paste, egg yolks, salt, mustard flour, dehydrated onion, spice, xanthan gum, dextrose, propylene glycol alginate, oleoresin paprika, natural flavor, dehydrated tomato paste, calcium disodium EDTA, chemically modified food starch.

CARBOHYDRATES (gm.)	ADDED SUGAR[3] (gm.)	FAT[4] (gm.)	FAT % CALORIES	SATURATED FAT (gm.)	CHOLESTEROL (mg.)	SODIUM (mg.)	VITAMIN A (% U.S.RDA)	VITAMIN C (% U.S.RDA)	IRON (% U.S.RDA)	CALCIUM (% U.S.RDA)	GLOOM
44	14	12	35	4	4	412	0	8	7	0	20
27	0	31	55	15	104	728	7	0	21	17	38
20	0	24	61	8	249	762	9	0	11	14	32
30	0	15	43	7	48	651	7	5	15	10	21
10	0	10	44	2	47	636	2	0	4	2	16
60	37	11	26	7	—	225	0	0	9	25	18
0	0	0	0	0	0	—	0	0	0	0	0
42	0	57	58	23	176	922	12	23	41	9	66
43	0	64	59	27	199	1206	20	23	41	22	76
31	0	27	51	13	96	827	14	5	22	20	35
29	0	21	48	9	74	543	3	5	22	4	26
24	0	13	52	7	14	160	0	4	3	0	17

BURGER KING

COMPLETE NUTRITIONAL VALUES[1] CONTINUED

	WEIGHT[2] (gm.)	CALORIES	PROTEIN (gm.)
✓ Hamburger	109	275	15
Hash Browns	61	162	2
Milk, whole, 8 fl. oz.	244	157	8
Onion Rings, regular	79	274	4
Pepsi, medium	366	159	0
Scrambled Egg Platter (eggs, croissant, hash browns)	195	468	15
Specialty Chicken Sandwich	230	688	26
Specialty Ham & Cheese Sandwich	230	471	24
Vanilla Shake, 10 fl. oz.	273	321	9
Whaler Sandwich	190	488	19
Whaler Sandwich with Cheese	201	530	21
Whopper	265	626	28
Whopper Jr.	136	322	15
Whopper with Cheese	288	709	33
Whopper Jr. with Cheese	147	364	17

1. A dash means that data not available.
2. To convert grams to ounces (weight), divide by 28.35; to convert grams to fluid ounces (volume), divide by 29.6.

CARL'S JR.

Based in Anaheim, California, Carl's Jr. is the "California cuisine" of the fast-food world. This chain serves a wide variety of foods with relatively low Gloom ratings in addition to typical unhealthful fast food. The restaurant offers modified table service—servers bring food to the table after patrons place their order at the counter.

For breakfast, Carl's Jr. has English Muffins. With butter and jelly

CARBOHYDRATES (gm.)	ADDED SUGAR³ (gm.)	FAT⁴ (gm.)	FAT % CALORIES	SATURATED FAT (gm.)	CHOLESTEROL (mg.)	SODIUM (mg.)	VITAMIN A (% U.S.RDA)	VITAMIN C (% U.S.RDA)	IRON (% U.S.RDA)	CALCIUM (% U.S.RDA)	GLOOM
29	0	12	39	5	37	509	3	5	15	4	17
13	0	11	61	5	2	193	0	—	—	—	15
11	0	9	67	6	35	119	7	6	0	30	10
28	0	16	53	3	0	655	0	0	4	12	25
40	40	0	0	0	0	—	0	0	0	0	5
33	0	30	58	11	370	808	7	4	15	10	40
56	0	40	52	8	82	1423	3	0	18	8	58
44	0	24	46	9	70	1534	15	12	18	19	39
49	35	10	28	6	—	205	0	0	0	29	16
45	0	27	50	6	84	592	1	0	12	5	35
46	0	30	51	8	95	734	5	0	12	11	39
42	0	38	55	13	94	842	12	23	27	8	47
30	0	17	48	6	41	486	6	10	16	4	22
43	0	45	57	18	117	1126	20	23	27	21	56
31	0	20	49	8	52	628	10	10	16	11	26

3. To convert grams of sugar to teaspoons of sugar, divide by 4.0.
4. To convert grams of fat to teaspoons of fat, divide by 4.4.

they contain 228 calories and 245 milligrams of sodium. Hold the toppings and you'll cut the calories significantly.

Steer clear of the sausage and bacon, and the cholesterol-laden omelettes and scrambled eggs. The California Omelette contains nearly six teaspoons of fat. If you want eggs, the plain scrambled eggs are the best choice. But you might want to try Hot Cakes and orange juice instead. The Sunrise Sandwiches are high in sodium (the company's data do not appear to be accurate), and the Hashed Brown Potatoes get 61 percent of their 280 calories from fat—a far cry from a plain, fat-free, Baked Potato.

"Why buy chicken for the health aspects and dip it in fat?" says Paul Mitchell, spokesperson for Carl's. So the chain "charbroils" the chicken for its Charbroiler Chicken Sandwich and serves it with lettuce, tomato, and barbecue sauce on a honey-wheat bun (not to be confused with whole wheat). It's heaping with sodium—1,380 milligrams—but gets only 28 percent of its 450 calories from fat.

For dinner, Carl's Jr. has a regular salad, as well as salad bars with some of their restaurants offering a low-calorie dressing. Many, if not all, Carl's salad bars include fresh fruit, a real plus that puts Carl's Jr. a cut above most of the competition. Stuffed baked potatoes, too, are only offered in some of their restaurants.

Roast beef lovers should certainly check out the California Roast Beef Sandwich. It has the lowest fat content of any fast-food roast beef sandwich we have seen. Note though that the roast beef is heavily processed. Yet it has a low Gloom rating of only 11. If more fast-food were like this, it would certainly be a lot easier to eat out.

All hamburgers at Carl's Jr. come with lettuce and tomato—a small addition of fiber that you won't find at many other places without paying extra. But a burger's a burger the world around and there's nothing wildly different about the burger situation at Carl's Jr., except that it's higher in fat. In a study conducted by CSPI of hamburger meat used by nine restaurant chains, Carl's Jr. was the fattiest, just nosing out Jack in the Box. Carl's hamburger meat is 38 percent fattier than the leanest (D'Lites).

The best burger deal nutritionally is the Happy Star Burger, which is also the center of the children's package. This burger, served with mustard, ketchup, and pickles, yields 330 calories, 670 milligrams of sodium, and gets 35 percent of its calories from fat. This compares to a standard burger at McDonald's that has 506 milligrams of sodium and gets 39 percent of its 263 calories from fat. The bigger the burger, of course, the gloomier the picture. The Super Star Hamburger contains 780 calories, nearly 60 percent of them from the 50 grams of fat (11 teaspoons). Obviously, you can cut the calories, fat, and sodium by getting all these burgers without the garnishes.

Despite the healthy image that Carl's Jr. seeks to convey, beef fat is the major ingredient of the frying fat, according to Paul Mitchell.

If you choose to have a large shake, make sure you have someone to share it with. The Carl's Jr. Shake provides 490 calories and is loaded with sugar—we estimate about 14 teaspoons per shake. And the fries, well, they're the highest in sodium of all we've seen.

According to spokesperson Mitchell, Carl's Jr. plans to revise and update its nutrition and ingredient information. Some nutrition information is distributed through the restaurants. As of June 1986, the information was four years old and did not reflect many changes in the menu. Amended to remove outdated information, that list follows. Though Carl's Jr. would not provide comprehensive ingredient information, some details follow the nutrition chart.

CARL'S JR. INGREDIENTS

Main Items

Chicken: boneless skinless chicken breast with rib meat, barbecue sauce.

Fish: cod, bleached wheat flour, water, chemically modified food starch, corn flour, whey, salt, natural flavor, soybean oil.

Side Dishes

American cheese: American cheese, water, milk fat, sodium citrate, sodium aluminum phosphate (basic), salt, sodium phosphate, sorbic acid, artificial color.

Breaded onion rings: onions, wheat flour, water, baking powder, sodium benzoate, artificial color.

Honey wheat bun: enriched bleached flour, water, corn syrup, soybean or lard or beef fat, yeast, whey, salt, dough conditioners (sodium stearoyl lactylate, potassium bromate), barley malt, calcium sulfate, ammonium sulfate, mono- and diglycerides, calcium propionate, lecithin.

Sausage: pork, water, salt, corn syrup solids, spices, sugar, dextrose, monosodium glutamate, BHT, propyl gallate, citric acid.

Seeded bun (4½ inches): enriched bleached flour (flour, niacin, ferrous sulfate, thiamin mononitrate, riboflavin), water, corn syrup, vegetable and/or animal shortening (may contain soybean oil and/ or partially saturated lard), yeast, whey, salt, dough conditioners (sodium stearoyl-2-lactylate, potassium bromate, barley malt), yeast nutrients (calcium sulfate, ammonium sulfate), monoglycerides, cal-

cium propionate. May contain sesame or poppy seeds.

Fats

Frying shortening: animal fat, vegetable oil mixture (probably 95-percent beef fat).

Beverages

Chocolate shake base: corn sweeteners, cocoa, chemically modified starch, caramel color, artificial colors including Yellow Dye Number 5, sodium propionate, salt, cellulose gum, natural flavor.

Strawberry shake base: corn sugar and invert syrups, artificial strawberry flavor, citric acid, sodium benzoate.

Vanilla ice-milk mix: milk, skim milk, sugar, corn sweeteners, nonfat milk solids, stabilizer-emulsifier (guar gum, calcium sulfate, carrageenan, polysorbate 60, dextrose, whey, salt), artificial flavor, annatto coloring.

Vanilla shake base: corn sugar and invert syrups, artificial vanilla flavor, caramel color, benzoic acid.

Condiments

Barbecue sauce: water, brown sugar, soy sauce, tomato paste, cider vinegar, Worcestershire sauce, salt, monosodium glutamate, granulated garlic, spice, xanthan gum.

Soy sauce: water, wheat, soybeans, salt, sodium benzoate.

Worcestershire sauce: diluted vinegar, sugar, corn syrup, soy sauce, salt, caramel color, garlic, spices.

CARL'S JR.

COMPLETE NUTRITIONAL VALUES[1]

	WEIGHT[2] (gm.)	CALORIES	PROTEIN (gm.)
American Cheese	—	70	4
Bacon 'n Cheese Omelette	—	290	23
Bacon, 2 strips	—	70	4
✓ Baked Potato, plain	—	167	4
Baked Potato, stuffed	— no data —		
Blue Cheese Dressing, 2 oz.	57	160	2
Butter, 1 tbsp.	—	108	0
California Omelette	—	310	20
✓ California Roast Beef Sandwich	—	300	25
Carrot Cake	—	350	4
Charbroiler Chicken Sandwich	—	450	26
Charbroiler Steak Sandwich	—	630	30
Cheese Omelette	—	280	19
English Muffin with Butter & Jelly	—	228	5
Famous Star Hamburger	—	530	24
Filet of Fish Sandwich, fried	—	570	20
French Fries, regular	—	250	3
Happy Star Hamburger	—	330	20
Hashed Brown Potatoes	100	280	2
Hot Dog	— no data —		
Hot Cakes with Syrup & Butter	—	480	7
Hot Chocolate	—	110	4
Low-cal Italian Dressing, 2 oz.	57	90	0
Old Time Star Hamburger	—	450	24
Onion Rings	—	330	5

CARBOHYDRATES (gm.)	ADDED SUGAR[3] (gm.)	FAT[1] (gm.)	FAT % CALORIES	SATURATED FAT (gm.)	CHOLESTEROL (mg.)	SODIUM (mg.)	VITAMIN A (% U.S.RDA)	VITAMIN C (% U.S.RDA)	IRON (% U.S.RDA)	CALCIUM (% U.S.RDA)	GLOOM
1	0	6	77	—	15	120	2	0	0	10	7
2	0	28	87	—	470	660	6	0	10	25	33
0	0	6	77	—	10	220	0	0	2	0	9
33	0	2	11	—	0	6	0	43	13	—	2
					— no data —						
2	0	16	90	—	30	230	0	0	0	2	21
14	0	12	100	—	35	149	10	0	0	0	15
3	0	24	70	—	630	550	6	0	15	30	28
34	0	7	21	—	60	505	8	10	30	20	11
44	14	18	46	—	45	375	4	0	8	4	26
55	0	14	28	—	55	1380	2	4	12	10	28
54	0	33	47	—	85	700	8	4	25	10	41
2	0	22	71	—	460	440	6	0	10	25	25
34	7	9	36	—	25	245	2	0	10	15	13
38	0	32	54	—	70	705	10	4	25	10	40
61	0	27	43	—	40	790	6	4	15	25	36
25	0	15	54	—	5	460	0	10	2	8	21
33	0	13	35	—	40	670	4	0	20	8	20
6	0	19	61	—	15	260	0	0	4	0	26
					— no data —						
80	34	15	28	—	15	530	0	0	15	20	26
20	15	2	16	—	0	12	0	4	4	10	4
0	0	10	100	—	0	360	0	0	0	0	17
45	0	20	40	—	60	625	8	0	30	6	26
39	0	17	46	—	15	75	2	0	10	2	20

CARL'S JR.

COMPLETE NUTRITIONAL VALUES[1] CONTINUED	WEIGHT[2] (gm.)	CALORIES	PROTEIN (gm.)
Orange Juice	—	80	1
✓ Salad, regular	—	210	11
Sausage, 1 patty	—	110	7
✓ Scrambled Eggs	—	150	10
Shakes, large	—	490	15
Soft Drinks, regular	—	240	0
Sour Cream	—	45	1
Sunrise Sandwich with Bacon	—	410	20
Sunrise Sandwich with Sausage	—	450	23
Super Star Hamburger	—	780	43
Sweet Roll with Butter	—	420	8
Swiss Cheese	—	70	4
Thousand Island Dressing, 2 oz.	57	240	0
Western Bacon Cheeseburger	—	670	35
Zucchini, fried	—	311	4

1. A dash means that data not available.
2. To convert grams to ounces (weight), divide by 28.35; to convert grams to fluid ounces (volume), divide by 29.6.

CHURCH'S FRIED CHICKEN

San Antonio-based Church's is number two in fast-food chicken sales, serving fried chicken meals with a jalapeño pepper. The bright green pepper, presumably, will distract many consumers from the fact that the chicken nuggets are made from "composite" chicken, not from whole pieces.

The minute you dunk your food in a fryer full of hot grease you're going to add fat and calories. Since virtually everything Church's

CARBOHYDRATES (gm.)	ADDED SUGAR[3] (gm.)	FAT[4] (gm.)	FAT % CALORIES	SATURATED FAT (gm.)	CHOLESTEROL (mg.)	SODIUM (mg.)	VITAMIN A (% U.S.RDA)	VITAMIN C (% U.S.RDA)	IRON (% U.S.RDA)	CALCIUM (% U.S.RDA)	GLOOM
20	0	0	0	0	0	0	8	160	2	2	0
33	0	4	17	—	0	695	80	45	15	10	9
0	0	9	74	—	25	235	0	0	2	0	12
1	0	12	72	—	380	110	2	0	8	4	13
90	54	8	15	—	25	350	0	0	6	60	17
61	61	0	0	0	0	45	0	0	0	2	8
2	0	4	80	—	11	10	4	0	0	2	4
28	0	24	53	—	310	780	6	0	15	20	32
28	0	27	54	—	125	790	2	0	15	20	35
38	0	50	58	—	155	785	10	4	35	10	59
57	9	18	39	—	20	450	4	0	15	8	26
1	0	5	64	—	15	125	2	0	0	10	6
8	0	24	90	—	20	320	0	0	0	0	34
42	0	40	54	—	90	1330	4	0	25	20	54
32	0	19	55	—	18	516	2	5	9	4	27

3. *To convert grams of sugar to teaspoons of sugar, divide by 4.0.*
4. *To convert grams of fat to teaspoons of fat, divide by 4.4.*

serves is so dunked, the food usually falls near the 60-percent-of-calories-from-fat mark. That's except for the coleslaw, of course, which gets 76 percent of its calories from the two teaspoons of fat in the fatty dressing. These choices are a far cry from the 30-percent-maximum target level set by several health organizations, such as the National Cancer Institute, the American Heart Association, and the National Academy of Sciences.

Considering the rest of the menu, the french fries look like a great deal, at a "measly" 45 percent of the 256 calories from fat. Okra and liver would be good choices, were they not heavily breaded and deep-fried.

"Best choices" at Church's are few and far between. While you probably don't want to make a meal of the jalapeño peppers, corn on the cob, and dinner rolls, these foods are lowest in fat and calories. Church's, like several other chains, is developing a nonfried chicken product, which may be available in late 1986.

Church's, with over 1,600 outlets, is the second biggest chicken-oriented chain, but still miles behind the 6,396-unit Kentucky Fried Chicken.

Limited nutrition information follows. Church's does not provide information about vitamins, iron, and calcium, nor does it disclose the sodium content of french fries. Church's would not part with ingredient information except when one spokesperson informed CSPI (after a third request), "I have not found any of our products to contain FD&C

CHURCH'S FRIED CHICKEN
COMPLETE NUTRITIONAL VALUES[1]

	WEIGHT[2] (gm.)	CALORIES	PROTEIN (gm.)
Apple Pie, 3 oz.	85	300	2
✓ Catfish, fried, 3 pieces	63	201	12
Chicken Nuggets, regular, 6 pieces	108	330	18
✓ Chicken Nuggets, spicy, 6 pieces	108	312	19
✓ Cole Slaw	85	83	1
✓ Corn on the Cob, buttered, 9 oz.	256	165	5
Dinner Roll	28	83	2
French Fries, regular (3 oz.)	85	256	4
Fried Chicken Breast	93	278	21
✓ Fried Chicken Leg	56	147	13
Fried Chicken Thigh	93	305	19
Fried Chicken Wing	97	303	22

Yellow Number 5 (dye)." Our investigation of some restaurants in Washington, D.C., found that the frying oil contains partially saturated soybean oil and methyl silicone (to prevent foaming or spattering).

CHURCH'S FRIED CHICKEN INGREDIENTS

Condiments

Bar-b-que sauce: water, corn sweeteners, tomato paste, distilled vinegar, sugar, chemically modified food starch, salt, soybean oil, spices and natural flavors, natural smoke flavor, onion powder, xanthan gum, citric acid, 0.1-percent sodium benzoate, lemon juice powder, caramel color.

Mustard sauce: water, distilled vinegar, sugar, corn syrup, mustard seed, salt, chemically modified food starch, tomato paste, tamarind extract, honey powder, pineapple juice powder, 0.1-percent sodium benzoate, monosodium glutamate, xanthan gum, turmeric, extractive of turmeric, natural and artificial flavor.

Sweet n' sour sauce: water, corn syrup, distilled vinegar, tomato paste, sugar, chemcially modified food starch, spice, honey powder, salt, xanthan gum, pineapple juice powder, tamarind extract, 0.1-percent sodium benzoate, turmeric, natural and artificial flavor, extractive of turmeric.

CARBOHYDRATES (gm.)	ADDED SUGAR[3] (gm.)	FAT* (gm.)	FAT % CALORIES	SATURATED FAT (gm.)	CHOLESTEROL (mg.)	SODIUM (mg.)	VITAMIN A (% U.S.RDA)	VITAMIN C (% U.S.RDA)	IRON (% U.S.RDA)	CALCIUM (% U.S.RDA)	GLOOM
31	14	19	56	—	—	—	—	—	—	—	24
11	0	12	54	—	—	453	—	—	—	—	18
22	0	19	51	—	—	750	—	—	—	—	28
20	0	17	50	—	—	546	—	—	—	—	24
6	0	7	76	—	—	—	—	—	—	—	8
29	0	3	18	—	—	—	—	—	—	—	4
15	0	2	17	—	—	—	—	—	—	—	2
31	0	13	45	—	—	—	—	—	—	—	15
9	0	17	56	—	—	560	—	—	—	—	24
5	0	9	53	—	—	286	—	—	—	—	12
9	0	22	64	—	—	448	—	—	—	—	28
9	0	20	59	—	—	583	—	—	—	—	27

CHURCH'S FRIED CHICKEN

COMPLETE NUTRITIONAL VALUES[1] CONTINUED	WEIGHT[2] (gm.)	CALORIES	PROTEIN (gm.)
Gizzards, fried	— no data —		
Hush Puppy	23	78	1
Jalapeño Pepper	17	4	0
Liver, fried	— no data —		
Okra, fried	— no data —		
Pecan Pie	85	367	4

1. A dash means that data not available.
2. To convert grams to ounces (weight), divide by 28.35; to convert grams to fluid ounces (volume), divide by 29.6.

DAIRY QUEEN

In the old days, Minneapolis-based Dairy Queen was known for its soft-serve ice cream and not as a fast-food restaurant. As of 1984, when hot dogs made up one quarter of its $1.4 billion in sales, it was obviously more than an ice-cream store—or 4,800 ice-cream stores.

In fact, Dairy Queen now sells many typical fast foods: fish, hamburgers, and french fries among them. All of these, combined with the famous soft serve, keep Dairy Queen in the top ten largest chains.

Because of its limited menu, Dairy Queen is not the best choice for consumers who care about health. Based almost entirely on hamburgers, hot dogs, soft drinks (Mr. Misty), and soft ice cream, the menu is expanded by different sizes and added toppings. A Hamburger becomes a Double or Triple Hamburger; so you end up with sandwiches that contain four, six, and ten teaspoons of fat, respectively. While chicken and fish grace the menu, these offerings are fried and also high in fat—a Chicken Sandwich has more fat (nine teaspoons) than a Double Cheeseburger. The Super Hot Dog with Cheese is super indeed—super high in sodium, with more than 1,605 milligrams (plenty for an entire day), and eight teaspoons of fat. Just reading

CARBOHYDRATES (gm.)	ADDED SUGAR[3] (gm.)	FAT[4] (gm.)	FAT % CALORIES	SATURATED FAT (gm.)	CHOLESTEROL (mg.)	SODIUM (mg.)	VITAMIN A (% U.S.RDA)	VITAMIN C (% U.S.RDA)	IRON (% U.S.RDA)	CALCIUM (% U.S.RDA)	GLOOM
— no data —											
12	0	3	33	—	—	55	—	—	—	—	4
1	0	0	0	0	0	243	6	3	3	0	2
— no data —											
— no data —											
44	32	20	48	—	—	—	—	—	—	—	27

3. To convert grams of sugar to teaspoons of sugar, divide by 4.0.
4. To convert grams of fat to teaspoons of fat, divide by 4.4.

about this gem may set your arteries aquiver. The newest Dairy Queen choice, breaded and fried beef nuggets, are also unlikely to be a dieter's choice.

The Triple Cheeseburger at Dairy Queen is less disastrous than a comparable burger at Wendy's, but that's about the best you can say for it. As with any restaurant offering a limited menu, order small, avoid extra sauces, and add a slice of tomato and a lettuce leaf when you can.

Dairy Queen has a policy of frying foods in highly saturated fat (90-percent beef fat, according to the company). However, our tests discovered one renegade outlet in Boston that at least temporarily was cooking its french fries in an unsaturated, all-vegetable shortening. This deviation from standard practice is a useful reminder that franchises don't always follow their marching orders.

Compared to most of the main-meal items, Dairy Queen's soft ice cream (or more likely, ice milk) is benign. In a regular-size cone, fat provides only one fourth of the calories. Sugar, however, is present in ample quantity—about eight teaspoons. That adds up to a Gloom rating of 11. Needless to say, dipping the cone in chocolate syrup adds calories, fat, and Gloom points.

The high-calorie shockeroo on the Dairy Queen menu is the large

Chocolate Malt: 1,060 calories crammed into 20 ounces of beverage. Dairy Queen refuses to disclose the sugar content of its products, but we estimate that this product contains about 25 teaspoons of sugar! Sometimes we think that Dairy Queen is really the Sugar King in disguise. The only silver lining in this waistline-bulger is the 700 milligrams of calcium, 70 percent of one's daily quota.

DAIRY QUEEN

COMPLETE NUTRITIONAL VALUES[1]

	WEIGHT[2] (gm.)	CALORIES	PROTEIN (gm.)	
Banana Split	383	540	9	
Buster Bar	149	460	10	
Chicken Sandwich	220	670	29	
Chocolate Malt, large, 20 fl. oz.	588	1060	20	
Chocolate Malt, regular, 14 fl. oz.	418	760	14	
Chocolate Malt, small, 10 fl. oz.	291	520	10	
Chocolate Shake, large, 20 fl. oz.	588	990	19	
Chocolate Shake, regular, 14 fl. oz.	418	710	14	
Chocolate Shake, small, 10 fl. oz.	291	490	10	
Chocolate Sundae, large, 8.4 fl. oz.	248	440	8	
Chocolate Sundae, regular, 6 fl. oz.	177	310	5	
Chocolate Sundae, small, 3.5 fl. oz.	106	190	3	
Dilly Bar	85	210	3	
Dipped Chocolate Cone, large	234	510	9	
Dipped Chocolate Cone, regular	156	340	6	
Dipped Chocolate Cone, small	92	190	3	
Double Delight	255	490	9	
Double Hamburger	210	530	36	
Double Hamburger with Cheese	239	650	43	

To best survive a trip to Dairy Queen, we suggest you stick to the fish sandwich, single hamburger, and small ice-cream cone, and avoid everything else.

DAIRY QUEEN INGREDIENTS

Frozen dessert (ice milk): nonfat milk, milk fat, sugar, corn sweeteners, whey, unspecified stabilizer and emulsifiers, artificial flavoring, artificial coloring.

CARBOHYDRATES (gm.)	ADDED SUGAR[3] (gm.)	FAT[4] (gm.)	FAT % CALORIES	SATURATED FAT (gm.)	CHOLESTEROL (mg.)	SODIUM (mg.)	VITAMIN A (% U.S.RDA)	VITAMIN C (% U.S.RDA)	IRON (% U.S.RDA)	CALCIUM (% U.S.RDA)	GLOOM
103	30	11	18	—	30	150	15	25	10	25	**16**
41	33	29	57	—	10	175	2	0	6	10	**38**
46	0	41	55	—	75	870	0	15	2	0	**53**
187	100	25	21	—	70	360	20	0	30	70	**40**
134	72	18	21	—	50	260	15	0	25	45	**29**
91	49	13	23	—	35	180	10	0	15	35	**21**
168	116	26	24	—	70	360	20	0	20	70	**43**
120	83	19	24	—	50	260	15	0	15	45	**31**
82	57	13	24	—	35	180	10	0	10	35	**21**
78	54	10	20	—	30	165	8	0	8	25	**18**
56	38	8	23	—	20	120	4	0	6	20	**14**
33	23	4	19	—	10	75	2	0	2	10	**8**
21	15	13	56	—	10	50	2	0	2	10	**16**
64	50	24	42	—	30	145	8	0	8	25	**33**
42	34	16	42	—	20	100	4	0	4	15	**22**
25	21	9	43	—	10	55	2	0	2	10	**13**
69	45	20	37	—	25	150	6	0	8	20	**28**
33	0	28	48	—	85	660	2	0	35	10	**34**
34	0	37	51	—	95	980	8	0	35	35	**46**

DAIRY QUEEN

COMPLETE NUTRITIONAL VALUES¹ CONTINUED

	WEIGHT² (gm.)	CALORIES	PROTEIN (gm.)	
DQ Sandwich	60	140	3	
Fish Sandwich, fried	170	400	20	
Fish Sandwich with Cheese	177	440	24	
Float	397	410	5	
Freeze	397	500	9	
French Fries, regular	71	200	2	
French Fries, large	113	320	3	
Hot Dog	100	280	11	
Hot Dog with Cheese	114	330	15	
Hot Dog with Chili	128	320	13	
Hot Fudge Brownie Delight	266	600	9	
Mr. Misty Float	411	390	5	
Mr. Misty Freeze	411	500	9	
Mr. Misty Kiss	89	70	0	
Mr. Misty, large	439	340	0	
Mr. Misty, regular	330	250	0	
Mr. Misty, small	248	190	0	
Onion Rings, 3 oz.	85	280	4	
Parfait	283	430	8	
Peanut Buster Parfait	305	740	16	
✓Single Hamburger	148	360	21	
Single Hamburger with Cheese	162	410	24	
Soft Ice Cream, 4 oz. (without cone)	113	180	4	
Soft Ice Cream Cone, large	213	340	9	
Soft Ice Cream Cone, regular	142	240	6	

CARBOHYDRATES (gm.)	ADDED SUGAR[3] (gm.)	FAT[4] (gm.)	FAT % CALORIES	SATURATED FAT (gm.)	CHOLESTEROL (mg.)	SODIUM (mg.)	VITAMIN A (% U.S.RDA)	VITAMIN C (% U.S.RDA)	IRON (% U.S.RDA)	CALCIUM (% U.S.RDA)	GLOOM
24	15	4	26	—	5	40	0	0	0	6	7
41	0	17	38	—	50	875	0	0	4	6	27
39	0	21	43	—	60	1035	2	0	2	15	33
82	74	7	15	—	20	85	4	0	6	20	17
89	45	12	22	—	30	180	8	0	10	30	19
25	0	10	45	—	10	115	0	25	6	0	11
40	0	16	45	—	15	185	0	4	4	2	21
21	0	16	51	—	45	830	0	0	8	8	26
21	0	21	57	—	55	990	2	0	8	15	32
23	0	20	56	—	55	985	0	0	10	8	31
85	45	25	38	—	20	225	6	0	10	20	35
74	66	7	16	—	20	95	4	0	4	20	16
91	80	12	22	—	30	140	8	0	8	30	23
17	17	0	0	0	0	trace	0	0	0	0	2
84	84	0	0	0	0	trace	0	0	0	0	11
63	63	0	0	0	0	trace	0	0	0	0	8
48	48	0	0	0	0	trace	0	0	0	0	6
31	0	16	51	—	15	140	0	0	25	10	18
76	40	8	17	—	30	140	8	6	8	25	14
94	80	34	41	—	30	250	6	0	10	25	49
33	0	16	40	—	45	630	2	0	20	10	22
33	0	20	44	—	50	790	4	0	20	20	28
27	21	6	30	4	15	65	4	0	4	15	9
57	43	10	26	—	25	115	8	0	8	25	16
38	30	7	26	—	15	80	4	0	4	15	11

DAIRY QUEEN

COMPLETE NUTRITIONAL VALUES[1] CONTINUED	WEIGHT[2] (gm.)	CALORIES	PROTEIN (gm.)	
✓ Soft Ice Cream Cone, small	85	140	3	
Strawberry Shortcake	312	540	10	
Super Hot Dog	175	520	17	
Super Hot Dog with Cheese	196	580	22	
Super Hot Dog with Chili	218	570	21	
Triple Hamburger	272	710	51	
Triple Hamburger with Cheese	301	820	58	

1. A dash means that data not available.
2. To convert grams to ounces (weight), divide by 28.35; to convert grams to fluid ounces (volume), divide by 29.6.

D'LITES

D'Lites is one of the new boys on the fast-food block. D'Lites is four years old, and at its peak, the chain included 100 outlets. But financial problems in 1986 forced it back to a mere 10 outlets around Atlanta, Georgia.

D'Lites whole emphasis is on providing fast, nutritious food. To a great extent, they succeed. A varied menu makes it a safe bet for nutritious choices.

Among the better choices, restaurant patrons can order multigrain buns rather than white. The hefty ten-ounce baked potatoes don't need fat-laden toppings to be filling, and D'Lites restaurants feature fine, extensive salad bars with low-calorie dressings. Both the cheese and the mayonnaise are special low-fat versions.

The chain offers a Litely Breaded Chicken Filet (170 calories, less than two teaspoons of fat) as an alternative to its Chicken Filet Sandwich (280 calories, 2½ teaspoons of fat). Even the Chicken Filet Sandwich has less than half the fat and calories of Arby's Chicken Breast Sandwich. D'Lites fish, too, is lightly breaded, making it relatively low in calories and fat. The Litely Breaded Chicken Filet

CARBOHYDRATES (gm.)	ADDED SUGAR[3] (gm.)	FAT[4] (gm.)	FAT % CALORIES	SATURATED FAT (gm.)	CHOLESTEROL (mg.)	SODIUM (mg.)	VITAMIN A (% U.S.RDA)	VITAMIN C (% U.S.RDA)	IRON (% U.S.RDA)	CALCIUM (% U.S.RDA)	GLOOM
22	18	4	26	—	10	45	2	0	2	10	7
100	50	11	18	—	25	215	8	20	10	25	19
44	0	27	47	—	80	1365	0	0	15	15	43
45	0	34	53	—	100	1605	2	0	8	25	53
47	0	32	51	—	100	1595	0	0	15	15	51
33	0	45	57	—	135	690	4	0	50	10	51
34	0	50	55	—	145	1010	8	0	50	35	59

3. *To convert grams of sugar to teaspoons of sugar, divide by 4.0.*
4. *To convert grams of fat to teaspoons of fat, divide by 4.4.*

contains 430 milligrams of sodium, and, according to company data, the Litely Breaded Fish Filet comes through with a remarkably low 95 milligrams. The Hot Ham & Cheese Sandwich, while high in sodium (1,160 milligrams), gets only 26 percent of its calories from fat.

According to a test commissioned by CSPI, D'Lites' hamburger meat is significantly leaner than that used by eight larger competitors. D'Lites' meat, after cooking, is 17-percent fat. Other companies used meat that was 20- to 24-percent fat, after cooking.

D'Lites Jr. has the lowest Gloom rating (9) in the hamburger category. D'Lites' quarter-pound hamburger sandwich is far lower in fat and sodium than McDonald's version; the two contain about equal amounts of protein. The highest-fat item, the Double D'Lite Burger, contains much less fat than other companies' double hamburgers. In other words, unless you eat three orders of bacon, you generally won't go too far wrong at D'Lites. You can, though, get "very lean" meat at some supermarkets that is somewhat leaner than what D'Lites uses.

D'Lites is hardly flawless though. There are fat-filled Mexiskins (64 percent of the calories are from fat) and Potato Skins (60 percent). The Baked Potato with Bacon & Cheddar contains 5 teaspoons of fat and 1,260 milligrams of sodium. By contrast, a plain baked potato has about 10 milligrams of sodium.

The vegetarian burger, a unique product in a world of fast-food look-alikes, is made from texturized soy protein, celery, peas, and produce mix (carrots, shredded lettuce, and peppers), with alfalfa sprouts on pita bread. While the vegie burger is fairly low in calories, nearly half of them come from fat. Compare it to the D'Lites' quarter pounder, which contains only ten additional calories (280), of which 39 percent come from fat. The vegetarian burger is, however, nearly half again as heavy as the quarter pounder and contains much more fiber. According to a D'Lites spokesperson, the Vegetarian D'Lite has not been a great success and is not offered at some outlets.

D'Lites makes its french fries seem oh-so-special by saying they are cooked in 100-percent pure vegetable oil. What they don't say is that at least one third of the heavily hydrogenated fat is saturated. D'Lites should do better.

Three cheers for a stab at Cream of Broccoli Soup, but why must it contain 2 teaspoons of fat and nearly 1,100 milligrams of sodium? These factors make the soup less than "d'lite-ful."

A D'Lites spokesperson says the company "periodically" updates

D'LITES

COMPLETE NUTRITIONAL VALUES[1]

	WEIGHT[2] (gm.)	CALORIES	PROTEIN (gm.)
✓ ¼ lb. D'Lite Burger	119	280	25
¼ lb. Fish Filet Sandwich	167	390	22
Bacon, 2 strips	8	40	2
Bacon Cheeseburger	148	370	32
✓ Baked Potato, plain	217	230	6
Baked Potato with Bacon & Cheddar	329	490	25
Baked Potato with Broccoli & Cheddar	367	410	15
✓ Chicken Filet Sandwich	150	280	23
Chocolate D'Lite	156	203	6

its nutrition information and that every year the products are evaluated to see if they can be modified to fit the D'Lites concept better. Nutrition information for some of the products is dispensed at D'Lites counters. Ingredient information is difficult to come by, however. The multigrain bun, developed especially for the restaurant, is a deep secret. The company is loath to reveal its contents and will only advertise it as a higher-fiber product. Whether the fiber comes from wood pulp, as it does in some supermarket breads, or wheat, the patron can't be sure.

The worst news about D'Lites is its precarious financial situation, due in part to stiff competition from chains that offer "lite" as well as greasy menu calories. In August, 1986, it began reorganizing under bankruptcy laws and sharply cut back its operation. At the very least, D'Lites keeps the big chains thinking about nutrition. It would be a shame if it went under.

D'LITES INGREDIENTS

Frying oil: partially hydrogenated vegetable shortening (soybean; may contain up to 2-percent cottonseed), methyl silicone stabilizer.

CARBOHYDRATES (gm.)	ADDED SUGAR³ (gm.)	FAT⁴ (gm.)	FAT % CALORIES	SATURATED FAT (gm.)	CHOLESTEROL (mg.)	SODIUM (mg.)	VITAMIN A (% U.S.RDA)	VITAMIN C (% U.S.RDA)	IRON (% U.S.RDA)	CALCIUM (% U.S.RDA)	GLOOM
19	0	12	39	—	95	240	0	0	25	4	14
29	0	21	48	—	50	520	0	0	8	4	27
1	0	4	90	—	10	200	0	0	0	0	7
20	0	18	44	—	110	730	0	0	25	20	24
50	0	1	4	0	0	trace	0	72	8	0	1
52	0	20	37	—	45	1260	0	72	15	35	31
51	0	16	35	—	15	820	0	126	15	30	22
24	0	11	35	—	45	760	0	0	10	4	19
36	20	4	17	—	16	70	4	0	0	20	7

D'LITES

COMPLETE NUTRITIONAL VALUES[1] CONTINUED

	WEIGHT[2] (gm.)	CALORIES	PROTEIN (gm.)
Cream of Broccoli Soup	236	180	8
Double D'Lite Burger	190	450	44
French Fries, large	114	320	4
French Fries, regular	92	260	3
Ground Beef, 1.2 oz. cooked	34	90	10
Ground Beef, 2.5 oz. cooked	71	170	20
Ham, extra lean	85	100	18
Hot Ham 'n Cheese Sandwich	137	280	27
✓ Jr. D'Lite	82	200	15
Lite Cheese, 1 slice	21	53	5
Lite Mayonnaise, 1 tbsp.	14	40	0
Lite Multi-Grain Bun	48	110	5
Lite Tartar Sauce, 1 tbsp.	15	60	0
Lite White Sesame Seed Bun	48	110	5
✓ Litely Breaded Chicken Filet	86	170	20
✓ Litely Breaded Fish Filet	87	190	16
Mexican Potato	369	510	27
Mexiskins (per skin)	37	99	4
Potato Skins (per skin)	37	90	3
✓ Salad Bar, typical choices, 10.5 oz.	286	130	10
Soup D'Lite, 9 fl. oz.	265	130	14
✓ Vegetarian D'Lite Sandwich	188	270	16

1. *A dash means that data not available.*
2. *To convert grams to ounces (weight), divide by 28.35; to convert grams to fluid ounces (volume), divide by 29.6.*

CARBOHYDRATES (gm.)	ADDED SUGAR[3] (gm.)	FAT[4] (gm.)	FAT % CALORIES	SATURATED FAT (gm.)	CHOLESTEROL (mg.)	SODIUM (mg.)	VITAMIN A (% U.S.RDA)	VITAMIN C (% U.S.RDA)	IRON (% U.S.RDA)	CALCIUM (% U.S.RDA)	GLOOM
21	0	7	35	—	10	1080	15	0	0	30	**17**
19	0	22	44	—	190	290	0	0	40	6	**24**
42	0	15	42	—	1	120	0	40	6	0	**17**
34	0	12	42	—	1	100	0	32	4	0	**14**
0	0	5	50	2	55	30	0	0	10	0	**5**
0	0	10	53	4	95	55	0	0	15	0	**10**
1	0	3	27	—	40	800	0	0	4	0	**10**
26	0	8	26	—	50	1160	0	0	10	15	**19**
19	0	7	32	—	55	210	0	0	20	4	**9**
2	0	3	51	—	10	310	4	0	0	15	**5**
1	0	4	90	—	5	85	0	0	0	0	**6**
19	0	2	16	—	0	190	0	0	8	4	**4**
2	0	6	90	—	4	150	0	0	0	0	**9**
18	0	2	16	—	0	190	0	0	6	4	**4**
6	0	7	37	—	35	430	0	0	4	0	**11**
10	0	10	47	—	50	95	0	0	0	0	**11**
61	0	18	32	—	60	1000	0	72	30	20	**26**
6	0	7	64	—	13	227	0	0	5	4	**10**
6	0	6	60	—	4	174	0	0	2	2	**8**
9	0	6	42	—	0	230	90	111	10	20	**7**
10	0	4	28	—	70	530	25	0	15	10	**8**
20	0	14	47	—	0	610	20	0	25	6	**19**

3. To convert grams of sugar to teaspoons of sugar, divide by 4.0.
4. To convert grams of fat to teaspoons of fat, divide by 4.4.

DOMINO'S PIZZA

Ann Arbor-based Domino's has been around for more than 25 years, but if you've only heard of it recently, you're not alone. From 1980 to 1985, the company grew by 500 restaurants each year. In early 1986 there were 2,816 of them, all claiming to deliver pizzas in 30 minutes or less, all the pizzas kept hot by the special Domino's "hot box" wrapping.

Nutritionists—who sometimes feel as if they're always criticizing foods—love to note that pizza, though commonly considered junk food, isn't really junk at all. At its best, pizza is a balanced meal that teenagers actually eat. The crust fills a requirement for complex carbohydrates (albeit refined flour), the tomato sauce and some of the toppings count for vegetables, and cheese adds calcium and protein. A typical commercial pizza, however, is hardly a cornucopia of vegetables. Despite the tomato sauce, two large slices of Domino's cheese or pepperoni pizza provide only four percent of the U.S. Recommended Daily Allowance (U.S. RDA) for vitamin A and even less for vitamin C.

While some upscale pizza parlors may compete by loading their pizzas with tons of cheese and toppings, Domino's dishes up a pizza of more moderate proportions. As a result, the consumer gets a fairly

DOMINO'S PIZZA

COMPLETE NUTRITIONAL VALUES[1]

	WEIGHT[2] (gm.)	CALORIES	PROTEIN (gm.)
✓12" Cheese Pizza, 2 slices	140	340	18
12" Pepperoni Pizza, 2 slices	140	380	20
16" Cheese Pizza, 2 slices	160	400	24
16" Pepperoni Pizza, 2 slices	170	440	24

1. A dash means that data not available.
2. To convert grams to ounces (weight), divide by 28.35; to convert grams to fluid ounces (volume), divide by 29.6.

nutritious meal—not as high in fat as those cheese-heavy products. Two slices of a 16-inch Cheese Pizza contain 400 calories; only 18 percent of them are from fat. Top the pizza with mushrooms, green peppers, and onions, and you are doing yourself a good turn. Top it with pepperoni, sausage, anchovies, or extra cheese, and you're adding unnecessary fat, sodium, and calories to the product. Two slices of a 16-inch Cheese Pizza contain 800 milligrams of sodium; pepperoni alone boosts the sodium by 280 milligrams. Add sausage and olives and anchovies and you'll be adding more sodium than you want to think about. A healthier modification would be to have cheese on only half the pizza, which Domino's will do upon request. The tomato-sauce-topped pizza—with mushrooms and green pepper—will be extra low in fat and sodium, and you'll finish dinner without that usual stuffed feeling.

A brief list of nutritional data follows. Domino's expected to have a more complete listing by fall 1986 (see the address in the Appendix). The company has not yet formally released ingredient information.

DOMINO'S INGREDIENTS

Cheese: blend of low-moisture part-skim mozzarella (part-skim milk, culture, rennet, salt, calcium chloride) and semisoft part-skim cheese (part-skim milk, culture, rennet, salt, calcium chloride).

Dough: enriched flour (bromated), vegetable shortening, salt, sugar, yeast.

Tomato sauce: tomatoes, salt, sugar, spices and herbs, grated natural cheese, garlic powder.

CARBOHYDRATES (gm.)	ADDED SUGAR[3] (gm.)	FAT[4] (gm.)	FAT % CALORIES	SATURATED FAT (gm.)	CHOLESTEROL (mg.)	SODIUM (mg.)	VITAMIN A (% U.S.RDA)	VITAMIN C (% U.S.RDA)	IRON (% U.S.RDA)	CALCIUM (% U.S.RDA)	GLOOM
52	0	6	16	—	10	660	4	0	20	30	**12**
48	0	12	28	—	30	880	0	0	20	30	**21**
58	0	8	18	—	40	800	4	0	30	40	**15**
56	0	14	29	—	60	1080	4	0	20	40	**24**

3. To convert grams of sugar to teaspoons of sugar, divide by 4.0.
4. To convert grams of fat to teaspoons of fat, divide by 4.4.

HARDEE'S

Hardee's, headquartered in Rocky Mount, North Carolina, wants to take on all the competition. Chicken, they got. Burgers, they got. Roast beef, they got.

And biscuits? Hardee's wasn't first on the block, but when it comes to biscuits, Hardee's can make and sell them. Biscuits with egg, with bacon and egg, with jelly, with ham, with ham and egg, with steak, with steak and egg, with sausage, and with sausage and egg. Even plain!

And all of them loaded with fat and calories. The Biscuit Gravy is a milk-based sauce with sausage bits. It will add 144 calories (59 percent from fat) to a biscuit's 257 calories. The Biscuit with Egg offers 383 calories, about half from fat. And, hold onto your seat, the Sausage & Egg Biscuit bulges with 521 calories and eight teaspoons of fat, making it the fattiest item on Hardee's menu. It has a Gloom rating of 47.

If Hardee's serves food that's good for you, biscuits aren't included. Instead, for breakfast have a glass of orange juice and an egg (total Gloom of 7); adding hash rounds adds another couple of hundred calories and 18 Gloom points—still well below a biscuit with egg, with or without meat.

For dinner, go for the Roast Beef Sandwich, which has a Gloom of 20. The roast beef is significantly leaner than the hamburger meat, though not quite as lean as roast beef served at Carl's Jr. or Roy Rogers. The Roast Beef Sandwich also rates better than the Turkey Club Sandwich (Gloom = 34) and Chicken Fillet Sandwich (Gloom = 38) sandwiches. (Incidentally, Hardee's rates the sodium content of the Chicken Fillet Sandwich at 360 milligrams; our tests found 1,307 milligrams. This sort of mistake is only one of many we found in fast-food companies' brochures.)

The Fisherman's Fillet Sandwich gets 39 percent of its calories from fat (low by Hardee's standards—even the prepackaged Chef Salad is more than 50-percent fat). Hardee's fries foods in highly saturated beef fat mixed with a little cottonseed oil. This means that a normally prudent choice of fish yields a sandwich as high in beef fat as a hamburger.

In the hamburger department, the regular Cheeseburger has 309 calories and 825 milligrams of sodium. The regular Hamburger has only 276 calories and 589 milligrams of sodium. But when you hit the Big Deluxe Hamburger Sandwich, Quarter-Pound Cheeseburger, or Bacon Cheeseburger, you're hitting grease city. Each of these hovers near the 40 mark on the Gloom scale and provides six to seven teaspoons of fat.

Hardee's, founded in 1961, has built an empire of over 2,000 outlets, but it is still only number five on the fast-food sales chart, half a billion dollars a year and a thousand units behind Wendy's. Hardee's, though, seems to have its sights set much higher. It is mounting an aggressive marketing campaign. New TV ads poke fun at its larger competitors. (One radio jingle has the audacity to assert that its quarter-pound hamburger is "not fatty.") It has also struck a deal with the 7-Eleven convenience store chain. Hardee's will test the sales of hamburgers and biscuits in ten 7-Elevens in Missouri. (Similarly, Church's is offering fried chicken in a dozen other 7-Elevens in the South.) If the test succeeds, Hardee's could expand quickly to many of the 7,500, 7-Elevens. We hope that at some point Hardee's marketing whizzes hear about nutrition and try to market new products that include fresh fruits, salads, and low-fat entrées.

"Company policy dictates that the specific ingredients of our products cannot be made public," Hardee's told us. But they did provide a list of foods that contain several additives about which many people are particularly concerned. Friendly clerks provided us with other ingredients.

HARDEE'S INGREDIENTS

Main Items

Chicken fillet: (served with mayonnaise and lettuce on a bun). *Chicken*—rib meat, water, salt, sodium phosphates. *Batter*—water, bleached wheat flour, salt, corn flour, spices, monosodium glutamate, natural flavor. *Breaded with*—bleached wheat flour, corn flour, salt, spice dextrose, leavening (monocalcium phosphate, sodium bicarbonate), sodium alginate, whey, soy flour, nonfat milk, natural flavor, eggs.

Fish: (served on a bun with tartar sauce and lettuce and cheese). *Breaded cod*—cod, bleached wheat flour, water, corn flour, chemically modified food starch, potatoes (processed with sulfites as a preservative), salt, leavening (sodium acid pyrophosphate, sodium bicarbonate), partially hydrogenated soybean oil and cottonseed oil, sugar, yeast, spice. *American cheese*—water, cream, enzyme-modified cheese, sodium citrate, salt, sodium phosphate, acetic acid, sorbic acid, lecithin, artificial colors.

Hot dog: (served on a bun with mustard, onions, and chili). *Hot dog*—beef and pork, water, salt, corn syrup, dextrose, spice, sodium erythorbate, paprika, sodium nitrite, natural flavor. *Chili*—beef, water, chili seasoning (spices, yellow corn flour, dehydrated onion, salt, structured soy flour, monosodium glutamate, dextrose, hydrolyzed plant protein, spice extractive encapsulated in chemically modified food starch), tomato paste, textured vegetable protein (soy flour, caramel color).

Turkey club: (served on a bun with mayonnaise, lettuce, tomato, and bacon). *Turkey breast*—water, salt, sodium phosphate.

Side Dishes

Bacon: bacon cured with water, salt, sodium phosphates, smoke flavoring, sugar, dextrose, sodium erythorbate, sodium nitrite.

Biscuit: enriched flour (wheat flour, salt, sodium bicarbonate, monocalcium phosphate, sodium aluminum phosphate, calcium carbonate, niacin, iron, thiamin mononitrate, riboflavin), shortening made from partially hydrogenated soybean and cottonseed oils, buttermilk (cultured lowfat milk, salt, carrageenan, locust bean gum).

Bun: enriched bromated flour (bleached wheat flour, malted barley, potassium bromate, niacin, iron, thiamin mononitrate, riboflavin), water, corn syrup, soybean oil, yeast, salt, calcium propionate, dough conditioner (vegetable mono-and diglycerides, vegetable ethoxylated mono- and diglycerides), yeast nutrients (calcium sulfates, ammonium chloride).

Gravy mix: sausage, wheat flour, nondairy creamer, corn syrup solids, partially hydrogenated soybean oil, sodium caseinate, sugar, potassium phosphate, mono-and diglycerides, sodium aluminosilicate, sodium hexametaphosphate, sodium calcium alginate, salt, artificial coloring, artificial flavoring, spices, yeast, caramel color.

Hash rounds: potatoes, shortening (soybean oil, palm oil, cottonseed oil), beef fat, salt, dextrose, natural flavors, disodium dihydrogen phosphate.

Sausage: whole boned hog, salt, spices, sugar, monosodium glutamate.

Fats

Shortening: blend of beef fat and cottonseed oil (93-percent animal, 7-percent vegetable).

Desserts

Apple turnover: Dough—wheat flour, lard, shortening, soybean, hydrogenated palm oil, water, crust improver, sugar, flour, salt, butter, soda, sodium propionate, dough conditioner (L-cysteine, high fructose corn syrup, salt, artificial butter flavor, flour, cane sugar, salt, hydrogenated butterfat, lecithin, vanillin). *Filling*—water, high fructose corn syrup, evaporated apples (processed with sulfites as a preservative), chemically modified food starch, spices, salt, butter flavoring; nonflavoring ingredients: propylene glycol, xanthan gum, dextrose, polysorbate 80, vegetable-based artificial coloring.

Cookies: enriched flour (wheat flour, iron, niacin, thiamin mononitrate, riboflavin, granulated sugar), chocolate chips (chocolate, lecithin, salt, artificial flavor),

HARDEE'S

COMPLETE NUTRITIONAL VALUES[1]

	WEIGHT[2] (gm.)	CALORIES	PROTEIN (gm.)
¼ lb. Cheeseburger	183	511	29
Apple Turnover	87	282	3
Bacon, 3 strips, & Egg Biscuit	114	405	13
Bacon Cheeseburger	206	556	32
Big Cookie	54	278	3
Big Deluxe Hamburger Sandwich	208	503	29

shortening (contains one or more of partially hydrogenated vegetable oils: soybean, cottonseed, or palm), margarine (mono- and diglycerides, invert syrup, whole eggs, molasses, salt, natural and artificial flavor, baking soda, sodium, aluminum phosphate).

Icing for cinnamon-raisin buns: sugar, water, corn syrup, stearic acid, titanium dioxide, salt, agar, potassium sorbate, citric acid, natural and artificial flavors, guar gum, pectin, dextrose, sodium hexametaphosphate.

Beverages

Shakes: milk, nonfat dry milk, cream, sugar, corn syrup, whey solids, cellulose gum, mono- and diglycerides, guar gum, carrageenan, artificial flavor, artificial color.

Condiments

Mayonnaise: soybean oil, distilled vinegar, egg yolks, corn syrup, whole eggs, salt, water, calcium disodium EDTA.

Mustard: water, distilled vinegar, mustard seed, salt, turmeric, spice extractives, paprika.

Tartar Sauce: soy oil, pickles, corn syrup, vinegar, egg yolk, water, dehydrated onion, salt, mustard, 0.1-percent potassium sorbate, extractives of paprika, flavoring, calcium disodium EDTA.

Individual Ingredients

Corn flour, corn syrup, corn starch, and/or corn sugar are ingredients of: breaded chicken breast, strawberry shake, chocolate shake, vanilla shake, chocolate chip cookie, apple turnovers, hash rounds, cinnamon and raisin icing, breaded fish portions, frankfurters, breaded breakfast steaks, BBQ sauce, breaded chicken fillets, horseradish sauce, mayonnaise, coffee creamer, strawberry jam, grape jelly, sausage gravy, gourmet Italian salad dressing, blue cheese salad dressing, Thousand Island dressing, French salad dressing.

Monosodium glutamate is an ingredient of: BBQ sauce, mushrooms and sauce, sausage, breaded breakfast steaks, Thousand Island dressing, sausage gravy.

Sodium nitrate and/or sodium nitrite are ingredients of: sandwich ham, breakfast ham, country ham, bacon, frankfurters.

Yellow Dye Number 5 is an ingredient of: gourmet Italian salad dressing, Thousand Island dressing, French salad dressing, dill pickle chips.

Other artificial colors or food dyes are ingredients of: blue cheese salad dressing, orange soft drink, strawberry shake, shredded cheddar cheese, liquid coffee creamer, margarine, sausage gravy mix.

CARBOHYDRATES (gm.)	ADDED SUGAR[3] (gm.)	FAT (gm.)	FAT % CALORIES	SATURATED FAT (gm.)	CHOLESTEROL (mg.)	SODIUM (mg.)	VITAMIN A (% U.S.RDA)	VITAMIN C (% U.S.RDA)	IRON (% U.S.RDA)	CALCIUM (% U.S.RDA)	GLOOM
35	0	28	50	—	—	1112	0	0	25	19	40
37	20	14	44	—	—	216	0	0	5	2	21
30	0	26	57	—	—	823	3	3	6	14	35
34	0	33	53	—	—	888	5	3	26	15	42
33	19	15	50	—	—	258	0	4	6	2	23
32	0	29	52	—	—	903	4	3	26	15	38

HARDEE'S

COMPLETE NUTRITIONAL VALUES¹ CONTINUED

	WEIGHT² (gm.)	CALORIES	PROTEIN (gm.)
Biscuit	74	257	4
Bisuit Gravy	113	144	5
Biscuit with Egg	158	383	11
Biscuit with Jelly	100	324	5
Canadian Sunrise Biscuit	159	482	21
✓Cheeseburger	116	309	14
Chef Salad	336	277	23
Chicken Fillet Sandwich	192	510	27
Cinnamon 'n' Raisin Biscuit	75	276	3
Country Ham Biscuit	96	328	14
✓Egg, fried, small	34	77	5
Fisherman's Fillet Sandwich	196	469	25
French Fries, large	121	406	5
French Fries, regular	71	239	3
Ham & Egg Biscuit	184	458	19
✓Hamburger	96	276	14
Hash Rounds	71	200	2
Hot Dog	120	346	12
Hot Ham 'n' Cheese Sandwich	148	376	23
Jelly Packet	18	49	0
Milk, whole, 8 fl. oz.	244	161	9
Milkshake, 11 fl. oz.	326	391	11
Mushroom 'n' Swiss Hamburger Sandwich	205	512	32
Orange Juice, 6 fl. oz.	184	81	0
✓Roast Beef Sandwich	129	312	20

CARBOHYDRATES (gm.)	ADDED SUGAR[3] (gm.)	FAT[*] (gm.)	FAT % CALORIES	SATURATED FAT (gm.)	CHOLESTEROL (mg.)	SODIUM (mg.)	VITAMIN A (% U.S.RDA)	VITAMIN C (% U.S.RDA)	IRON (% U.S.RDA)	CALCIUM (% U.S.RDA)	GLOOM
32	—	12	43	—	—	521	0	0	11	8	19
10	—	10	59	—	—	440	1	0	10	2	14
35	—	22	52	—	—	819	15	0	18	18	31
47	15	13	36	—	—	653	1	1	15	15	22
33	—	30	55	—	—	1121	0	0	23	14	42
35	0	13	37	—	—	825	18	0	8	12	21
10	0	16	52	—	—	517	13	17	14	21	20
42	0	26	46	—	—	1307	22	22	27	8	38
30	—	16	53	—	—	346	0	0	3	9	22
28	—	18	49	—	—	1038	0	0	16	8	29
1	0	6	74	—	—	54	6	5	0	1	7
47	0	20	39	—	—	1013	6	0	12	14	31
47	0	22	49	—	—	306	0	28	8	2	27
28	0	12	46	—	—	180	0	17	5	1	15
37	—	26	51	—	—	1585	17	0	24	21	42
21	0	15	50	—	—	589	0	0	14	3	22
20	0	13	59	—	—	310	0	6	6	0	18
26	—	22	57	—	—	768	0	0	14	4	32
37	0	15	36	—	—	1067	4	0	21	21	25
13	12	0	0	0	0	3	0	0	0	0	2
12	0	9	50	6	27	127	7	3	1	30	10
63	43	10	24	—	—	241	0	0	4	45	17
44	0	23	41	—	—	1051	4	0	23	11	34
20	0	0	0	0	0	0	8	140	0	0	0
30	0	12	36	—	—	826	2	5	18	9	20

HARDEE'S COMPLETE NUTRITIONAL VALUES' CONTINUED	WEIGHT¹ *(gm.)*	CALORIES	PROTEIN *(gm.)*
Sausage Biscuit	114	426	14
Sausage & Egg Biscuit	162	521	16
Shrimp 'n' Pasta Salad	329	362	14
✓ Side Salad	117	21	1
Steak Biscuit	141	491	13
Steak & Egg Biscuit	162	527	20
Turkey Club Sandwich	194	426	24

1. A dash means that data not available.
2. To convert grams to ounces (weight), divide by 28.35; to convert grams to fluid ounces (volume), divide by 29.6.

JACK IN THE BOX

 The Southwest's Jack in the Box offers high fat in just-about-everything—burgers, breakfast, nachos. Only four items (the shakes, Club Pita, orange juice, and buttermilk dressing) get fewer than 30 percent of their calories from fat. The rest of the offerings rank in the 40- to 50-percent range with a few—such as the breakfast "crescents"—that go even higher. No wonder the Gloom ratings climb so high. But let's walk bravely through the doors of the fifteenth largest fast-food chain and search for the best of the offerings.

If you find yourself hungry and near a Jack in the Box at breakfast time, aim for the Breakfast Jack (egg, ham, and cheese on a bun), which has a Gloom rating of 24. The Pancake Breakfast registers a towering 55 on the Gloom scale, but by using just a little of the syrup and by setting the bacon aside, you could greatly reduce the calorie, sugar, fat, and sodium content. Your best bet for breakfast is probably milk, orange juice, and either pancakes or the Breakfast Jack. Skip the crescent sandwiches and scrambled eggs.

Two cheers for Jack in the Box's choice of milk: Its standard

CARBOHYDRATES (gm.)	ADDED SUGAR³ (gm.)	FAT⁴ (gm.)	FAT % CALORIES	SATURATED FAT (gm.)	CHOLESTEROL (mg.)	SODIUM (mg.)	VITAMIN A (% U.S.RDA)	VITAMIN C (% U.S.RDA)	IRON (% U.S.RDA)	CALCIUM (% U.S.RDA)	GLOOM
29	—	28	60	—	—	831	0	0	18	9	**39**
34	—	35	60	—	—	1033	15	0	22	17	**47**
11	0	29	72	—	—	941	34	33	19	10	**36**
4	0	trace	4	—	0	42	28	35	4	2	**0**
46	0	28	52	—	—	1108	0	0	21	10	**42**
41	—	31	53	—	—	973	15	0	32	15	**41**
32	0	22	46	—	—	1185	16	8	12	4	**34**

3. To convert grams of sugar to teaspoons of sugar, divide by 4.0.
4. To convert grams of fat to teaspoons of fat, divide by 4.4.

contains 2-percent milk fat, 30 less calories worth of fat than the 3.3-percent whole milk that other chains provide.

A lunch or dinner at Jack in the Box could start with orange juice, milk, or a shake. Then add a Club Pita, a combination of ham, turkey, lettuce, and tomato in a pita bread pocket. This sandwich derives only 27 percent of its 284 calories from fat (let's be generous and temporarily ignore the 953 milligrams of sodium). Don't be overly impressed by the presence of a little lettuce and tomato, though. This sandwich provides only five percent of the U.S. RDA of vitamin A and seven percent of the RDA of vitamin C, half as much as a McD.L.T. and far less than a carrot stick and a few sips of orange juice.

The second-lowest-fat dinner entrée is the Sirloin Steak Dinner (including steak, french fries, salad, and garlic roll). This provides 37 Gloom points, a relatively moderate rating.

If you're thinking hamburger, think small and plain. The regular burger yields only 17 Gloom points. The Jumbo Jack has twice the Gloom rating, and the best thing we can say about it is that it's not so "jumbo." In our tests of large burgers made at nine different chains, the Jumbo Jack was the smallest.

The larger, specialty burgers head for the Gloom stratosphere. Typical is the Ham & Swiss Burger. Its 638 calories, nine teaspoons of fat, and 1,330 milligrams of sodium create quite a mouthful, one that registers 51 on the Gloom scale.

In the taco department, go with either the regular or super, depending upon your appetite. The Taco Salad is higher in vitamins and minerals, but also substantially higher in fat and sodium. The cheese-covered Supreme Nachos are rich in calcium, but they really blow your fat (nine teaspoons) and sodium (1,782 milligrams) quotas out of the water. Speaking of water, you better ask for a couple of glasses of water to wash down these salty chips, then head for a restaurant that has a salad bar.

JACK IN THE BOX

COMPLETE NUTRITIONAL VALUES[1]

	WEIGHT[2] (gm.)	CALORIES	PROTEIN (gm.)
Apple Turnover	119	410	4
Bacon Cheeseburger Supreme	231	724	34
Bacon, 2 slices	—	70	3
Blue Cheese Dressing	—	210	0
✓ Breakfast Jack	126	307	19
Buttermilk House Dressing	—	290	0
Canadian Crescent	134	452	19
Cheese Nachos	170	571	15
✓ Cheeseburger	113	323	16
Chicken Supreme	228	601	31
Chocolate Shake, 10.8 fl. oz.	322	330	11
✓ Club Pita	165	284	22
French Fries, regular	66	221	2
Grape Jelly	—	38	0

Jack in the Box has refused to release ingredient information. Nor would the company respond to specific questions about Yellow Dye Number 5 and the type of fat it uses for frying. However, clerks told us that all foods are fried in beef fat.

In July 1986, Jack in the Box executives acceded to demands by the attorneys general of California and other states for ingredient disclosure. Ask store managers for this information and complain to your state's attorney general if the manager doesn't deliver.

JACK IN THE BOX INGREDIENTS

Frying shortening: beef fat (possibly mixed with a little vegetable oil).

Pancakes: Aunt Jemima frozen batter: enriched flour, sugar, dextrose, sodium aluminum sulfate, hydrogenated soy oil, salt, polysorbate, sodium erythorbate, liquid soybean oil.

CARBOHYDRATES (gm.)	ADDED SUGAR³ (gm.)	FAT⁴ (gm.)	FAT % CALORIES	SATURATED FAT (gm.)	CHOLESTEROL (mg.)	SODIUM (mg.)	VITAMIN A (% U.S.RDA)	VITAMIN C (% U.S.RDA)	IRON (% U.S.RDA)	CALCIUM (% U.S.RDA)	GLOOM
45	29	24	53	—	15	350	0	0	8	0	36
44	0	46	57	—	70	1307	13	5	27	31	59
0	0	6	77	2	10	226	0	0	2	—	9
11	—	18	47	—	0	735	—	—	—	—	32
30	0	13	37	—	203	871	9	0	17	17	21
6	—	29	19	—	0	555	—	—	—	—	43
25	0	31	62	—	226	851	11	5	19	12	40
49	0	35	55	—	37	1154	10	5	8	37	49
32	0	15	41	—	42	749	6	2	15	16	22
39	0	36	54	—	60	1582	9	7	17	24	52
55	36	7	19	—	25	270	0	0	4	35	14
30	0	8	27	—	43	953	5	7	14	8	17
27	0	12	47	—	8	164	0	5	3	1	15
9	8	0	0	0	0	3	0	0	0	0	1

JACK IN THE BOX

COMPLETE NUTRITIONAL VALUES[1] CONTINUED

	WEIGHT[2] (gm.)	CALORIES	PROTEIN (gm.)
Ham & Swiss Burger	239	638	36
✓ Hamburger	98	276	13
Jumbo Jack	205	485	26
Jumbo Jack with Cheese	272	630	32
Ketchup	—	10	0
Moby Jack	137	444	16
Mushroom Burger	179	477	28
Onion Rings	108	382	5
Orange Juice	—	80	1
Pancake Breakfast with Bacon & Syrup	232	630	16
Pasta Seafood Salad	14	394	15
Sausage Crescent	156	584	22
Scrambled Eggs Breakfast	267	720	26
Sirloin Steak Dinner	334	699	38
Strawberry Shake, 11 fl. oz.	328	320	10
Supreme Crescent	146	547	20
Supreme Nachos	298	718	23
Swiss & Bacon Burger	180	643	33
✓ Taco, regular	81	191	8
Taco Salad	358	377	31
Taco, super	135	288	12
Thousand Island Dressing	—	250	0
Vanilla Shake, 10.7 fl. oz.	317	320	10

1. A dash means that data not available.
2. To convert grams to ounces (weight), divide by 28.35; to convert grams to fluid ounces (volume), divide by 29.6.

CARBOHYDRATES (gm.)	ADDED SUGAR[3] (gm.)	FAT[4] (gm.)	FAT % CALORIES	SATURATED FAT (gm.)	CHOLESTEROL (mg.)	SODIUM (mg.)	VITAMIN A (% U.S.RDA)	VITAMIN C (% U.S.RDA)	IRON (% U.S.RDA)	CALCIUM (% U.S.RDA)	GLOOM
37	0	39	54	—	117	1330	9	16	34	23	51
30	0	12	38	—	29	521	1	2	15	7	17
38	0	26	48	—	64	905	7	9	39	10	34
45	0	35	50	—	110	1665	15	8	25	25	52
2	—	0	180	—	0	99	—	—	—	—	1
39	0	25	50	—	47	820	6	0	12	16	34
30	0	27	51	—	87	906	8	5	30	22	36
39	0	23	54	—	27	407	0	5	8	3	31
20	0	0	0	0	0	0	8	160	2	2	0
79	45	27	39	—	85	1670	10	45	15	10	49
32	0	22	50	—	48	1570	47	35	33	21	35
28	—	43	66	—	187	1012	11	0	16	17	55
55	0	44	55	—	260	1110	15	20	30	25	56
75	0	27	35	—	75	969	3	13	53	22	37
55	35	7	20	—	25	240	0	0	2	35	13
27	0	40	65	—	178	1053	11	0	15	15	52
66	0	40	50	—	55	1782	20	14	18	41	59
31	0	43	60	—	99	1354	8	5	26	23	57
16	0	11	51	—	21	406	8	0	6	10	15
10	0	24	56	—	102	1436	23	11	24	28	35
21	0	17	54	—	37	765	12	3	9	15	25
9	—	24	32	—	0	560	—	—	—	—	37
57	35	6	17	—	25	230	0	0	0	35	12

3. *To convert grams of sugar to teaspoons of sugar, divide by 4.0.*
4. *To convert grams of fat to teaspoons of fat, divide by 4.4.*

KENTUCKY FRIED CHICKEN

Unlike most other fast-food giants, Kentucky Fried Chicken (KFC), the third biggest chain, concentrates on one thing: chicken. More than 6,000 KFCs span the globe, offering a menu that has changed very little since Colonel Sanders himself peddled door-to-door in the '50s. In 1986 KFC was bought by PepsiCo, Pizza Hut, and Taco Bell. Americans buy about 300 million pounds of KFC's chicken per year. The chicken starts out lean, but it doesn't end up that way.

The menu is short and sweet—chicken and grease. With a few exceptions, that's the extent of the KFC menu. But you knew that when you drove in. Visiting KFC is like eating at Baskin-Robbins—you don't go there because you're dieting. Fortunately for KFC fans, the fat used for frying is a vegetable oil (partially saturated soybean oil, which may contain up to five-percent cottonseed or corn oil) that is much less saturated than beef fat.

A simple menu requires a simple explanation. Order Original Recipe and you'll save calories—78 on the chicken breast alone. The Extra Crispy Chicken contains one to two teaspoons more fat per piece than the Original Recipe. KFC's Extra Spicy Chicken is the same as Extra Crispy, except for added spices in which the chicken is marinated.

Dinner packages could carry health warnings from the surgeon general. Getting more than half their calories from fat is typical for these dinners. The Extra Crispy dinners contain several teaspoons more fat than the Original Recipe dinners. Most dinners also contain about 1,500 milligrams of sodium, or about half of what is considered a prudent daily maximum.

In their own diminutive way, Kentucky nuggets are just as bad as the dinners. A large order of nine nuggets yields 1,260 milligrams of sodium and gets 57 percent of its calories from fat (a total of six teaspoons). The nuggets are made of processed chicken (like McNuggets), rather than whole pieces of chicken. Colonel Sanders, if he were still involved with the chain, would be ashamed of this slippage in quality.

Despite these figures (and more in the charts), company spokesperson Billie Brown wrote, "We don't agree with your statement that our menu items contain high levels of fat. Eaten in moderation, a meal of Kentucky Fried Chicken is wholesome and nutritious. . . ." Perhaps once KFC's roasted chicken, now in test markets, is distributed nationally, Brown's claim will contain some truth.

All that said, it is still possible to convert a trip to KFC into a healthful dining experience. Peel the skin from your chicken and you'll save yourself loads of calories, fat, and sodium. Order mashed potatoes instead of fries and you save 200 calories. Choose the corn on the cob rather than coleslaw. It may cost you 40 calories, but it has a better Gloom rating—only 16 percent of the calories come from fat, and it has virtually no sodium versus 171 milligrams in the coleslaw. You can reduce the fat further by asking for corn without the imitation butter. By the way, if you've never eaten fast-food corn, it's not bad, but don't expect a fresh-from-the-field taste. Some restaurants have baked beans, one of the few excellent fast-food sources of dietary fiber and a good choice when you can find them. The beans have a Gloom rating of just 5. Finally, according to KFC's data, the fries contain much less vitamin C than McDonald's.

Kentucky Fried Chicken deserves at least a small pat on the back for offering one of the only foods in fast-food-land that is rich in vitamin A: liver. You can probably guess the reason why our pat is a small one. The chicken livers are heavily breaded and deep-fried; sometimes it's hard to find the liver amid the breading. The added fat, coupled with the naturally occurring cholesterol, means that this otherwise extraordinarily nutritious food gets put on the "now and then" list. KFC has also experimented with "Mean Greens" (boiled collard, turnip, and mustard greens), but is discontinuing this flavorful vitamin-rich choice.

In February 1985, KFC told us that none of its products contained Yellow Dye Number 5. Later that year, the company revealed that the potato salad did, indeed, contain the dye. In late 1985, sulfites were present in the mashed potato mix, although "the suppliers are exploring possible substitutes." These problems aside, we applaud KFC for including breakdowns of saturated and polyunsaturated fats in its nutrition brochure.

KENTUCKY FRIED CHICKEN INGREDIENTS

Main Items:
Seasoning for spicy chicken: salt, monosodium glutamate, spices, garlic powder.

Side Dishes
Biscuits: self-rising flour, shortening (soybean and cottonseed oils), buttermilk.

Cole Slaw: cabbage; *salad dressing:* Miracle Whip (soybean oil, water, vinegar, sugar, egg yolks, starch, chemically modified food starch, salt, mustard flour, spice, paprika, natural flavor), sugar, tarragon vinegar, soybean oil, salt; carrots; onions.

Mean greens: collard, turnip, and mustard greens; salt, liver, hickory smoke flavor [may have additional ingredients].

Spicy rice: rice, liver, hot sauce, butter, seasoning, Worcestershire sauce.

Fats
Fat used for frying: 100-percent vegetable oil (partially saturated soybean oil, which may contain up to five-percent cottonseed or corn oil).

Desserts
Strawberry shortcake: water, strawberries, sugar, flour, partially saturated shortening (may contain coconut oil, palm kernel oil, soybean oil, beef fat, corn oil, or palm oil), corn syrup, eggs, chemically modified food starch, nonfat milk, whey, egg whites, leavening (baking soda, sodium acid pyrophosphate, monocalcium phosphate), salt, soy flour, mono- and diglycerides, imitation vanilla, polyglycerol esters of fatty acids, polysorbate 60, cellulose gum, carrageenan, citric acid, sodium citrate, artificial color, propylene

KENTUCKY FRIED CHICKEN

COMPLETE NUTRITIONAL VALUES[1]

	WEIGHT[2] (gm.)	CALORIES	PROTEIN (gm.)	
Biscuit	75	269	5	
✓Chicken, roasted	— no data —			
✓Cole Slaw	79	105	1	
✓Corn on the Cob	143	176	5	
Extra Crispy or Spicy Drumstick	60	173	13	
Extra Crispy or Spicy Side Breast	98	354	18	
Extra Crispy or Spicy Thigh	112	371	20	
Extra Crispy or Spicy Wing	57	218	12	
✓Greens	— no data —			
Kentucky Fries	119	268	5	
Kentucky Nuggets, 6 pieces	96	276	17	
Liver, fried	— no data —			
✓Mashed Potatoes	80	59	2	
Mashed Potatoes with Gravy	86	62	2	

glycol monoesters, disodium phosphate, lecithin, xanthan gum, potassium sorbate.

Pudding (vanilla): skim milk, water, sugar, saturated coconut oil, chemically modified food starch, sodium caseinate, dextrose, salt, natural and artificial flavors, potassium sorbate, calcium carrageenan, sodium stearoyl lactylate, xanthan gum, polysorbate 60, sorbitan monostearate, guar gum, sodium acid pyrophosphate, artificial color.

Condiments

Barbeque sauce: water, sugar, vinegar, tomato paste, salt, paprika, chemically modified food starch, soybean oil, liquid brown sugar, spice, dehydrated garlic, hickory smoke flavor, mustard flour, dehydrated onion, natural and artificial flavor, xanthan gum, sodium benzoate.

Hot sauce: water, vinegar, sugar, tomato paste, salt, soybean oil, brown sugar, natural flavor, chemically modified corn starch, paprika, spices, onion powder, garlic powder, hydrolyzed vegetable protein, gum arabic, 0.1-percent sodium benzoate, xanthan gum, caramel color.

Sweet 'n sour sauce: sugar, vinegar, water, pineapple juice concentrate, chemically modified food starch, soybean oil, salt, liquid brown sugar, hydrolyzed vegetable protein, dehydrated onion, spice, natural flavor, Worcestershire sauce, sodium benzoate, oleoresin paprika.

CARBOHYDRATES (gm.)	ADDED SUGAR[3] (gm.)	FAT* (gm.)	FAT % CALORIES	SATURATED FAT (gm.)	CHOLESTEROL (mg.)	SODIUM (mg.)	VITAMIN A (% U.S.RDA)	VITAMIN C (% U.S.RDA)	IRON (% U.S.RDA)	CALCIUM (% U.S.RDA)	GLOOM
32	—	14	47	—	—	521	0	0	8	9	**21**
— no data —										
12	0	6	50	1	4	171	5	31	1	3	**7**
32	0	3	16	1	0	10	5	4	4	1	**3**
6	0	11	57	3	65	346	0	0	3	2	**15**
17	0	24	60	6	67	797	0	0	5	3	**34**
14	0	26	64	7	121	766	0	0	7	5	**36**
8	0	16	64	4	63	437	0	0	3	2	**21**
— no data —										
33	0	13	43	3	2	81	0	5	5	2	**15**
13	0	17	57	4	71	840	0	0	4	1	**27**
— no data —										
12	0	1	9	trace	0	228	0	0	2	2	**3**
10	0	1	20	trace	0	297	0	0	2	2	**5**

KENTUCKY FRIED CHICKEN

COMPLETE NUTRITIONAL VALUES¹ CONTINUED	WEIGHT² (gm.)	CALORIES	PROTEIN (gm.)
✓ Original Recipe Drumstick	58	147	14
Original Recipe Side Breast	95	276	20
Original Recipe Thigh	96	278	18
Original Recipe Wing	56	181	12

1. A dash means that data not available.
2. To convert grams to ounces (weight), divide by 28.35; to convert grams to fluid ounces (volume), divide by 29.6.

LONG JOHN SILVER'S

As a fish and chicken restaurant, Long John Silver's (LJS) offers lots of choices, but you have to pick your way carefully through the menu to find a healthful one.

Look past the 1,180-calorie three-piece fried Fish Dinner and the 1,037-calorie four-piece Chicken Planks Dinner. Forget the fish dinners that contain more than 2,000 milligrams of sodium—including the Breaded Shrimp Platter and Fish & More. These are among the fattiest fast-food meals, with each having upward of one-quarter cup (12 teaspoons) of pure fat per meal. All these—among others—prove that the nutrition news at LJS can be very bad.

The most healthful meal on the menu is the Ocean Chef Salad. It contains shrimp and surimi, plus some tomatoes and carrots. Surimi is simulated crab made from whitefish, crab meat, and a flock of additives. It's a popular item in Japan, and probably is okay—*if* consumers know they're getting an imitation product and are given the ingredients. Thirty-one percent of the salad's calories come from fat. The Ocean Chef Salad has about half the calorie and less than one third the fat content of the Seafood Salad.

LJS, the biggest seafood chain in the country, offers a line of breaded items that corresponds to the batter-cooked foods but with fewer calories—240 fewer in the case of the three-piece Kitchen-

CARBOHYDRATES (gm.)	ADDED SUGAR[3] (gm.)	FAT[4] (gm.)	FAT % CALORIES	SATURATED FAT (gm.)	CHOLESTEROL (mg.)	SODIUM (mg.)	VITAMIN A (% U.S.RDA)	VITAMIN C (% U.S.RDA)	IRON (% U.S.RDA)	CALCIUM (% U.S.RDA)	GLOOM
3	0	9	54	2	81	269	0	0	3	1	11
10	0	17	56	5	96	654	0	0	4	5	24
8	0	19	62	5	122	517	3	0	6	3	25
6	0	12	61	3	67	387	1	0	3	4	17

3. To convert grams of sugar to teaspoons of sugar, divide by 4.0.
4. To convert grams of fat to teaspoons of fat, divide by 4.4.

Breaded Fish Dinner. If you do get the batter-fried items, it's worth noting that the batter can be removed relatively easily and discarded.

An LJS spokesperson says the chain is developing some excellent baked and broiled fish dishes. While these entrées were available in only some of LJS's 1,370 outlets in early 1986, the broiled fish appears especially promising, according to a spokesperson. The company expects to offer a full lineup of broiled seafood by the end of the decade, including salmon, halibut, cod, shrimp, and scallops. Let's hope they'll be accompanied by a baked potato and (hold on to your seat) a green vegetable.

So choose the Ocean Chef Salad or the baked or broiled fish if they're available in the outlet you go to. Pass up the french fries and Hush-puppies in favor of a "natural-grain" bun and the corn on the cob (with 176 calories), available in some "shoppes." The corn is normally drenched in imitation butter, but you can get it plain. The barbecue and honey-mustard sauces contain about one third of the calories found in tartar sauce, with virtually no fat (an ounce of tartar sauce contains 3 teaspoons of fat and 119 calories).

Long John Silver's has introduced its version of chicken nuggets, but has not yet released nutrition data. The nuggets are "formed" pieces of deep-fried chicken like those at McDonald's and Roy Rogers. They appear to be more heavily breaded than some other brands, but perhaps less salty. They taste as you would expect heavily processed breaded, deep-fried chicken to taste. Skip it. Instead, get the chicken planks, which are boneless strips of white meat, coated with batter, and (what else?) deep-fried.

We commend LJS for providing the french fries without added salt. Other chains should adopt this sensible policy. Anyone who wants salt can easily add it. In addition, LJS fries its foods in vegetable oil, rather than beef fat.

Long John Silver's provides a brochure that lists limited nutrition information about its major, nationally distributed products. Pick one up at a restaurant or send away for it. Because the company has not measured vitamin, iron, and calcium levels, our Gloom ratings are a few points higher than they would otherwise be.

Unfortunately, the text of the brochure rates as one of the most deceptive pieces of food industry literature that we have seen. It's just brimming with words like "nutritious," "health food," "nutrient dense," and "fish is better for you than a burger." The pamphlet cites several studies linking fish to a lower rate of heart disease. It also implies that LJS's products, not just fish in general, "offer a wealth of nutrients per number of calories." The catch is that all the references are to raw or plainly cooked fish, not to the batter-fried, greasy affairs, containing as much fat as protein, that LJS dishes out—together with fried potatoes and fried hush puppies. The scientists who conducted the various studies would choke if they saw the double-digit fat values of LJS's fish dinners. The brochure will be somewhat closer to the truth once the baked and broiled fish dishes are available.

LONG JOHN SILVER'S

COMPLETE NUTRITIONAL VALUES[1]

	WEIGHT[2] (gm.)	CALORIES	PROTEIN (gm.)
Apple Pie, 4 oz.	113	280	2
Batter-Fried Fish, 1 piece	85	202	13
Batter-Fried Shrimp Dinner	—	711	17

LONG JOHN SILVER'S INGREDIENTS

LJS does not disclose the ingredients of its products except for pies and salad dressings that are labeled.

Main Items

"Surimi seafood": Alaskan pollock, snow crab meat, turbot, wheat starch, egg whites, salt, hydrolyzed vegetable protein, artificial color (made of a natural substance).

Side Dish

Corn on the cob: corn, imitation butter (partially hydrogenated soybean oil, artificial flavor, lecithin, coconut oil, artificial color, methyl silicone).

Desserts

Apple pie: apples, flour, sugar, partially saturated shortening (may contain soybean oil, cottonseed oil, corn oil, lard, beef fat, or palm oil), corn syrup, water, chemically modified food starch, dextrose, salt, spices.

Lemon meringue pie: water, sugar, corn syrup, flour, partially saturated shortening (may contain soybean oil, cottonseed oil, lard, beef fat, or palm oil), chemically modified food starch, margarine (partially saturated soybean and cottonseed oils, water, salt, mono- and diglycerides, lecithin, artificial flavor and color, vitamin A palmitate), lemon flavor (citric acid, lemon juice, lemon oil), salt, egg whites, dextrose, agar, sodium citrate, locust bean gum, sodium phosphate, artificial color, cream of tartar, natural and artificial flavors.

Pecan pie: corn syrup, sugar, flour (malted barley flour and potassium bromate), eggs, pecans, partially saturated shortening (may contain soybean oil, cottonseed oil, corn oil, lard, beef fat, or palm oil), margarine (partially saturated soybean and cottonseed oils, water, salt, mono- and diglycerides, lecithin, artificial coloring and flavoring, vitamin A palmitate), water, salt, dextrose, coconut, natural and artificial vanilla flavor.

Condiments

Blue cheese dressing: soybean oil, blue cheese, vinegar, water, eggs, salt, corn syrup, xanthan gum, sour cream solids, spices, garlic.

Lite Italian dressing: water, vinegar, salt, sugar, soybean oil, garlic, gums (arabic, guar, and xanthan), propylene glycol alginate, spices, dehydrated bell peppers, Yellow Dye Numbers 5 and 6.

Sea salad dressing: soybean oil, water, vinegar, corn syrup, pickle relish, onion, eggs, green bell peppers, tomato paste, sugar, salt, milk powder, spices, lemon juice, propylene glycol alginate, paprika, and 0.1-percent sodium benzoate.

Thousand Island dressing: soybean oil, vinegar, corn syrup, relish, water, eggs, sugar, tomato paste, salt, spices, propylene glycol alginate, paprika, onion, calcium disodium EDTA, beet powder.

CARBOHYDRATES (gm.)	ADDED SUGAR[3] (gm.)	FAT[4] (gm.)	FAT % CALORIES	SATURATED FAT (gm.)	CHOLESTEROL (mg.)	SODIUM (mg.)	VITAMIN A (% U.S.RDA)	VITAMIN C (% U.S.RDA)	IRON (% U.S.RDA)	CALCIUM (% U.S.RDA)	GLOOM
43	15	11	35	—	10	247	—	—	—	—	18
11	0	12	53	—	31	673	—	—	—	—	20
60	0	45	57	—	127	1297	—	—	—	—	67

LONG JOHN SILVER'S

COMPLETE NUTRITIONAL VALUES¹ CONTINUED	WEIGHT² (gm.)	CALORIES	PROTEIN (gm.)
Batter-Fried Shrimp, 1 piece	17	47	2
Breaded Clams, 1 order	132	526	17
Breaded Oyster, 1 piece	21	60	2
Breaded Shrimp Platter	—	962	20
Breaded Shrimp, 1 order	134	388	12
Carbonated Drink, 10 fl. oz.	—	120	0
Catsup	11	12	0
Cherry Pie	113	294	3
Chicken Nuggets Dinner, 6-piece	—	699	23
✓Chicken Plank, 1 piece	63	152	9
Chicken Planks Dinner, 3-piece	—	885	32
Chicken Planks Dinner, 4-piece	—	1037	41
Clam Chowder, 6.6 oz.	187	128	7
Clam Dinner	—	955	22
✓Cole Slaw, drained on fork	99	182	1
✓Corn on the Cob	150	176	5
Crackers, 4 pieces	12	50	1
Diet Carbonated Drink, 10 fl. oz.	—	0	0
Fish & Chicken	—	935	36
Fish & Fryes, 2 pieces of fish	—	651	30
Fish & Fryes, 3 pieces of fish	—	853	43
Fish & More	—	978	34
Fish Dinner, fried, 3-piece	—	1180	47
Fish Sandwich Platter	—	835	30
Fryes	85	247	4

CARBOHYDRATES (gm.)	ADDED SUGAR² (gm.)	FAT⁴ (gm.)	FAT % CALORIES	SATURATED FAT (gm.)	CHOLESTEROL (mg.)	SODIUM (mg.)	VITAMIN A (% U.S.RDA)	VITAMIN C (% U.S.RDA)	IRON (% U.S.RDA)	CALCIUM (% U.S.RDA)	GLOOM
3	0	3	57	—	17	154	—	—	—	—	5
58	0	31	53	—	2	1170	—	—	—	—	48
6	0	3	45	—	5	65	—	—	—	—	4
93	0	57	53	—	122	2007	—	—	—	—	90
33	0	23	53	—	96	1229	—	—	—	—	40
30	30	0	0	0	0	—	—	—	—	—	4
3	—	0	0	0	0	136	—	—	—	—	2
46	15	11	34	—	10	251	—	—	—	—	18
54	0	45	58	—	25	853	—	—	—	—	60
10	0	8	47	—	0	515	—	—	—	—	14
72	0	51	52	—	25	1918	—	—	—	—	78
82	0	59	51	—	25	2433	—	—	—	—	92
15	0	5	35	—	17	611	—	—	—	—	12
100	0	58	55	—	27	1543	—	—	—	—	85
11	0	15	74	—	12	367	—	—	—	—	23
29	0	4	28	—	—	—	—	—	—	—	5
8	0	2	36	—	—	145	—	—	—	—	4
0	0	0	0	0	0	—	—	—	—	—	0
73	0	55	53	—	56	2076	—	—	—	—	84
53	0	36	50	—	75	1352	—	—	—	—	54
64	0	48	51	—	106	2025	—	—	—	—	74
82	0	58	53	—	88	2124	—	—	—	—	89
93	0	70	53	—	119	2797	—	—	—	—	109
84	0	42	45	—	75	1402	—	—	—	—	63
31	0	12	44	—	13	6	—	—	—	—	14

LONG JOHN SILVER'S

COMPLETE NUTRITIONAL VALUES[1] CONTINUED	WEIGHT[2] (gm.)	CALORIES	PROTEIN (gm.)	
Hushpuppies, 2 pieces	48	145	3	
✓ Kitchen-Breaded Fish, 1 piece	57	122	9	
Kitchen-Breaded Fish Dinner, 2-piece	—	818	26	
Kitchen-Breaded Fish Dinner, 3-piece	—	940	35	
Milk, whole, 8 fl. oz.	244	157	8	
Noncarbonated Drink, 10 fl. oz.	300	120	0	
✓ Ocean Chef Salad	—	229	27	
Oyster Dinner	—	789	17	
Pumpkin Pie	113	251	4	
Scallop Dinner	—	747	17	
Seafood Platter	—	976	29	
Seafood Salad	408	426	19	
Seafood Sauce	34	34	0	
Tartar Sauce	30	119	0	
Thousand Island Dressing	30	141	0	

1. A dash means that data not available.
2. To convert grams to ounces (weight), divide by 28.35; to convert grams to fluid ounces (volume), divide by 29.6.

McDonald's

Nineteen million people a day can't all be wrong. There's a reason to go to McDonald's—maybe more than one. And they all add up to some $11 billion in annual sales.

Accessibility has something to do with it. Nearly 7,000 pairs of golden arches adorn American streetcorners, interstates, and shopping malls. Two thousand more pairs of arches have sprouted up

CARBOHYDRATES (gm.)	ADDED SUGAR[3] (gm.)	FAT[4] (gm.)	FAT % CALORIES	SATURATED FAT (gm.)	CHOLESTEROL (mg.)	SODIUM (mg.)	VITAMIN A (% U.S.RDA)	VITAMIN C (% U.S.RDA)	IRON (% U.S.RDA)	CALCIUM (% U.S.RDA)	GLOOM
18	—	7	43	—	1	405	—	—	—	—	13
8	0	6	44	—	25	374	—	—	—	—	10
76	0	46	51	—	76	1526	—	—	—	—	69
84	0	52	50	—	101	1900	—	—	—	—	79
11	0	9	52	—	33	119	—	—	—	—	11
30	30	0	0	0	0	—	—	—	—	—	4
13	0	8	31	—	64	986	—	—	—	—	18
78	0	45	51	—	55	763	—	—	—	—	61
34	13	11	39	—	35	242	—	—	—	—	17
66	0	45	54	—	37	1579	—	—	—	—	71
85	0	58	53	—	95	2161	—	—	—	—	91
22	0	30	63	—	113	1086	—	—	—	—	45
9	0	0	0	0	0	358	—	—	—	—	4
5	0	11	83	—	—	—	—	—	—	—	14
5	0	14	89	—	8	263	—	—	—	—	21

3. To convert grams of sugar to teaspoons of sugar, divide by 4.0.
4. To convert grams of fat to teaspoons of fat, divide by 4.4.

overseas, with expansion proceeding at a fast and furious rate. A new McDonald's restaurant opens its doors somewhere on this globe every 15 hours. Walk through any one of them and you find the standard for the fast-food french fry, a decent cup of coffee, and a hamburger not more than ten minutes old.

McDonald's has long been the leader among fast-food restaurants. It broke open the breakfast market. It showed that burger joints could also fry chicken. It has the most massive advertising campaigns, its half a billion dollars annually. This promotional barrage makes Mc-Donald's the single most advertised brand in the world.

McDonald's was also first with the special package for children—the "happy meal" usually consists of a hamburger or cheeseburger, regular fries, and a drink, although any patron can put together a meal of choice to fill the happy-meal box. That allows the customer to choose among natural fruit juices and possibly low-fat milk.

McDonald's menu has come a long way from its burger, fries, and shake or soft drink days. For instance, if you chose a plain English Muffin and fruit (or tomato) juice for breakfast you'd have a low-fat 271-calorie "meal" with a little more than 300 milligrams of sodium. Ask them to hold the butter and you're even better off. On the other hand, you could choose a Biscuit with Sausage & Egg and begin your day with a meal that gets 61 percent of its 585 calories from fat and contains 1,301 milligrams of sodium.

The lunch and dinner menu offers some surprises. While fish and chicken are often touted as healthful foods, McDonald's fish sandwich and chicken nuggets get a high percentage of their calories from fat—more than 50 percent, putting them in the same ballpark as the Big Mac. In fact, the McNuggets or Filet-o-Fish Sandwich each have about twice as much fat as the regular hamburger.

Though arch-competitors Burger King and Popeyes make chicken nuggets out of whole pieces of chicken, McDonald's white-meat nuggets are made of processed chicken, ground-up chicken skin, salt, and additives to hold the works together. McNuggets, with a Gloom of 27, are much higher in fat and calories than Burger King's Chicken Tenders. No wonder some people call them Chicken McNasties.

The meat that McDonald's uses is 20-percent fat, after frying. That's almost identical to Burger King, Wendy's, and Roy Rogers. However, it's significantly fattier than D'Lites' burgers (17-percent fat after frying).

McDonald's latest marketing success is the McD.L.T. In early 1986, the chain publicized this one product with over five million ad bucks a week, totaling over $100 million. (What we would give to have that kind of money for a health-education campaign!) The ads feature that cool slice of tomato and bit of lettuce, but sales might not be so swift if customers were reminded that the sandwich contains ten teaspoons of fat, four times as much as the regular hamburger and twice as much as the Quarter-Pounder. Almost 60 percent of the calories in a McD.L.T. come from the fat. Its Gloom rating is a sorry 54. Despite the highly touted tomato, the sandwich's 680 calories provide only ten percent of the recommended daily intake of vitamin A and 15 percent of vitamin C. That doesn't prevent the company from printing tray liners promoting the nutritional quality of the sandwich. While they eat, diners can look at a full color photo of the McD.L.T. and read, "Give yourself a boost today with the tasty goodness and nutritional benefits of McDonald's McD.L.T. sandwich." They don't mention that the "boost" might be toward heart disease.

If you're at McDonald's, order a "happy meal" for yourself and the children. Wash it down with orange or grapefruit juice, or low-fat milk, to get the most nutrition and the least calories, fat, and sodium for your McDollar.

Extremely slow to jump on the salad bandwagon, McDonald's has introduced several types of prepackaged salads (shrimp, chef, garden vegetable), beginning with outlets in Atlanta, Chicago, Columbus (Ohio), Milwaukee, St. Louis, and Washington. A choice of five dressings, including a low-calorie vinaigrette, is available. So far, the company has not released nutrition data on the salads. The shrimp salad delivers about 2 ounces of tiny shrimp, five ounces of iceberg lettuce, a couple of slices each of tomato, egg, and cucumber, plus a bit of shredded carrots. The salads, which weigh 7 to 9 ounces, may be a far cry from the all-you-can-eat salad bars, but at least they offer McDonald's patrons a decent alternative to the greasy fare.

McDonald's is testing a grilled, skinless Chicken L.T. Sandwich that is packaged like its McD.L.T. The Chicken L.T. should be much lower in fat than McNuggets, unless the unbreaded chicken breast is drenched in fatty McSauce. Let's keep our fingers crossed on this one. McDonald's is also testing pizza in several cities. Pizza Hut and Domino's: Beware!

McDonald's fries its french fries in 95-percent beef fat (mixed with a little vegetable oil). Eggs are fried in butter. But the company switched in mid-1986 to a combination of corn oil and cottonseed oil for its chicken, fish, hash browns, and pies. This change, a great gift to consumers' arteries, was a responsible reaction to public pressure.

In response to the public's concern about sodium, McDonald's has sought to reduce sodium levels. Bonnie Liebman, CSPI's nutrition director, found that McDonald's reduced the average sodium content of its foods by 15 percent between 1984 and 1985. Nevertheless, sodium is still a major flaw in many of McDonald's foods. Recall that an adult should consume no more than 1,100 to 3,300 milligrams a day, and that seven- to ten-year-old children should consume no more than 600 to 1,800 milligrams a day. An Egg McMuffin, with its salty cheese, provides 885 milligrams. The new McD.L.T. offers 1,030 milligrams. A Biscuit with Sausage has 1,145. Obviously, there's lots of room for improvement.

McDonald's has long been forthcoming with nutrition information about its products. One of the company's pamphlets was even honest enough to acknowledge, "There are strengths and weaknesses to McDonald's menu.... Our menu is generally low in [vitamin A]. Vitamine E, folic acid, and fiber are also generally low." Pamphlets listing nutrition and ingredient information are available at outlets.

McDONALD'S INGREDIENTS

Main Items

Beef patty: 100-percent beef.

Chicken McNuggets: (white meat, dark meat, skin, salt, sodium phosphate) breaded with water, enriched flour (niacin, iron, thiamin mononitrate, riboflavin, corn flour, modified corn starch, salt, leavening (bicarbonate of soda, sodium acid pyrophosphate, sodium aluminum phosphate, monocalcium phosphate, calcium lactate), spices, whey, wheat starch, monosodium glutamate. Fried in vegetable shortening.

Filet for Filet-O-Fish: cod fish, breaded with wheat flour (bleached), water, modified corn starch, yellow corn flour, salt, whey, dextrose, cellulose gum, paprika and turmeric extract color, natural flavoring. Fried in vegetable shortening.

Hot cakes: water, enriched wheat flour (niacin, iron, thiamin mononitrate, riboflavin, corn flour, whey powder, leavening (bicarbonate of soda, sodium aluminum phosphate, monocalcium phosphate), dextrose, partially hydrogenated vegetable shortening (soybean oil) with mono- and diglycerides, nonfat dry milk, salt, wheat starch, sugar, dried whole eggs, dried egg whites, lecithin.

Pork sausage: pork, water, salt, spices, corn syrup, dextrose, MSG, BHA, propyl-

gallate, citric acid.

Side Dishes

Bacon: circular bacon, smoke flavoring added, cured with water, salt, sugar, natural hickory-smoked flavoring, sodium phosphate, sodium erythorbate, sodium nitrite.

Buns (regular hamburger bun): enriched wheat flour (niacin), iron, thiamin mononitrate, riboflavin, water, sugar, shortening (lard and/or partially hydrogenated soybean and/or cottonseed oil), yeast, salt, dough conditions (potassium bromate, sodium stearoyl-2-lactylate, L-cysteine), calcium sulfate, yeast food (calcium chloride, ammonium chloride), sesame seeds, calcium propionate (preservative).

Buttermilk biscuits: enriched bleached wheat flour (niacin, thiamin mononitrate, riboflavin), partially hydrogenated vegetable oil (palm kernel, soybean, cottonseed, and/or palm), leavening (baking powder, sodium bicarbonate, sodium aluminum phosphate, monocalcium phosphate), sugar salt. Prepared at stores with fresh buttermilk.

Biscuit dressing: partially hydrogenated soybean oil, lecithin, artificial flavor, TBHQ (preservative), artificial color, methylsilicone. (Used to prepare buttermilk biscuits.)

Canadian style bacon: sliced Canadian style bacon with natural juices, fully cooked, smoked cured with water, salt, dextrose, corn syrup, sodium phosphate, sodium erythorbate, sodium nitrite.

Cheese: American cheese, water, milkfat, sodium citrate, kasal, salt, sodium phosphate, sorbic acid (preservative).

English muffins: Enriched wheat flour (unbleached wheat flour, malted barley, niacin, reduced iron, thiamin mononitrate, riboflavin, water, yeast, corn syrup, salt, shortening (may contain one or more of the following: lard or partially hydrogenated soybean and/or cottonseed oil), vinegar, calcium propionate (preservative), soy flour, farina and/or corn meal, whey solids, dough conditioners (mono- and diglycerides, sodium stearoyl-2-lactylate, polysorbate), yeast nutrients (ammonium chloride, calcium sulfate, potassium bromate).

French fries: potatoes, a blend of partially hydrogenated beef and vegetable shortening (beef fat, cottonseed oil), dextrose, sodium acid pyrophosphate added to preserve natural color. Fried in beef fat and vegetable shortening.

Hash browns: potatoes, a blend of partially hydrogenated beef shortening and vegetable oil, salt, corn flour, wheat flour, dextrose, sodium acid pyrophosphate (to promote color retention), spice. Fried in vegetable shortening.

Fats

Butter *(for cooking eggs and buttering inside of English muffins and biscuits):* salt.

Shortening blends: *For French Fries:* beef shortening, partially hydrogenated vegetable shortening (cottonseed oil), monoglyceride citrate, propyl gallate (preservative). *For Chicken McNuggets, Filet-O-Fish, Hash Browns, hot pie, desserts:* partially hydrogenated corn oil, cottonseed oil, hydrogenated cottonseed oil, monoglyceride citrate, propyl gallate (preservative).

Desserts

Birthday cakes: *Chocolate cake:* sugar, enriched bleached flour (niacin, iron, thiamin mononitrate, riboflavin, skim milk, fresh whole eggs, partially hydrogenated vegetable shortening (soybean and/or cottonseed oil), cocoa, corn syrup, fresh egg whites, baking powder (sodium acid pyrophosphate, baking soda, corn starch, monocalcium phosphate, calcium sulfate), salt, vanillin, propylene glycol esters, mono- and diglycerides, lactylic stearate. *Yellow cake:* sugar, enriched bleached flour (niacin, iron, thiamin mononitrate, riboflavin, fresh whole eggs, whey, corn syrup, partially hydrogenated vegetable shortening (soybean, and/or cottonseed oils), mono- and diglycerides, fresh egg whites, baking powder (sodium acid pyrophosphate, baking soda, corn starch, monocalcium phosphate, calcium sulfate), salt, vanillin, annatto extract (color). *White icing:* sugar, partially hydrogenated vegetable shortening, skim milk, corn syrup, mono- and diglycerides, corn starch, salt, vanillin.

Breakfast danish pastry: *Apple danish:* enriched flour (malted barley flour, niacin, iron, thiamin mononitrate, riboflavin, apples, sugar, partially hydrogenated vegetable shortening (soybean and/or cottonseed oil), corn syrup, fresh whole eggs, skim milk, modified food starch, water, mono- and diglycerides, yeast, salt, fresh egg whites, cinnamon, dextrin, lemon juice, vanillin, dried apples, agar, propylene glycol alginate, xanthan gum, gelatin, citric acid, annatto extract, ascorbic acid, carob bean gum, calcium carrageenan. *Cinnamon raisin danish:* enriched flour (malted barley flour, niacin, iron, thiamine mononitrate, riboflavin, sugar, partially hydrogenated vegetable shortening (soybean and/or cottonseed oil), corn syrup, fresh whole eggs, water, skim milk, raisins, cinnamon, mono- and diglycerides, yeast salt, modified food starch, fresh egg whites, baking powder (sodium acid pyrophosphate, baking soda, corn starch, monocalcium-phosphate, calcium sulfate), dextrin, vanillin, agar, annatto extract, gelatin. *Iced cheese danish:* enriched flour (malted barley flour, niacin), iron, thiamin mononitrate, riboflavin, Neufchatel cheese, sugar, partially hydrogenated vegetable shortening (soybean and/or cottonseed oil), fresh whole eggs, corn syrup, skim milk, water, mono- and diglycerides, yeast, salt, fresh egg whites, lemon juice, vanillin, natural flavors, agar, xanthan gum, annatto and turmeric extracts, gelatin. *Raspberry danish:*

enriched flour (malted barley flour, niacin, iron, thiamin mononitrate, riboflavin, corn syrup), partially hydrogenated vegetable shortening (soybean and/or cottonseed oil), sugar, raspberries, fresh whole eggs, modified food starch, dried apples, skim milk, water, mono- and diglycerides, yeast, salt, fresh egg whites, dextrin, citric acid, vanillin, agar, propylene glycol alginate, xanthan gum, annatto extract, gelatin, artificial color, ascorbic acid, carob bean gum, carrageenan.

Chocolaty Chip Cookies: enriched wheat flour containing niacin, reduced iron, thiamin mononitrate, and riboflavin, sugar, animal and/or vegetable shortening (beef fat and/or partially hydrogenated soybean, coconut, palm kernel and/or palm oils), sweet chocolate (lecithin, vanillin), butter, whey, molasses, cocoa, salt, leavening (sodium bicarbonate, sodium acid pyrophosphate, monocalcium phosphate), emulsifiers (lecithin, sorbitan monostearate, polysorbate 60), cocoa (processed with alkali), dextrose, artificial flavor.

Hot caramel sundae topping: corn syrup, sweetened condensed whole milk, butter, disodium phosphate, salt, pectin, artificial flavors.

Hot fudge sundae topping: sweetened condensed skim milk, sugar, water, vegetable shortening (contains partially hydrogenated palm oil), cocoa, dextrin, sodium alginate, disodium phosphate, salt, vanillin, potassium sorbate (preservative).

Hot pie desserts: apple fruit, juice, sugar, cornstarch, oleo, spices, salt, citric acid (preservative). In a crust consisting of flour, shortening (beef shortening, soybean oil with BHA, propyl gallate and citric acid to protect flavor), water, salt, sugar, dextrose, whey solids, vegetable gums, sodium bicarbonate, citric acid, modified cornstarch, flavoring, L-cysteine. Fried in vegetable shortening.

McDonaldland Cookies: enriched wheat flour containing niacin, reduced iron, thiamin mononitrate, and riboflavin, sugar, animal and/or vegetable shortening (beef fat and/or lard and/or partially hydrogenated soybean oil), corn syrup, salt, leavening (sodium bicarbonate, sodium acid pyrophosphate, monocalcium phosphate), lecithin, artificial flavor.

Soft serve: Cones: flour, sugar, starch, partially hydrogenated vegetable shortening (may contain one or more of the following oils: soybean, cottonseed, or palm), salt, baking soda, annatto, vanillin. *Soft serve mix:* whole milk, sucrose, cream, nonfat milk solids, corn syrup solids, mono- and diglycerides, guar gum, vanillin, carrageenan, cellulose gum, annatto extract.

Strawberry sunday topping: Strawberries, sugar, water, natural flavors, corn syrup, citric acid, pectin, locust bean gum, sodium benzoate or potassium sorbate (preservative), artificial color, calcium chloride.

Beverages

Hot chocolate drink base: sugar, sweetened condensed skim milk, water, partially hydrogenated vegetable shortening (soybean oil), cocoa (Dutch processed) salt, chocolate liquor, disodium phosphate, artificial flavors, lecithin,

McDonald's

Complete Nutritional Values[1]

	WEIGHT* (gm.)	CALORIES	PROTEIN (gm.)
Apple Pie, 3 oz.	85	253	2
Barbeque Sauce	32	60	0
Big Mac	200	570	25

cream, potassium polysorbate.

Milkshakes: *Milkshake mix:* whole milk, sucrose, nonfat milk solids, corn syrup solids, cream, guar gum, dextrose, sodium hexametaphosphate, carrageenan, vanillin, cellulose gum. *Chocolate flavored syrup:* corn syrup, water, cocoa, sugar, malt, salt, sodium benzoate or potassium sorbate (preservative), citric acid, vanillin. *Strawberry syrup artificially flavored:* corn syrup, water, sugar, strawberry juice concentrate, citric acid, sodium benzoate (preservative), propylene glycol, artificial colors, flavor. *Vanilla syrup artificially flavored:* corn syrup, water, sugar, propylene glycol, caramel color, citric acid, sodium benzoate (preservative), vanillin.

Orange drink: water, corn sweetener, sugar, citric acid, concentrated orange juice, natural and artificial flavors, glycerylabietate, vegetable gum, processed vegetable oil, glycerine, artificial color, preserved with sodium benzoate.

Condiments

Barbecue sauce: corn syrup, water, tomato paste, red wine vinegar, vinegar, salt, food starch-modified, spice, soybean oil, dextrose, natural flavor, xanthan gum, natural hickory smoke flavor, sugar, dehydrated garlic, sodium benzoate (preservative), monosodium glutamate, wheat, soybeans caramel color, dehydrated onion.

Big Mac sauce: soybean oil, chopped pickle, sugar, vinegar, egg yolks, water, dehydrated onions, mustard flour, salt, xanthan gum, potassium sorbate and EDTA (preservatives), dehydrated garlic, oleoresin paprika, hydrolyzed vegetable protein, spice, natural flavor.

Dill pickle slices: cucumbers, water, salt, vinegar, sodium benzoate (preservative), natural flavoring, alum, polysorbate 80, turmeric.

Hot cake syrup: corn syrup, sugar, water, natural flavor, artificial maple flavor, potassium sorbate, (preservative), caramel color.

Hot mustard sauce: corn syrup, vinegar, water, soybean oil, mustard seed, spices and natural flavorings, salt, egg yolks, modified food starch, turmeric, sodium benzoate (preservative), paprika, xanthan gum, guar gum, carrageenan, annatto extract, poppy seeds, caramel color, EDTA.

Ketchup: tomatoes, corn syrup, distilled vinegar, salt, natural flavorings.

Mayonnaise: soybean oil, whole eggs, egg yolks, vinegar, water, salt, sugar, lemon juice, natural flavors. EDTA.

Mustard: vinegar, water, mustard seed, salt, turmeric, paprika, spices.

Strawberry preserves: sugar, strawberries, pectin, citric acid.

Sweet & sour sauce: corn syrup, water, apricot concentrate, vinegar, soybean oil, salt, food starch-modified, dehydrated Worcestershire sauce (with monosodium glutamate), xanthan gum, natural flavor, spice, wheat, soybeans, sugar, sodium benzoate (preservative), dehydrated garlic, dehydrated onion.

Tartar sauce: soybean oil, chopped dill pickles, egg yolks, vinegar, fresh onions, water, sugar, salt, mustard powder, capers, xanthan gum, and parsley. Preserved with potassium sorbate.

CARBOHYDRATES (gm.)	ADDED SUGAR[3] (gm.)	FAT[1] (gm.)	FAT % CALORIES	SATURATED FAT (gm.)	CHOLESTEROL (mg.)	SODIUM (mg.)	VITAMIN A (% U.S.RDA)	VITAMIN C (% U.S.RDA)	IRON (% U.S.RDA)	CALCIUM (% U.S.RDA)	GLOOM
29	11	14	51	—	12	398	0	0	4	1	23
14	—	0	6	—	0	309	1	0	1	0	4
39	0	35	55	—	83	979	8	5	27	20	45

MCDONALD'S

COMPLETE NUTRITIONAL VALUES[1] CONTINUED

	WEIGHT[2] (gm.)	CALORIES	PROTEIN (gm.)	
Biscuit with Bacon, Egg, & Cheese	145	483	17	
Biscuit with Sausage	121	467	12	
Biscuit with Sausage, Egg	175	585	20	
Biscuit, plain	85	330	5	
Caramel Sundae	165	361	7	
Cheeseburger	114	318	15	
Cherry Pie	88	260	2	
Chicken McNuggets, 6 pieces	109	323	19	
Chocolate Shake, 10.2 fl. oz.	291	383	10	
Chocolaty Chip Cookies, 1 box	69	342	4	
Coke, 12 fl. oz.	341	144	0	
Diet Coke, 12 fl. oz.	341	1	0	
Egg McMuffin	138	340	19	
✓ English Muffin with Butter	63	186	5	
Filet-O-Fish	143	435	15	
Fries, regular	68	220	3	
Grapefruit Juice, 6 fl. oz.	183	75	1	
✓ Hamburger	100	263	12	
Hash Brown Potatoes	55	144	1	
Honey	14	50	0	
Hot Fudge Sundae	164	357	7	
Hot Mustard Sauce	30	63	1	
Hotcakes with Syrup & Butter	214	500	8	
McD.L.T.	244	680	30	
McDonaldland Cookies	67	308	4	

CARBOHYDRATES (gm.)	ADDED SUGAR[3] (gm.)	FAT[4] (gm.)	FAT % CALORIES	SATURATED FAT (gm.)	CHOLESTEROL (mg.)	SODIUM (mg.)	VITAMIN A (% U.S.RDA)	VITAMIN C (% U.S.RDA)	IRON (% U.S.RDA)	CALCIUM (% U.S.RDA)	GLOOM
33	—	32	59	—	263	1269	13	3	14	0	47
35	—	31	60	—	48	1145	1	0	11	8	46
36	—	40	61	—	285	1301	8	0	19	12	56
37	—	18	50	—	9	786	4	0	7	7	29
61	42	10	25	—	31	145	6	6	1	20	17
29	0	16	45	—	41	743	7	3	16	17	23
32	14	14	47	—	13	427	2	0	3	1	23
15	0	20	56	5	62	512	0	4	7	1	26
66	42	9	21	4	30	300	7	0	5	32	17
45	18	16	43	8	18	313	2	2	9	3	24
36	36	0	0	0	0	—	0	0	0	0	5
0	0	0	0	0	0	—	0	0	0	0	0
31	0	16	42	—	259	885	12	0	16	23	24
30	0	5	26	—	15	310	3	1	8	12	9
36	0	26	53	—	47	799	4	0	14	13	35
26	0	12	47	—	9	109	0	21	3	1	13
18	0	trace	0	0	0	2	0	120	0	0	0
28	0	11	39	—	29	506	2	3	16	8	16
15	0	9	56	3	4	325	0	7	2	1	14
12	12	0	0	0	0	2	0	0	0	0	2
58	41	11	27	—	27	170	5	4	3	21	18
11	10	2	30	trace	3	259	0	0	1	1	5
94	40	10	19	—	47	1070	5	8	12	10	27
40	0	44	58	—	101	1030	10	15	35	25	54
49	22	11	32	—	10	358	0	2	8	1	19

MCDONALD'S

COMPLETE NUTRITIONAL VALUES[1] CONTINUED

	WEIGHT[2] (gm.)	CALORIES	PROTEIN (gm.)	
Milk, low-fat (2.0%-butterfat), 8 fl. oz.	244	121	8	
Milk, whole (3.3%-butterfat), 8 fl. oz.	244	150	8	
Orange Drink, 12 fl. oz.	341	162	0	
Orange Juice, 6 fl. oz.	183	80	1	
Quarter Pounder	160	427	25	
Quarter Pounder with Cheese	186	525	30	
✓Salads, prepackaged	— no data —			
Sausage	53	210	10	
Sausage McMuffin	115	427	18	
Sausage McMuffin with Egg	165	517	23	
✓Scrambled Eggs	98	180	13	
Soft Serve Cone	115	189	4	
Sprite, 12 fl. oz.	341	144	0	
Strawberry Shake, 10.2 fl. oz.	290	362	9	
Strawberry Sundae	164	320	6	
Sweet & Sour Sauce	32	64	0	
Vanilla Shake, 10.2 fl. oz.	291	352	9	

1. A dash means that data not available.
2. To convert grams to ounces (weight), divide by 28.35; to convert grams to fluid ounces (volume), divide by 29.6.

CARBOHYDRATES (gm.)	ADDED SUGAR[3] (gm.)	FAT[4] (gm.)	FAT % CALORIES	SATURATED FAT (gm.)	CHOLESTEROL (mg.)	SODIUM (mg.)	VITAMIN A (% U.S.RDA)	VITAMIN C (% U.S.RDA)	IRON (% U.S.RDA)	CALCIUM (% U.S.RDA)	GLOOM
12	0	5	35	—	18	125	10	4	0	30	5
11	0	8	49	0	33	125	6	4	0	30	9
35	35	2	13	0	0	—	0	0	0	0	7
19	0	0	0	0	0	2	8	140	0	0	0
29	0	24	50	9	81	718	3	4	24	10	31
31	0	32	54	13	107	1220	12	5	27	26	43
— no data —											
1	0	19	80	7	39	423	0	0	5	2	24
30	—	26	55	10	59	942	8	2	13	17	37
32	—	33	57	13	287	1045	13	0	19	20	44
3	0	13	65	5	514	205	13	2	14	6	14
31	17	5	25	2	24	109	4	0	1	18	8
36	36	0	0	0	0	—	0	0	0	0	5
62	40	9	22	4	32	207	8	7	1	32	15
54	37	9	24	3	25	90	6	5	2	17	14
15	trace	0	4	0	0	186	4	0	1	0	2
60	39	8	21	4	31	201	7	5	1	33	15

3. To convert grams of sugar to teaspoons of sugar, divide by 4.0.
4. To convert grams of fat to teaspoons of fat, divide by 4.4.

POPEYES

Popeyes, the twenty-third largest restaurant chain with 540 outlets, hails from Louisiana and provides a slightly different experience for the eater's taste buds. What a surprise it is to experience tastes at a fast-food restaurant other than greasy or salty. Popeyes is a cross between authentic Cajun cooking and Kentucky Fried Chicken. Don't ask us what Popeye has to do with this chain; canned spinach is certainly not offered. Popeyes does not reveal (or has never tested) the nutrient content of its products, so our discussion of its products is necessarily limited.

Popeyes starts out as a source of fried chicken, which it offers in mild and spicy versions. (KFC does the same in some outlets.) This chicken is probably as greasy as any other fried chicken. The chicken nuggets, however, are an interesting variation from some other brands. First, they're made of whole pieces of real chicken, not that processed stuff that McDonald's, Kentucky Fried Chicken, and several other chains use. Second, unlike other companies' nuggets, they're mildly spicy. If you're put off by hot spices, don't be put off by Popeyes motto, "raging cajun flavor." The spices ain't so ragin'.

Popeyes also offers rice with red beans, a nice touch. The rice, of course, is white, but the red beans offer some dietary fiber. This dish appears to be quite low in fat. Popeyes also serves corn on the cob. Don't forget to ask that any margarine be served on the side. Incidentally, at one outlet we were told that the corn would take 35 minutes to prepare. So much for fast food.

POPEYES INGREDIENTS

Main Item

Beans: water, beans, ham (cured in salt water), natural smoke flavoring, sugar, brown sugar, sodium phosphate, onion, monosodium glutamate, seasoning.

Condiments

Bar-b-que sauce: water, tomato paste, sugar, distilled vinegar, corn syrup, salt, natural hickory smoke flavor, starch, soy sauce, spices, caramel color, sodium benzoate and potassium sorbate added as preservatives.

Cajun mustard sauce: corn syrup, water, distilled vinegar, brown sugar, chopped figs, soy sauce, mustard flour, chemically modified food starch, soybean oil, salt, sodium benzoate and potassium sorbate added as preservatives, carotenal (coloring), natural flavorings.

Sweet and sour sauce: water, corn syrup, pineapple, brown sugar, sugar, distilled vinegar, soy sauce, starch, molasses, sodium benzoate and potassium sorbate added as preservatives, spices.

ROY ROGERS

A subsidiary of the Marriott Corp., Roy Rogers has 540 restaurants in southern and eastern states doing more than $500 million worth of business a year.

With roast beef sandwiches on the menu, it's a burger joint one better. Much better, actually. Granted, the Hamburger Sandwiches are higher in fat than at most other restaurants (60 percent for the 563-calorie cheeseburger, for example, compared to 54 percent for Mc-Donald's Quarter-Pounder with Cheese). A hamburger and fries (fried in a relatively saturated fat) gets you 724 calories, 50 Gloom points, and one step closer to poor health.

But the roast beef gives you a chance to have your beef and nutrition too. The large Roast Beef Sandwich provides 360 calories, just 21 Gloom points and allows you to stick with your 30-percent-fat goal. According to a study sponsored by the Center for Science in the Public Interest, the beef in these sandwiches is only 1.7-percent fat by weight. Now that's lean! For the sake of comparison, the roast beef used by Hardee's and Arby's contains 13- to 14-percent fat. Roy Rogers' roast beef is a remarkably rare treat in the fast-food world and excellent proof that people willingly eat food that's good for them. Only Carl's Jr., on the West Coast, offers a roast beef sandwich that is a bit lower in fat than Roy Roger's.

Low in fat, however, does not automatically mean low in sodium. The highest sodium fast food of all the chains we surveyed is Roy Rogers' large Roast Beef Sandwich with Cheese: 1,953 milligrams of sodium or one whole teaspoon. The fat-laden RR Bar Burger is only slightly lower, at 1,826 milligrams. Fries and a shake will add 447 milligrams more to a meal. Come on Roy, partner, you can do better than that!

If you think a baked potato is a natural side dish to roast beef, order yours without the trimmings, or with margarine only. The more trimmings they pile on, the more calories you eat, topping out with a Taco Beef 'n Cheese potato at 463 calories (compared to plain with margarine at 274). The so-called taco potato has a Gloom rating of 29, compared to a rating of 1 for a plain eight-ounce Baked Potato. (Potatoes may not be served during summer months.)

Roy's fine salad bar helps you balance any meal in an as-nutritious-as-home manner. The self-service display contains about 15 items, plus condiments. Its only drawback is that it lacks fresh fruit. Remember to go easy on the dressing, bacon bits, and croutons, which can add surprisingly large amounts of fat and sodium to an otherwise marvelously nutritious and delicious salad.

Besides burgers and roast beef, Roy Rogers offers regular fried chicken and chicken nuggets. The nuggets, like those sold at McDonald's, are made up of processed chicken. Roy Rogers has not published nutrition information on the nuggets, but they taste as if they're going to break the salt barrier and it's hard to remove the breading. Better to stick to the regular fried chicken and to remove some of the breading.

Roy's breakfast menu, like that at most other fast-food restaurants, is enough to give you apoplexy. Egg & Biscuit Platters to boggle the mind—with ham, with bacon, with sausage. Gloom ratings range from 35 to 53. The Breakfast Crescent Sandwiches, which are offered with the same salty meats, have fat contents up to 67 percent of calories and 9 teaspoons per serving. Their Gloom ratings range from 37 to 56. The hash browns are actually individual little pieces of potato, many with the potato skins showing. Though Roy Rogers does not provide nutrition information on the hash browns, our taste buds vote for them over McDonald's coagulated mass of shredded potatoes.

Pancakes will keep you on the right track—stay away from salty meat by ordering the plain Pancake Platter with butter and you will get

ROY ROGERS

COMPLETE NUTRITIONAL VALUES[1]

	WEIGHT[2] (gm.)	CALORIES	PROTEIN (gm.)
Apple Danish	71	249	5
Bacon Bits, 1 tsp.	—	24	4
Bacon Cheeseburger	180	581	32
Baked Potato, Hot Topped, Bacon 'n Cheese	248	397	17
Baked Potato, Hot Topped, Broccoli 'n Cheese	312	376	14

one third sodium, with just 30 percent of the calories from fat.

When asked about ingredients in the food, a Roy Rogers spokesperson responded vaguely by saying that "most" of the products are free of "any added or residual ingredients from processing," and that "low levels of flavor enhancers such as MSG are present in chicken and roast beef seasonings." We were delighted to discover while drinking a strawberry milkshake that the straw became clogged with small pieces of real strawberries. The company uses a blend of beef and vegetable fats for frying.

ROY ROGERS INGREDIENTS

Main Items
Roast beef: 100-percent beef.

Fats
Frying oil: beef fat, vegetable oil (soybean and cottonseed, sometimes containing palm or safflower oil).

Beverages
Vanilla shake mix: whole milk, cream, nonfat dry milk, sucrose, fructose, whey powder, stabilizer, vanilla flavor.

Condiments
Barbecue sauce: water, sugar, vinegar, corn syrup, tomato paste, salt, chemically modified food starch, spices including paprika, natural mesquite smoke flavor, onion powder, beet powder, monosodium glutamate, caramel color, natural flavorings, garlic powder, propylene glycol alginate, pectin, sodium benzoate and potassium sorbate added as preservatives.

Mustard sauce: prepared mustard (distilled vinegar and water, mustard seed, salt, turmeric spices), water, sugar, vinegar, spices including paprika, chemically modified food starch, salt, sodium benzoate and potassium sorbate added as preservatives.

Sweet 'n sour sauce: water, sugar, vinegar, chemically modified food starch, pineapple juice, malto-dextrin, sodium diacetate, salt, turmeric, caramel color, sodium benzoate and potassium sorbate added as preservatives, artificial and natural flavors, extractives of paprika.

CARBOHYDRATES (gm.)	ADDED SUGAR[3] (gm.)	FAT[4] (gm.)	FAT % CALORIES	SATURATED FAT (gm.)	CHOLESTEROL (mg.)	SODIUM (mg.)	VITAMIN A (% U.S.RDA)	VITAMIN C (% U.S.RDA)	IRON (% U.S.RDA)	CALCIUM (% U.S.RDA)	GLOOM
32	5	12	42	—	15	255	2	0	7	10	**16**
38	0	1	38	trace	0	210	0	0	0	0	**3**
25	0	39	61	—	103	1536	8	0	25	34	**54**
33	0	22	49	—	34	778	3	9	12	15	**30**
40	0	18	43	—	0	523	4	14	14	21	**23**

ROY ROGERS

COMPLETE NUTRITIONAL VALUES[1] CONTINUED

	WEIGHT[2] (gm.)	CALORIES	PROTEIN (gm.)
Baked Potato, Hot Topped, Sour Cream 'n Chives	297	408	7
Baked Potato, Hot Topped, Taco Beef 'n Cheese	359	463	22
Baked Potato, Hot Topped with Margarine	236	274	6
✓ Baked Potato, plain	227	211	6
Biscuit	63	231	4
Breakfast Crescent Sandwich	127	401	13
Breakfast Crescent Sandwich with Bacon	133	431	15
Breakfast Crescent Sandwich with Ham	165	557	20
Breakfast Crescent Sandwich with Sausage	162	449	20
Broccoli, ½ cup	—	20	3
Brownie	64	264	3
Caramel Sundae	145	293	7
Cheddar Cheese, ¼ cup	—	112	6
Cheese Danish	71	254	5
Cheeseburger	173	563	30
Cherry Danish	71	271	4
Chicken Breast	126	324	32
Chicken Breast & Wing	169	466	42
✓ Chicken Leg	47	117	12
Chicken Nuggets	— no data —		
Chicken Thigh	98	282	20
Chicken Thigh & Leg	146	399	32
Chicken Wing	43	142	10
Chinese Noodles, ¼ cup	—	55	2
Chocolate Shake, 11.25 fl. oz.	319	358	8

CARBOHYDRATES (gm.)	ADDED SUGAR² (gm.)	FAT⁴ (gm.)	FAT % CALORIES	SATURATED FAT (gm.)	CHOLESTEROL (mg.)	SODIUM (mg.)	VITAMIN A (% U.S.RDA)	VITAMIN C (% U.S.RDA)	IRON (% U.S.RDA)	CALCIUM (% U.S.RDA)	GLOOM
48	0	21	46	—	31	138	10	26	13	10	**23**
45	0	22	42	—	37	726	5	22	21	15	**29**
48	0	7	24	—	0	161	6	56	9	2	**9**
48	0	0	1	—	0	trace	0	45	9	2	**1**
26	—	12	47	—	0	575	0	0	2	6	**20**
25	—	27	61	—	148	867	10	0	9	16	**37**
26	—	30	62	—	156	1035	10	0	9	16	**42**
25	—	42	67	—	189	1192	11	0	12	17	**56**
26	—	29	59	—	168	1289	10	0	10	16	**43**
4	0	0	0	0	0	7	23	116	4	4	**0**
37	18	11	39	—	10	150	0	0	15	3	**16**
52	32	8	26	—	23	193	8	0	3	20	**14**
1	0	9	72	—	—	195	—	—	—	—	**12**
31	5	12	43	—	11	260	2	0	6	4	**17**
27	0	37	60	—	95	1404	7	0	20	34	**51**
32	5	14	48	—	11	242	4	0	6	4	**19**
7	0	19	52	—	324	601	2	0	6	4	**24**
11	0	29	55	—	376	867	2	0	9	5	**37**
2	0	7	52	—	64	162	1	0	3	1	**8**
					— no data —						
7	0	20	63	—	89	505	1	0	5	2	**25**
9	0	26	60	—	153	667	2	0	8	3	**33**
3	0	10	62	—	52	266	1	0	3	2	**13**
7	0	3	45	—	0	100	0	0	0	0	**4**
61	39	10	26	—	37	290	9	0	3	29	**18**

ROY ROGERS

COMPLETE NUTRITIONAL VALUES¹ CONTINUED

	WEIGHT¹ (gm.)	CALORIES	PROTEIN (gm.)	
Coke, 12 fl. oz.	341	145	0	
✓ Cole Slaw	99	110	1	
Crescent Roll	70	287	4	
Croutons, 2 tbsp.	—	132	6	
Cucumbers, 5–6 slices	—	4	0	
Diet Coke, 12 fl. oz.	341	1	0	
Egg & Biscuit Platter	165	394	17	
Egg & Biscuit Platter with Bacon	173	435	20	
Egg & Biscuit Platter with Ham	200	442	24	
Egg & Biscuit Platter with Sausage	203	550	23	
French Fries, large	113	357	5	
French Fries, regular	85	268	4	
Hamburger Sandwich	143	456	24	
Hash Brown Potatoes	— no data —			
Hot Chocolate, 6 fl. oz.	178	123	3	
Hot Fudge Sundae	151	337	7	
Macaroni	100	186	3	
Milk, 8 fl. oz.	244	150	8	
Orange Juice, 7 fl. oz.	207	99	2	
Orange Juice, 10 fl. oz.	296	136	2	
Pancake Platter, with Syrup & Butter	165	452	8	
Pancake Platter with Bacon, Syrup, & Butter	173	493	10	
Pancake Platter with Ham, Syrup, & Butter	200	506	14	
Pancake Platter with Sausage, Syrup, & Butter	203	608	14	
✓ Potato Salad	100	107	2	

CARBOHYDRATES (gm.)	ADDED SUGAR³ (gm.)	FAT⁴ (gm.)	FAT % CALORIES	SATURATED FAT (gm.)	CHOLESTEROL (mg.)	SODIUM (mg.)	VITAMIN A (% U.S.RDA)	VITAMIN C (% U.S.RDA)	IRON (% U.S.RDA)	CALCIUM (% U.S.RDA)	GLOOM
37	37	0	0	0	0	22	0	0	0	0	5
11	0	7	56	—	0	261	7	135	1	3	8
27	0	18	56	—	0	547	0	0	4	5	26
31	0	0	0	0	0	453	—	—	—	—	5
1	0	0	0	0	0	2	0	0	0	0	0
0	0	0	0	0	0	52	0	0	0	0	1
22	—	27	61	—	284	734	11	0	13	12	35
22	—	30	61	—	294	957	11	0	13	12	40
23	—	29	58	—	304	1156	11	0	14	12	41
22	—	41	67	—	325	1059	11	0	16	12	53
43	0	18	46	—	56	221	0	21	4	3	22
32	0	14	45	—	42	165	0	16	3	2	16
27	0	28	56	—	73	495	2	0	19	9	34
— no data —											
22	17	2	15	—	35	125	0	0	0	8	6
53	37	13	33	—	23	186	10	0	5	26	19
19	0	11	52	—	0	603	0	0	2	1	19
11	0	8	49	—	33	120	6	4	0	30	9
23	0	trace	2	—	0	2	9	163	0	0	0
31	0	trace	2	—	0	3	13	224	0	0	0
72	30	15	30	—	53	842	22	0	11	9	28
72	30	18	33	—	63	1065	22	0	12	9	34
72	30	17	31	—	73	1264	22	0	13	9	35
72	30	30	44	—	94	1167	22	0	14	10	47
11	0	6	51	—	0	696	5	2	2	1	14

ROY ROGERS

COMPLETE NUTRITIONAL VALUES[1] CONTINUED	WEIGHT[2] (gm.)	CALORIES	PROTEIN (gm.)
✓ Roast Beef Sandwich	154	317	27
Roast Beef Sandwich with Cheese	182	424	33
Roast Beef Sandwich, large	182	360	34
Roast Beef with Cheese, large	211	467	40
RR Bar Burger	208	611	36
Shredded Carrots, ¼ cup	25	12	1
Sliced Beets, ¼ cup	50	16	1
Strawberry Shake, 11 fl. oz.	312	315	8
Strawberry Shortcake	205	447	10
Strawberry Sundae	142	216	6
Vanilla Shake, 10.8 fl. oz.	306	306	8

1. *A dash means that data not available.*
2. *To convert grams to ounces (weight), divide by 28.35; to convert grams to fluid ounces (volume), divide by 29.6.*

TACO BELL

The fastest growing limited-menu restaurants are Mexican, and Taco Bell, owned by PepsiCo, leads the pack. In 1985, the restaurant sold $1.14 billion worth of its not-very-spicy Mexican-style food. About half of all Mexican-style fast food is eaten at Taco Bell. Although the eighth largest fast-food chain is 25 years old and has over 2,100 outlets, it has never managed to publish a brochure describing the nutrient content of its products.

Visiting a restaurant that offers Mexican-style foods offers a break from the hamburger and fried chicken joints, even if it's not quite like visiting Mexico. The menu, like a hamburger or roast beef restaurant's, is built on ground beef, cheese, tomatoes, and lettuce. But instead of a big fluffy bun, you get a plain or fried tortilla; instead of

CARBOHYDRATES (gm.)	ADDED SUGAR[3] (gm.)	FAT[4] (gm.)	FAT % CALORIES	SATURATED FAT (gm.)	CHOLESTEROL (mg.)	SODIUM (mg.)	VITAMIN A (% U.S.RDA)	VITAMIN C (% U.S.RDA)	IRON (% U.S.RDA)	CALCIUM (% U.S.RDA)	GLOOM
29	0	10	29	—	55	785	2	0	23	9	17
30	0	19	41	—	77	1694	8	0	24	34	34
30	0	12	30	—	73	1044	2	0	26	9	21
30	0	21	40	—	95	1953	8	0	27	34	38
28	0	39	58	—	115	1826	10	0	21	34	57
2	0	0	0	0	0	7	100	3	0	0	0
4	0	0	0	0	0	100	0	3	1	0	1
49	35	10	29	—	37	261	9	2	3	28	17
59	26	19	39	—	28	674	8	2	5	27	30
33	24	7	30	—	23	99	8	2	3	21	11
45	34	11	31	—	40	282	9	0	3	30	17

3. To convert grams of sugar to teaspoons of sugar, divide by 4.0.
4. To convert grams of fat to teaspoons of fat, divide by 4.4.

ketchup, you get a bland Mexican-style tomato sauce.

Before going any further, we must report that Taco Bell fries all its tortillas in coconut oil. This fat is much more highly saturated than beef fat and considerably more conducive to heart disease. It's inexcusable for a billion-dollar restaurant chain to be so oblivious to the health impact of its foods. We recommend not eating at Taco Bell until it makes a public announcement that it has switched to a less harmful oil.

Now, as we were saying, Taco Bell has one thing that most hamburger chains don't: beans. Beans are one of the best sources of dietary fiber and protein, with very little fat. At least that's how they start out. Mexican-style cooking invariably involves preparing beans with lard, and Taco Bell follows the custom. For your fill of fiber, choose the bean burrito (a flour tortilla, not fried, wrapped around beans and other ingredients), and keep your fingers crossed that it does not have too much lard. Without nutrition information, there's no way to know how much fat gets into the burrito or into other products.

Most of Taco Bell's products are variations on a fried tortilla, flat for tostadas and folded over for tacos. At Taco Bell a plain tostada, for instance, is a flat, fried tortilla, covered with some refried beans, shredded lettuce, and cheese. The more elaborate tacos and tostadas add ground beef, tomato, sour cream, and black olives. In any of these foods, the salad ingredients are fine; don't feel obligated to eat the entire fried tortilla or shell.

The snack department includes cinnamon crispas, the Taco Bell equivalent of the potato chip—fried flour tortillas sprinkled with cinnamon and sugar—and nachos—pieces of fried tortilla covered with cheese.

Probably your best bet at Taco Bell, if you want to avoid the fried items, is the new seafood salad. The salad includes shrimp and a "blend of Pacific whitefish and snow crab" on a bed of lettuce in a fried flaky shell, along with some cheese, olives, and tomatoes. The whitefish/snow crab item is surimi made by International Multifoods. Surimi is an imitation fish product, developed by the Japanese, that includes pollock, a little bit of crab meat, plus a bunch of additives to hold the stuff together.

Taco Bell does not offer baked potatoes, a salad bar, or even orange juice, and it is not open for breakfast.

As part of our survey of restaurants, we asked Taco Bell if any of their foods contained Yellow Dye Number 5, Red Dye Number 3, saccharin, or sodium nitrite. Taco Bell's director of quality assurance Mary Knoll Bloss responded, "yes." but nothing more specific. Bloss added, "It is not our practice to disclose such information to the public." Well, it's *our* practice not to patronize restaurants that won't say what their foods are made up of.

TACO BELL INGREDIENTS:

Main Item

Beans: water, beans, lard, salt.

Side Dishes

Surimi "seafood": pollock, water, sorbitol, snow crab meat, chemically modified food starch, corn starch, salt, potato starch, natural and artificial flavors, sodium tripolyphosphate, color added.

Corn tortilla: corn, water, traces of lime (calcium oxide).

Flour tortilla (for burrito and taco light): enriched flour, water, lard or partially hydrogenated soybean oil, salt, sodium stearoyl lactylate.

Flour tortilla (for enchirito): enriched flour, water, lard or partially hydrogenated soybean oil, salt, sodium stearoyl lactylate, Yellow Dye Number 5 and Red Dye Number 40.

Condiments

Green Sauce: crushed green hot pepper.

Red sauce: modified food starch, sugar, spices, salt, paprika, soybean oil, dehydrated jalapeños, garlic powder, citric acid, xanthan gum, sodium benzoate.

Fats

Frying oil: coconut oil.

WENDY'S

 Where's the beef? Right there with the fat in Wendy's Triple Cheeseburger.

But, whoa, say Wendy's executives. Less than one percent of sales are these triple burgers—so few that they've taken them off the national menu and any publicity to the contrary is hitting below the belt. On the other hand, if you call your local Wendy's restaurant, they'll probably tell you (as they told us) that they have the sandwich on the menu and they'll tell you the price. They might conceivably also tell you that it'll provide 60 percent of the U.S. RDA for iron and 35 percent of the U.S. RDA for calcium, but they definitely won't volunteer the fat content. Fat accounts for 59 percent of the 1,040 calories. The Triple Cheeseburger contains 15 teaspoons of fat, the highest of all fast foods. It is also the second highest in sodium, with 1,848 milligrams. Its Gloom rating of 85 indicates that this one product contains as much fat and sodium as many people should eat in an entire day.

But let's put the Triple Cheeseburger aside (and hope Wendy's does, too). How's the Double Cheeseburger? Still pretty excessive as far as we're concerned, weighing in at 630 calories and 48 Gloom points. If a sedentary middle-aged woman's diet contains 1,500 calories, she had better forget about fries if she wants to eat dinner. And she might well forgo the fries if she realized that most of their 280 calories come from the beef-fat shortening. If you crave a burger, but you're concerned about your health, stick to the regular Hamburger (Gloom of 20, when served on a multigrain bun) or the smaller burger in the kid's meal (Gloom = 11).

Rounding out the gloomy news about the third largest hamburger chain is the fact that Wendy's has been testing the sale of hot dogs in over 500 outlets around the country. Hot dogs, with or without the chili or cheese, are loaded with fat. Roughly 80 percent of a hot dog's calories come from fat.

But let's look on the good side of Wendy's for a moment, and there really is some good news to report. Let's talk salad. Wendy's salad bar is one of the best in the business, because it has fresh fruit. The choices range, depending on the season, from blueberries and canta-loupe to broccoli and cauliflower. For three bucks you can really load up on good eats. And don't be shy about getting refills. You can also get a small salad to go. The wide range of low-calorie dressings is a morale booster—it makes you feel good about eating there. Wendy's has run beautiful television and magazine ads touting its "light menu," a pleasant relief from the ads for french fries, and giant hamburgers.

Wendy's also offers a large, nutrient-rich baked potato that's big, hot, filling, and good for you. It provides 60 percent of the U.S. RDA for vitamin C and 15 percent of the iron allowance. At your request, Wendy's will heap the potatoes with all sorts of things, including vitamin- and mineral-rich, but fat-laden broccoli and cheese. The Baked Potato with Cheese (37 Gloom points) provides 35 percent of the U.S. RDA for calcium, but has more calories (590) than the Double Hamburger. The Baked Potato with Chicken à la King is a better selection. It gets only 15 percent of its 350 calories from fat and rates 14 on the Gloom scale—a good choice if you're looking for a quick meal in a spud.

If you're still hungry try the Chili. At Wendy's, Chili blows its typical greasy-spoon reputation—only 260 calories and two teaspoons of fat (yet its very high in sodium: 1,070 milligrams). This chili (Gloom = 17) and several chains' roast beef sandwiches are just about the only red-meat dishes that get less than 30 percent of their calories from fat.

The Chicken Sandwich is another reasonable choice with a Gloom score of just 15. Only 28 percent of this sandwich's calories come from fat, but sodium-watchers should be aware of the 500 milligrams of sodium. (On the other hand, a new chicken club sandwich, now in test markets, is loaded with fat from deep frying, bacon topping, and a smear of mayonnaise.)

The multigrain bun would appear to be a sight for sore eyes, but bleached flour is its main ingredient and it contains only a small percentage of whole grains. Still, it's a step in the right direction and, perhaps, Wendy's will dare to give its customers a real whole-grain bun one of these days. They should also be offering skim or low-fat milk at all their outlets.

Wendy's traditionally billed its 3,459 restaurants as adult-oriented eating places, and a spokesperson said they offered a children's package only as a convenience to parents. That changed in spring 1986, when the company wholeheartedly embraced the children's market with a $5-million promotion tied to Walt Disney characters— Gummi Bears. Children's meal packages are decorated with pictures of the bears, and premium options included posters, cups, or straws along with $1 coupons for Gummi Bear toys, according to *Advertising Age* magazine.

Many Wendy's outlets are now open for breakfast with such items as french toast, omelettes, and scrambled eggs, as well as orange juice and milk. Our pick of the omelettes is the version with mushrooms, green pepper, and onion (Gloom rating of 16). All the omelettes come with toast and little puck-shaped chunks of fried potatoes. As with so many other dishes, you can greatly improve the health value of a Wendy's breakfast, if you ask the clerk to put the condiments on the side. Otherwise, your bright yellow french toast (from Yellow Dye Number 5) is likely to be topped with a scoop of butter, and the regular toast may be drenched in butter. According to industry reports, Wendy's breakfast effort has not wowed the masses, and the company is likely to develop a new, quicker-to-prepare group of dishes.

Wendy's is in an interesting position in the fast-food industry. It's a giant—the fourth biggest chain—but still way behind McDonald's, Burger King, and Kentucky Fried Chicken and probably destined to stay behind, barring some daring moves. Wendy's produces some of the best fast foods, what with its Lite Menu featuring a fruit-adorned salad bar, baked potato, and chicken sandwich. However, it also markets some of the worst fast foods, namely its double and triple cheeseburgers. If Wendy's dropped the fattiest items from its menu, slashed sodium levels in the remaining products, and added several healthful meals based perhaps on fresh fruit, roast beef as lean as Roy Rogers', and a vegetarian sandwich, it would have the basis for a bold and convincing advertising campaign. Tasty, healthful meals, together with clean and convenient restaurants could prove to be an irresistible combination for families debating where to go for dinner.

WENDY'S INGREDIENTS

Main Items

Baked potato toppings: Bacon bits: real bacon cured with water, salt, sugar, sodium phosphates, smoke flavoring, sodium erythorbate, sodium nitrite, BHA, BHT. *Broccoli. Cheese sauce:* water, cheddar cheese, vegetable oil (soybean or cottonseed), chemically modified food starch, vinegar, sodium phosphate, Yellow Dye #5 artificial color, salt, propylene glycol monostearate with monoglycerides, sodium citrate, cellulose gum. *Freeze dried chives:* 100-percent chives. *Margarine:* liquid soybean oil, saturated soybean oil, water, salt, vegetable mono- and diglycerides, soybean lecithin (sodium benzoate added as a preservative), calcium disodium EDTA, citric acid, artificially flavored, colored with carotene, vitamin A palmitate added. *Sour cream:* pasteurized cream, nonfat milk solids, tapioca starch, locust bean gum, carrageenan, sodium citrate, enzymes. *Whipped margarine:* liquid and partially saturated soybean oil, water, salt, whey, vegetable lecithin, vegetable mono- and diglycerides, sodium benzoate, artificially flavored, colored with carotene, vitamin A palmitate added.

Chicken sandwich: Chicken breast: 100-percent boneless, skinless chicken breast. *Buttermilk:* pasteurized skim milk, cultured with streptococcus lactis. *Chicken breading:* wheat flour, salt, spices, garlic powder. *Liquid vegetable shortening:* partially saturated soybean oil, TBHQ (preservative), methyl silicone added.

Chili: Beef: 100-percent ground beef. *Chili base:* tomatoes, salt, citric acid, calcium chloride. *Chili beans:* beans, water, sugar, corn syrup, salt, natural flavorings, onion powder, calcium chloride. *Chili seasoning:* dehydrated onions, salt, spices, soybean oil, garlic powder.

Hamburger sandwich: Beef patty— 100-percent ground beef, salt (available without salt upon request). *White bun:* flour, water, sugar, soybean oil and/or partially saturated lard, yeast, salt, sodium stearoyl-2-lactylate, calcium stearoyl-2-lactylate, barley malt, potassium bromate, niacin, ferrous sulfate, thiamin hydrochloride, riboflavin. *Multigrain bun:* bleached white flour, water, corn syrup, lard, yeast, rolled wheat, wheat bran, salt, wheat gluten, soy flour, oatmeal, barley flakes, rye meal, corn flour, rice flour, caramel color, molasses, calcium propionate, sodium stearoyl-2-lactylate, calcium stearoyl-2-lactylate, malted barley, potassium bromate, mono calcium acid phosphate. *Sliced cheese (optional):* American cheese, water, cream, sodium citrate, enzyme-

WENDY'S COMPLETE NUTRITIONAL VALUES[1]	WEIGHT[2] *(gm.)*	CALORIES	PROTEIN *(gm.)*
Alfalfa Sprouts	56	20	2
American Cheese, 1 slice	18	70	4
American Cheese, imitation, 1 oz.	28	70	6
Bacon Bits, 1/7 oz.	4	10	1
Bacon Cheeseburger, White Bun	147	460	29
Bacon, 2 strips	18	110	5

modified cheese, salt, sodium phosphate, acetic acid, sorbic acid, lecithin.

Side Dishes

French fries: potatoes, partially saturated fats and oils (may contain beef fat, soybean oil, cottonseed oil, and palm oil), dextrose (corn syrup), sodium acid phosphate.

Fats

Shortening (solid): beef fat, cottonseed oil, monoglyceride citrate, propyl gallate, propylene glycol, dimethylpolysiloxane.

Condiments

Apple topping: water, corn sweeteners, sugar, dehydrated apples, apple juice concentrate, chemically modified food starch, natural and artificial flavors, salt, malic acid, spice, potassium sorbate and sodium benzoate added as preservatives, beta carotene (color).

Blueberry topping: corn sweeteners, blueberries, water, natural and artificial flavors, chemically modified food starch, citric acid, salt, and sodium benzoate and potassium sorbate added as preservatives.

Sweet and sour sauce: water, vinegar, sugar, pineapple concentrate, tomato paste, chemically modified food starch, salt, spices, sodium benzoate (preservative), artificial color, calcium disodium EDTA (preservative).

Sweet mustard: vinegar, honey, mustard seed, water, brown sugar, salt, chemically modified food starch, spices, soybean oil, dehydrated onion, dehydrated garlic, turmeric, zanthan gum.

Table syrup: corn syrup, sugar, water, high-fructose corn syrup, artificial flavor, caramel as artificial color, potassium sorbate added as a preservative, citric acid.

Additives

Sulfites may be an ingredient of: apple dumpling, apple topping for french toast.

Yellow Dye Number 5 is an ingredient of: french toast seasoning, golden Italian dressing, reduced calorie Italian dressing, pasta salad (component of dressing), cheese sauce for baked potato.

Yellow Dye Number 6 is an ingredient of: french toast seasoning, reduced calorie salad dressing.

Monosodium glutamate (MSG) is an ingredient of: Hidden Valley Ranch salad dressing, croutons, reduced-calorie bacon/tomato salad dressing, sausage (component of seasoning), fish (breading portion).

CARBOHYDRATES (gm.)	ADDED SUGAR[3] (gm.)	FAT[4] (gm.)	FAT % CALORIES	SATURATED FAT (gm.)	CHOLESTEROL (mg.)	SODIUM (mg.)	VITAMIN A (% U.S.RDA)	VITAMIN C (% U.S.RDA)	IRON (% U.S.RDA)	CALCIUM (% U.S.RDA)	GLOOM
2	0	—	0	—	0	—	8	0	4	0	0
0	0	6	77	—	15	260	4	0	0	10	8
1	0	5	64	—	0	—	10	0	0	20	4
0	0	trace	—	trace	5	95	0	0	0	0	1
23	0	28	55	—	65	860	8	0	20	15	36
0	0	10	82	—	15	445	0	0	0	0	16

WENDY'S

COMPLETE NUTRITIONAL VALUES[1] CONTINUED

	WEIGHT[*] (gm.)	CALORIES	PROTEIN (gm.)
Baked Potato with Bacon & Cheese	350	570	19
Baked Potato with Broccoli & Cheese	365	500	13
Baked Potato with Cheese	350	590	17
✓ Baked Potato with Chicken à la King	358	350	15
Baked Potato with Chili & Cheese	400	510	22
Baked Potato with Sour Cream & Chives	310	460	6
Baked Potato with Stroganoff & Sour Cream	406	490	14
✓ Baked Potato, plain	250	250	6
Bell Peppers, ¼ cup	20	4	0
Blue Cheese Dressing, 1 tbsp.	15	60	1
Blueberries, fresh, 1 tbsp.	14	8	0
Breadstick, 1 piece	4	20	0
Breakfast Sandwich	129	370	17
Broccoli, ½ cup	44	14	1
Bun, Multi-Grain	48	135	5
Bun, White	52	160	5
Cantaloupe, fresh, 2 oz.	57	4	0
Carrots, ¼ cup	28	12	0
Cauliflower, ½ cup	50	14	1
Celery Seed Salad Dressing, 1 tbsp., ½ fl. oz.	14	70	0
Cheddar Cheese, imitation, 1 oz.	28	90	6
Chicken, fried	— no data —		
✓ Chicken Sandwich, Multi-Grain Bun	128	320	25
Chili, 8 oz.	256	260	21
Chocolate Milk, 8 fl. oz.	224	210	8

CARBOHYDRATES (gm.)	ADDED SUGAR[3] (gm.)	FAT[4] (gm.)	FAT % CALORIES	SATURATED FAT (gm.)	CHOLESTEROL (mg.)	SODIUM (mg.)	VITAMIN A (% U.S.RDA)	VITAMIN C (% U.S.RDA)	IRON (% U.S.RDA)	CALCIUM (% U.S.RDA)	GLOOM
57	0	30	47	—	22	1180	15	60	15	20	41
54	0	25	45	—	22	430	35	150	15	25	26
55	0	34	52	—	22	450	20	60	15	35	37
59	0	6	15	—	20	820	2	60	15	6	14
63	0	20	35	—	22	610	15	60	20	25	25
53	0	24	47	—	15	230	10	60	15	4	26
60	0	21	39	—	43	910	6	60	20	8	30
52	0	2	7	—	0	trace	0	60	15	2	2
1	0	0	0	0	0	5	0	40	0	0	0
0	0	7	95	—	12	85	0	0	0	0	9
2	0	0	0	0	0	0	0	6	0	0	0
2	0	1	45	—	0	—	0	0	0	0	1
33	—	19	46	—	200	770	20	—	20	15	26
2	0	0	0	0	0	10	10	60	0	2	0
23	—	3	20	—	2	220	0	0	4	0	6
28	—	3	17	—	0	266	0	0	4	2	6
1	0	0	0	0	0	0	5	4	0	0	0
3	0	0	0	0	0	15	60	4	0	0	0
3	0	0	0	0	0	5	0	60	2	0	0
3	0	6	77	—	3	65	0	0	0	0	8
1	0	6	60	—	0	450	8	0	0	20	10
— no data —											
31	0	10	28	—	59	500	0	0	8	2	15
26	0	8	28	—	30	1070	20	10	25	8	17
26	13	8	34	—	30	150	6	4	0	30	11

WENDY'S

COMPLETE NUTRITIONAL VALUES[1] CONTINUED	WEIGHT[2] (gm.)	CALORIES	PROTEIN (gm.)	
Chow Mein Noodles, ¼ cup	11	60	1	
Cola, 12 fl. oz.	261	110	0	
Cole Slaw, ½ cup	60	90	0	
Cottage Cheese, ½ cup	105	110	13	
Croutons, 18 pieces	7	30	1	
Cucumbers, ¼ cup	26	4	0	
Danish	85	360	6	
Diet Cola, 12 fl. oz.	261	0	0	
Dill Pickles, 4 slices	9	1	0	
Double Cheeseburger, White Bun	215	630	45	
Double Hamburger, White Bun	197	560	41	
Eggs, hard-boiled, 1 tbsp.	9	14	1	
Fish Fillet, fried	— no data —			
French Fries, regular	98	280	4	
French Toast, 2 slices	135	400	11	
Frosty Dairy Dessert, small, 12 fl. oz.	243	400	8	
Fruit Flavored Drink, 12 fl. oz.	261	110	0	
Golden Italian Dressing, 1 tbsp.	15	45	0	
Green Peas, ½ cup	80	60	4	
✓ Hamburger, Kids' Meal	75	200	13	
Hamburger, Multi-Grain Bun	119	340	25	
Hamburger, White Bun	117	350	21	
Home Fries	103	360	4	
Hot Chocolate, 6 fl. oz.	201	100	1	
Hot Dogs	— no data —			

CARBOHYDRATES (gm.)	ADDED SUGAR[3] (gm.)	FAT[4] (gm.)	FAT % CALORIES	SATURATED FAT (gm.)	CHOLESTEROL (mg.)	SODIUM (mg.)	VITAMIN A (% U.S.RDA)	VITAMIN C (% U.S.RDA)	IRON (% U.S.RDA)	CALCIUM (% U.S.RDA)	GLOOM
6	0	3	45	—	0	80	0	0	2	0	4
29	29	0	0	0	0	15	0	0	0	0	4
3	0	8	80	—	0	70	0	30	0	2	8
3	0	5	41	—	15	425	0	0	0	6	9
4	0	1	30	—	0	90	0	0	0	0	2
1	0	0	0	0	0	0	0	6	0	0	0
44	7	18	45	—	—	340	4	0	10	2	25
0	0	0	0	0	0	20	0	0	0	0	0
0	0	0	0	0	0	125	0	0	0	0	2
24	—	40	57	—	140	835	4	0	35	14	48
24	—	34	55	—	125	575	0	0	35	4	40
0	0	1	64	—	40	10	0	0	0	0	1
— no data —											
35	0	14	45	5	15	95	0	20	6	0	16
45	0	19	43	—	115	850	10	0	10	8	29
59	40	14	32	—	50	220	10	0	6	30	21
28	28	0	0	0	0	10	0	140	0	0	2
3	—	4	80	—	0	260	0	0	0	0	8
9	0	0	0	0	0	90	10	20	8	0	1
11	0	8	36	—	20	265	0	0	10	2	11
20	—	17	45	—	67	290	0	0	15	2	20
27	—	18	46	—	65	410	0	0	25	4	22
37	0	22	55	—	20	745	0	8	4	2	34
17	13	3	27	—	—	145	0	0	2	2	7
— no data —											

WENDY'S

COMPLETE NUTRITIONAL VALUES[1] CONTINUED	WEIGHT[2] (gm.)	CALORIES	PROTEIN (gm.)
Jalapeño Peppers, 1 tbsp.	14	9	0
Ketchup, 1 tsp.	5	6	0
Lettuce, 1 piece	13	2	0
Lettuce, Iceberg, 1 cup	55	8	0
Lettuce, Romaine, 1 cup	55	10	0
Mayonnaise, 1 tbsp.	14	100	0
Mild Pepperoncini, 1 tbsp.	14	18	0
Milk, 8 fl. oz.	244	150	8
Mozzarella Cheese, imitation, 1 oz.	28	90	6
Mushrooms, ¼ cup	18	6	0
Mustard, 1 tsp.	5	4	0
Noncola Soft Drink, 12 fl. oz.	261	100	0
Oil, 1 tbsp.	15	130	0
Omelet #1—Ham & Cheese	114	250	18
Omelet #2—Ham, Cheese, & Mushroom	118	290	18
Omelet #3—Ham, Cheese, Onion, & Green Pepper	128	280	19
✓Omelet #4—Mushroom, Onion, & Green Pepper	114	210	14
Onion Rings, raw	10	4	0
Orange Juice, 6 fl. oz.	180	80	1
Oranges, fresh, 2 pieces, 2 oz.	57	10	0
Pasta Salad, ½ cup	99	134	4
Peaches, packed in syrup, 2 oz.	57	17	0
✓Pick-up Window Side Salad	510	110	8
Pineapple Chunks in juice, 4 oz.	125	80	0

CARBOHYDRATES (gm.)	ADDED SUGAR³ (gm.)	FAT⁴ (gm.)	FAT % CALORIES	SATURATED FAT (gm.)	CHOLESTEROL (mg.)	SODIUM (mg.)	VITAMIN A (% U.S.RDA)	VITAMIN C (% U.S.RDA)	IRON (% U.S.RDA)	CALCIUM (% U.S.RDA)	GLOOM
2	0	0	0	0	0	4	60	90	0	0	0
1	0	0	0	0	0	65	0	0	0	0	1
0	0	0	0	0	0	0	0	0	0	0	0
2	0	0	0	0	0	5	4	4	0	0	0
2	0	0	0	0	0	5	20	15	4	0	0
0	0	11	99	—	10	80	0	0	0	0	15
4	0	0	0	0	0	—	0	—	0	0	0
11	0	8	48	5	35	120	6	4	0	30	9
0	0	7	70	—	1	320	0	0	0	0	11
0	0	0	0	0	0	5	0	0	0	0	0
0	0	0	—	0	0	50	0	0	0	0	1
26	26	0	0	0	0	35	0	0	0	0	4
0	0	15	100	—	0	0	0	0	0	0	19
6	0	17	61	—	450	405	20	—	15	10	20
7	0	21	65	—	355	570	20	—	15	10	26
7	0	19	61	—	525	485	20	10	15	15	22
7	0	15	64	—	460	200	15	10	15	6	16
0	0	0	0	0	0	0	0	0	0	0	0
17	0	0	0	0	0	0	6	140	0	0	0
3	0	—	0	—	0	0	0	15	0	0	0
17	0	6	40	—	—	400	20	20	4	2	9
4	0	0	0	0	0	0	2	0	0	0	0
5	0	6	49	—	15	540	15	20	6	10	10
20	0	0	0	0	0	0	0	20	0	0	0

WENDY'S

COMPLETE NUTRITIONAL VALUES[1] CONTINUED

	WEIGHT[2] (gm.)	CALORIES	PROTEIN (gm.)
Ranch Salad Dressing, 1 tbsp.	15	80	0
Red French Salad Dressing, 1 tbsp.	15	70	0
Red Onions, 1 tbsp.	10	4	0
Reduced Calorie Bacon & Tomato Salad Dressing, ½ fl. oz.	15	45	0
Reduced Calorie Creamy Cucumber Salad Dressing, ½ fl. oz.	15	50	0
Reduced Calorie Italian Salad Dressing, ½ fl. oz.	15	25	0
Reduced Calorie Thousand Island Salad Dressing, ½ fl. oz.	15	45	0
Relish, ⅓ oz.	9	14	0
Saltine Crackers, 4 pieces	12	45	1
Sausage, 1 patty	45	200	9
Scrambled Eggs	91	190	14
Sunflower Seeds & Raisins, 1¼ oz.	36	180	7
Swiss Cheese, imitation, 1 oz.	28	80	6
Taco Salad	357	390	23
Thousand Island Salad Dressing, ½ fl. oz.	15	70	0
Toast with Margarine, 2 slices	69	250	6
Tomatoes, 1 oz.	28	6	0
Tomatoes, 1 slice	14	2	0
Triple Cheeseburger	400	1040	72
Turkey Ham, ¼ cup	36	46	7
Watermelon, fresh, 2 pieces, 2 oz.	57	18	0
Wine Vinegar, 1 tbsp.	15	2	0

1. A dash means that data not available.
2. To convert grams to ounces (weight), divide by 28.35; to convert grams to fluid ounces (volume), divide by 29.6.

CARBOHYDRATES (gm.)	ADDED SUGAR[3] (gm.)	FAT[4] (gm.)	FAT % CALORIES	SATURATED FAT (gm.)	CHOLESTEROL (mg.)	SODIUM (mg.)	VITAMIN A (% U.S.RDA)	VITAMIN C (% U.S.RDA)	IRON (% U.S.RDA)	CALCIUM (% U.S.RDA)	GLOOM
0	0	9	100	—	0	155	—	0	0	0	13
5	—	5	64	—	0	130	0	0	0	0	8
0	0	0	0	0	0	0	0	0	0	0	0
2	—	4	80	—	0	160	0	0	0	0	7
2	—	5	90	—	0	140	0	0	0	0	8
2	—	2	72	—	0	180	0	0	0	0	5
2	—	4	80	—	5	125	0	0	0	0	7
3	—	0	0	0	0	70	0	0	0	0	1
8	0	2	40	—	4	150	0	0	—	—	4
0	0	18	81	—	30	410	0	—	4	0	24
7	0	12	57	—	450	160	15	0	15	6	13
12	0	13	65	—	0	10	0	0	15	4	13
0	0	6	68	—	1	450	0	0	0	0	11
36	0	18	42	—	40	1100	35	35	25	20	27
2	—	7	90	—	8	115	0	0	0	0	10
35	0	9	32	—	0	410	6	0	15	2	14
1	0	0	0	0	0	0	4	10	0	0	0
0	0	0	0	0	0	0	2	4	0	0	0
35	0	68	59	—	225	1848	8	4	60	35	85
1	0	2	39	—	27	—	0	0	—	—	2
0	0	0	0	0	0	0	0	0	0	0	0
0	0	0	0	0	0	5	0	0	0	0	0

3. To convert grams of sugar to teaspoons of sugar, divide by 4.0.
4. To convert grams of fat to teaspoons of fat, divide by 4.4.

THE RESTAURANTS

Arby's
AFA Service Corporation
Suite 700
10 Piedmont Center
3495 Piedmont Rd., NE
Atlanta, GA 30305
404/262-2729

Arthur Treacher's
4959 Mahoning Ave.
Youngstown, OH 44515
216/792-2252

Burger King Corporation
Consumer Information
M/S 1441
P.O. Box 520783
General Mail Facility
Miami, FL 33152
305/596-7011

Carl's Jr.
P.O. Box 4349
Anaheim, CA 92803
714/535-4848

Church's Fried Chicken, Inc.
P.O. Box BH001
San Antonio, TX 78284
512/735-9392

D'Lites of America, Inc.
6075 The Corners Parkway
Suite 200
Norcross, GA 30092
404/448-0654

Domino's Pizza, Inc.
3001 Earhart Rd.
P.O. Box 997
Ann Arbor, MI 48106
313/668-4000

International Dairy Queen, Inc.
P.O. Box 35286
Minneapolis, MN 55435
612/830-0200

Jack in the Box
Foodmaker, Inc.
9330 Balboa Ave.
San Diego, CA 92123
619/571-2121

Kentucky Fried Chicken
Public Affairs Department
P.O. Box 32070
Louisville, KY 40232
502/456-8300

Long John Silver's
Jerrico, Inc.
P.O. Box 11988
Lexington, KY 40579
606/268-2000

McDonald's Corporation
Consumer Affairs
McDonald's Plaza
Oak Brook, IL 60521
312/887-3200

Pizza Hut, Inc.
Consumer Affairs Department
P.O. Box 428
Wichita, KS 67201
316/681-9000

Popeyes
1333 S. Clearview Pkwy.
Jefferson, LA 70121
504/733-4300

Roy Rogers Restaurants
Marriott Corporation
Marriott Dr.
Washington, DC 20058
202/897-1490

Taco Bell
16808 Armstrong Ave.
Irvine, CA 92714
714/863-4500

Wendy's International, Inc.
Consumer Affairs Department
4288 West Dublin Granville Rd.
P.O. Box 256
Dublin, OH 43017
614/764-3100

If you'd like the government to require fast food to bear ingredient and nutrition labeling, write:

**Commissioner
Food and Drug
Administration**
5600 Fishers La.
Rockville, MD 20857
301/443-1544

**Secretary of Agriculture
U.S. Department of
Agriculture**
Washington, DC 20250
202/447-8732

Our address is:

**Center for Science in
the Public Interest**
1501 16th St., NW
Washington, DC 20036
202/332-9110

FURTHER RESOURCES

A Practical New Guide to Healthy Living, Dr. J. W. Anderson, $8.95. The low-fat, high-fiber, high-carbohydrate guide for diabetics. *Dr. Anderson's HCF Diet,* $7, explains how the high-fiber, high-carbohydrate diet can fit into everyone's life, lowering cholesterol and increasing nutrient intake. To order by mail, include cost of book plus $1 postage per order. Include the title(s), your name, and address and send to HCF Foundation, P.O. Box 22124, Lexington, KY 40522.

Choices for a Healthy Heart, Joseph Piscatella, Workman Publishing, $10.95 (available Spring 1987). This book focuses on our major life-style factors—diet, exercise, stress, and smoking—and their effect on cardiac fitness. Includes 200 new heart-healthy recipes.

The Complete Eater's Digest and Nutrition Scoreboard, Michael F. Jacobson, Anchor Press, $9.95. A complete guide to food additives, nutrition and health, and a glimpse into the politics of food.

Don't Eat Your Heart Out Cookbook, Joseph Piscatella, Workman Publishing, $14.95. With 400 heart-healthy recipes and practical tips on how to change eating habits permanently, this book is an excellent resource for those seeking a diet low in cholesterol, fat, salt, sugar, and calories.

Jack Sprat's Legacy, Patricia Hausman, Richard Marek, $2.95. A lucid explanation of the link between high-fat diets and heart disease, breast cancer, and colon cancer. Available only by mail, send $3.95 to the Center for Science in the Public Interest, 1501-16th St. NW, Washington, DC 20036.

Jane Brody's Good Food Book, Jane Brody, W. W. Norton Co., $19.95. A wonderfully complete book containing a discussion of nutrition, the fundamentals of cooking, plus hundreds of recipes.

Roadside Empires, Stan Luxenberg, Viking, $17.95. A detailed look at the phenomenon of franchising with a special focus on fast-food chains.

Salt: The Brand Name Guide to Sodium Content, Bonnie Liebman *et al.,* Warner Books, $3.95. A handy guide to the sodium content of more than 5,000 foods comes along with an explanation of the link between sodium and hypertension. Includes low-salt recipes.

Available at bookstores or from the Center for Science in the Public Interest.

Some of the key trade journals that are loaded with information about the restaurant industry are: *Advertising Age, Ad Week, Nation's Restaurant News, Restaurant Business, Restaurant Hospitality,* and *Restaurants and Institutions.*

NOW THAT YOU'VE READ THE BOOK...

SEE THE POSTER!

The Fast-Food Eating Guide will make a colorful—and educational—addition to your kitchen or office wall. This information packed wall-chart compares the nutritional values of over 200 fast-food items and meals. Comparing the various products on this cheerfully illustrated chart may be the best way to get your child, patient, or self to pass up the junk and select the good stuff at fast-food restaurants.

The 18 x 24-inch wall chart comes in a standard paper version ($3.95) and in a durable, stain-resistant, plastic-laminated version ($7.95)—ideal if you dare to use the chart while eating a greasy meal.

READ THE NEWSLETTER

For the latest news on foods and health, join The Center for Science in the Public Interest (CSPI) and receive *Nutrition Action Healthletter.* This is the newsletter relied upon by consumers and journalists from coast to coast, because the information is original, it's no-holds-barred honest, and it's understandable.

With billion-dollar advertising blitzes telling you how wonderful the all-new Tongue Teasers are, *Nutrition Action Healthletter* gives you the real poop. Ten times a year, this nationally acclaimed, 16-page, illustrated newsletter provides tasty, nourishing recipes, debunks deceptive ads, and gives you the lowdown on vitamin supplements.

Beyond giving you the information that will improve your diet and health and save you money, CSPI serves as your personal lobbyist and watchdog in Washington. We've stopped numerous deceptive advertising campaigns, gotten restrictions on unsafe food additives, and obtained improved food labeling. We hope you'll join 75,000 other concerned citizens and become part of our membership family.

COUPON

✓Please send me

☐ CSPI's latest catalog of publications (no charge)

☐ 1-year membership in CSPI   ___@$19.95 = _____

☐ Fast-Food Eating Guide poster (paper)   ___@ $3.95 = _____

☐ Fast-Food Eating Guide laminated poster ___@ $7.95 = _____

☐ More copies of this book   ___@ $4.95 = _____

Postage & Handling ___@   .50 = _____

Total Enclosed _____

NAME

STREET   APT

CITY   STATE   ZIP

TOTAL AMOUNT ENCLOSED

Mail the coupon and a check for the total amount to:
Center for Science in the Public Interest.
1501 16th St., NW
Washington, D.C. 20036